Anna E. R. and Laura Furness

In memory of their grandfather

Alexander Ramsey

AUDUBON, BY HIMSELF

The Natural History Press, publisher for The American Museum of Natural History, is a division of Doubleday and Company, Inc. Directed by a joint editorial board made up of members of the staff of both the Museum and Doubleday, the Natural History Press publishes books and periodicals in all branches of the life and earth sciences, including anthropology and astronomy. The Natural History Press has its editorial offices at The American Museum of Natural History, Central Park West at 79th Street, New York, New York 10024, and its business offices at 501 Franklin Avenue, Garden City, New York 11530.

AUDUBON, BY HIMSELF

A Profile of John James Audubon,

From Writings Selected, Arranged and Edited

by ALICE FORD

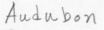

Published for

THE AMERICAN MUSEUM OF NATURAL HISTORY

The Natural History Press
Garden City, New York

Foreword

I

This self-portrait of John James Audubon would in a way take the place of the autobiography that he intended but never quite managed to leave us. It moves along, faithfully, from his birth in Haiti in 1785 to his final adventure at the mouth of the Yellowstone River in 1843. We hear from Audubon the witness, the plain-sailing philosopher, and the romantic's romantic. The dynamic sweep of his quests draws us with him across an ocean and a continent, through wilderness, along coasts and great rivers, and finally to Fort Union on the Dakota plains at the mouth of the Yellowstone. He recreates scenes of the frontier which even in his time was slipping away before the thrust of the westward movement.

Wonderful it is that at eighteen years of age Audubon the born storyteller could speak and write only beginner's English. Not until he passed his fortieth birthday did he publish his first paper, "Vieillot's Swallow," which James De Kay edited for the *Annals* of the Lyceum of Natural History, New York City. David Brewster of Edinburgh was the next in a line of editors. Then came the *Edinburgh New Philosophical Journal* which groomed several papers for its use.

Audubon was forty-six when circumstances forced him to become his own publisher of his *Ornithological Biography* (1831–39), the text for his folio *Birds*. Soon after his close friend the English zoologist, William Swainson, declined to be editor, Audubon hired a needy science professor of the University of Edinburgh, William Macgillivray. From 1831 until 1839 Macgillivray served as scientific editor and writing aide; to appreciate the proportions of his task, the reader need only turn to the appendices of this book and read the original manuscript version of "Pitting of Wolves." It is true that the present rendering differs a little from that of Macgillivray, who had to groom copy only a few doors away from Audubon and the latter's amanuensis and wife, Lucy. Yet it no more

diminishes the vitality and charm of the irrepressible style of the origi-
nator than did a virtual palimpsest of nineteenth-century hands that
bore down on the often wayward grammar, punctuation, paragraphing,
spelling and syntax. It may conceivably come closer, than any attempt
thus far, to the way in which Audubon would have written if English
had been his native tongue. On the evidence, truly, his written French
was none too much better. (The foreigner may amuse and titillate the
sentimentalist by his sound. Willingly? Surely not.)

Why did Macgillivray permit the words *muffle, flapper, hulk* and
other lapses stand, when Audubon meant to say *muzzle, flipper,*
and *hull?* Why did he pass over the cascading redundancies, *non
sequiturs,* misleading allusions, indefinite antecedents, and desperate
participles? Perhaps because of the sheer magnitude of the task before
him, and the fact that he himself was a writer only of necessity. Whatever the answer, there seemed no reason to preserve them here. Macgillivray barred a cruel passage that appeared in the manuscript of
"The Opossum," but, unaccountably, he did not censor those in "The
Racoon Hunt" and "Scipio the Bear." Present-day champions of the
cause of conservation and wildlife will not find them here.

The 1828 journal, fitfully kept, did not qualify for this selection. The
original is extinct; and the published version was bowdlerized, no
doubt, as heavily as the 1826 journal is well known to have been.

II

Even the quaint, often turgid nineteenth-century rendering of the
prose of Audubon is so readable, to his devotees above all, that it
continues to draw praise. It inspires analogies that would have been
soothing to this man who actually detested the act of writing. Not that
he heard no praise in his lifetime. The Shakespearean actress Fanny
Kemble wrote that Audubon's description of Niagara Falls, which he
read to her in fine declamatory style in the salon of her Boston host,
would have done credit to Lord Byron. One asks oneself if Poe might
not have been proud to claim "Death of a Pirate" for his own. Much as
Audubon admired the wilderness novels of James Fenimore Cooper, he
himself was far more the witness. In our day a noted connoisseur,
Sacheverell Sitwell, has said:

"In the aggregate, weighed in the balance of things imponderable, because
they cannot be compared, Audubon is of the importance of Herman Melville,
and *The Birds of America* is upon the scale of *Moby Dick.*"

Certainly the pursuit of the white killer-whale was not so much more venturesome than the pursuit "of all the birds of North America," or so much bolder than the resolve to paint them in the size of nature, and to report their life histories. In ways the analogy is applicable to both the art and prose of Audubon.

Many were his advisers and sources on the subject of scientific nomenclature. The oft-proclaimed fact that he lacked authority need not be repeated here. What needs to be stated is that, in these selections, the scientific names are omitted because Audubon himself rarely gave them, except in titles to biographies—names for the most part obsolete. To put modern nomenclature into his mouth would be to create a needless anachronism for readers who, almost certainly, have access to up-to-date guides for the names of these not-at-all unusual or uncommon species. Even a late Webster's International Dictionary will provide them. Who, though, would not prefer to know that when Audubon wrote of the "Pewee" he meant the Phoebe? Thanks to the American Museum of Natural History, such lapses have been brought into true focus by readers of the manuscript of this anthology.

No editor can blink faulty spelling, grammar, and syntax, with a good conscience, any more than he can—with a clear conscience—wickedly invent, improvise, or distort as he goes along. What he must have constantly in mind are the probable intentions of his author and the reasonable expectations, and pleasure, of the reader. If the narrative contains *lacunae* to which the editor can bring enlightenment, without going beyond a phrase or a sentence, it would seem his duty to fill them. Audubon was erratic as to variant spellings and capitalization, but on "Nature" and the common names of *wild* creatures—except perhaps for insect life—he usually conferred the dignity of capitals. We have tried, within the bounds of consistency, to follow his lead.

ALICE FORD

Washington, 1969

Acknowledgments

For permission to quote from their rare manuscript journals, I wish to thank the Houghton Library of Harvard College, Harvard University, and Mr. Henry Bradley Martin.

The National Audubon Society generously permitted quotation of their manuscript episode, "Pitting Wolves," and the American Philosophical Society their manuscript of "The Fair Incognito." Passages from *Audubon and His Journals* (1897) are quoted by courtesy of Charles Scribner's Sons. Those from *The Letters of John James Audubon, 1826–1838* are by courtesy of the Club of Odd Volumes which, in 1930, published correspondence owned then and now by the Houghton Library and the American Philosophical Society. The Henry Howland Papers are quoted with the permission of the Buffalo Museum of Science.

By making the original edition of *Ornithological Biography* and its episodes available, the New York Public Library and the New York Society Library contributed in an indispensable way.

Here I repeat my indebtedness to all those whose names are credited with the illustrations and by whose kind consent they appear.

The Natural History Press and its staff—and particularly Thomas S. Childs, Jr.—deserve utmost thanks and most special recognition.

Contents

PLATES

PART ONE

I

Reverie on the Mississippi

ON this rainy morning, when I cannot go ashore to hunt, I shall relate some incidents of my life as I drift down the river on a flat-boat.

My father, born in Les Sables d'Olonne, a fishing hamlet on the Bay of Biscay, was Lieutenant de Vaisseau Jean Audubon. He sailed as a sea captain to Saint Domingue, in the West Indies, where in 1785 I found light and life in the New World. During my earliest years there and in France he often brought me birds and flowers. With great eagerness he would point out the elegant movement of the birds, and the beauty and softness of their plumage. He called my attention to their show of pleasure or sense of danger, their perfect forms and splendid attire. He would speak of their departure and their return with the seasons, their haunts, and—most wonderful of all—their change of livery. He excited me, to make me study them and to raise my mind toward their great Creator. I gazed in ecstasy upon the pearly, shining eggs where they lay, in softest down or among dried leaves and twigs. I watched to see how Nature had provided each species with eyes, open at birth or closed for some time after . . . that I might trace the slow progress of the young birds towards perfection.

My mother, an extraordinarily beautiful woman, died shortly after my birth in Saint Domingue on April 26, 1785. I was removed to France when only three years old and received by that best of women, Anne Moynet Audubon, my foster mother, and raised and cherished to the utmost of her means. My father gave me and my half-sister Rose, two years my junior, an education appropriate to his purse. I studied mathematics at an early age and had many teachers of agreeable talents. The continual wars in which France was engaged forced me away, when only eleven. I entered the Navy and was received as cabin-boy at

Rochefort-sur-Mer, great naval training station—against my inclinations. My father had started, at a very early age, as cabin-boy on a merchant ship—with his father as captain—for the Grand Miquelon, Canada. His voyage was a hard one but it rendered him robust, active and fit to go through the world's rugged paths. When of age he commanded trading vessels to Saint Domingue. Taken prisoner at sea by the English, he gained his freedom from gaol in New York after a year or so, then joined the American Revolution. He was in several engagements in the American service and at the taking of Lord Cornwallis at Yorktown. Before his return to Europe he purchased a beautiful farm on the Schuylkill River and the Perkiomen Creek in Pennsylvania.

But to go back a little, one incident of childhood is perfect in my memory . . . one of the curious things which perhaps led me to love birds, and finally to study them with pleasure infinite. My foster mother had several beautiful parrots and some monkeys. One monkey was a full-grown male of a very large species. One morning "Pretty Polly" asked for her breakfast as usual: "Mignonne wants bread and milk." The monkey, probably thinking the bird presumed upon his rights in the scale of Nature, walked deliberately towards her and, with unnatural composure, killed her. My infant heart agonized at this cruel sight. I prayed a servant to beat the monkey, but he refused because he preferred him to the parrot. My long and piercing cries brought my mother rushing into the room. I was tranquillized, the monkey forever afterward chained, and Mignonne buried with all the pomp of a cherished one.

As I grew up I was fervently desirous of becoming acquainted with Nature. But the moment a bird was dead, no matter how beautiful it had been in life, the pleasure of possession became blunted for me. I wished to possess all the productions of Nature, but I wished to see life in them, as fresh as from the hands of their Maker. This was impossible. . . . I turned to my father, made known to him my disappointment, and he gave me a book of illustrations that put new life in my veins. Although the pages were not what I longed for, they gave me a desire to copy Nature. To Nature I went and tried to imitate her. But when, for many years, I saw that my drawings were worse than the ones I regarded as bad in the book, the difficulties irritated me but never for a moment destroyed the desire for perfect truth to Nature. The worse my drawings were the more beautiful did the originals appear. To have been torn from the study would have been as death; my time was entirely occupied with art. Hundreds of these rude sketches, drawn annually, made bonfires on my birthday for a long time. I did not abandon the idea of representing Nature.

My stepmother who was devotedly attached to me completely spoiled me, hid my faults, boasted to everyone of my youthful merits, and—worst of all—said frequently in my presence that I was the handsomest boy in France. All my wishes and idle notions were at once gratified. She went so far as actually to grant me *carte blanche* at all the confectionery shops in the town, and also in the village of Couëron, near Nantes, where we spent summers and eventually moved from the center of the city.

My father was of quite another, much more valuable turn of mind as to my welfare. He believed that the stores of the mind and not the power of gold coins render a man happy. He himself had suffered much from the want of education. The civil wars of France and Saint Domingue ravaged his wealth. He ordered me put to school, and to be taught also at home. "Revolutions too often take place in the lives of individuals, and they are apt to lose in one day the fortune they possessed," he was wont to say. "But talents and knowledge, sound mental training, honest industry can never fail nor be taken from anyone, once these valuable means are his." Therefore, all my mother's entreaties and tears notwithstanding, off to school I was sent. None but military schools were good in this period when thunders of Revolution roared over the land and blood soaked the earth. My private teachers were the only means of the least benefit. My father, long a seaman, and then in the French Republican Navy, wished me either to follow in his footsteps or to become an engineer. I studied drawing, geography, mathematics, fencing and the like, and also music for which I had considerable talent. Mathematics was hard dull work, I thought. Geography pleased me more. I was quite enthusiastic for dancing, and also for becoming commander of a corps of dragoons some day.

My father was mostly absent on duty, so that my mother let me do much as I pleased. Instead of applying closely to my studies I preferred to go with my friends in search of birds' nests, or to fish and shoot. I usually made for the field, my little basket filled with good eatables for lunch at school, but to burst with nests, eggs, lichens, flowers, and even pebbles from the shore of some rivulet by the time I came home at evening.

On my father's first return from long duty at sea he complimented me on my various collections. But when he inquired as to what else I had been doing, I, like a culprit, hung my head. After dinner he asked my sister Rose for some music and was so pleased with her improvement that he presented her with a beautiful book. For nearly a month I had not touched my violin, which lay stringless; I could not play when asked. After a silence he asked what drawings I had to show him. I had but few and those were not good ones. He looked at my stepmother, kissed my sister, and humming a tune left the room. Next morning at dawn he and I, with my trunk and violin, were off by carriage, behind a postilion. My parent took out his book and read in silence, leaving me entirely to my thoughts. Although he showed no anger he scarcely spoke to me on the way.

A few days later we entered the gates of Rochefort-sur-Mer. At the house where we alighted he smiled as the sentinel presented arms and murmured words to him that I did not catch. The place was furnished with servants, and everything seemed to go on as if the owner had not left it. We sat down and my father took one of my hands in his. "My beloved boy," he said, "thou art now safe. I have brought thee here that I may be able to pay constant attention to thy studies." Off we went together, I to see the docks, the fine ships-of-war, and to walk round the wall, he to his duties. I was presented to every officer we met; they noticed me more or less. But I perceived that I was like a prisoner-of-war on parole.

With young Vivien de la Plaine, son of a petty officer, I spent my leisure. While my father was in command of the corvette, *l'Instituteur,* we were on his training cruise for many young cabin-boys like ourselves. Then we were put ashore while he sailed for Falmouth and an exchange of prisoners with the English. One morning, having been set to a very arduous mathematical problem by a tutor, I gave him the slip, jumped from the window, and ran off through the Marine Secrétariat gardens. The unfledged bird may poise for a while on the edge of the nest or perhaps attempt to soar off on its winglets, but his imprudence may prove inimical; an older bird, its eye on him, pounces relentlessly on the young adventurer and grasps him in his talons. So it was with me. I had leaped from my cage and thought myself quite safe while I rambled. Then I saw a corporal coming towards me. I did not attempt to escape from this man whom I knew well. I was put aboard a pontoon in the river harbor and left amid a medley of culprits. I felt vile in their vile company, but I was released when my father returned from his tour of duty, and was again severely reprimanded.

After I failed in my examination for officer's training I returned to Nantes. My father retired from the Navy as Lieutenant de Vasseau, soon after. The family presently settled in our villa, *La Gerbetière,* at Couëron. I was within months of turning seventeen when my father [not anxious to see me lost with the best blood of France in the Napoleonic drive for conquest] outmanoeuvered the conscription by sending me to Mill Grove, his Pennsylvania farm. At eighteen and a half I was sent to America to make money—for such was my father's wish. But brought up in easy circumstances, I was ill-fitted for it. I landed in New York, caught the yellow fever after walking to a bank at Greenwich village to get money with a letter of credit; was packed off to Norristown by the ship captain; and was placed in the care of two Quaker boardinghouse ladies. To their ministrations I owe my life.

Miers Fisher, Quaker lawyer of Philadelphia and my father's agent —much admired by Washington for his integrity—came for me in his carriage and removed me to his country house on the road toward Trenton. To his daughter, of no mean appearance, I happened to take an unconquerable dislike. He was opposed to music of all descriptions, and dancing, and indeed to most of my amusements. He could not bear me to carry a gun or fishing-rod. At last I reminded him that it was a duty to install me on the estate to which my father had sent me.

At Mill Grove I was presented to the caretaker and tenant farmer, William Thomas, also a Quaker. He was to dole out what was considered sufficient for a young gentleman's quarterly allowance.

Mill Grove was ever to me a blessed spot. The mill was also a source of joy to me. In a cave above the Perkiomen Creek, where the Pewees were wont to build, I never failed to find quietude and delight. For one year I was as happy as the young bird that, having left its parents' sight, carols merrily while hawks watch it for easy prey.[*1]

The nest of the plain-colored Pewee flycatcher [Phoebe] was fastened to the rock over the arched entrance. Although it was empty it was still clean, as if the absent owner intended to revisit it with the return of spring.

One morning in April when the air still had the piercing chill of winter I entered the cave and heard a rustling above my head. Two birds flew off. The Pewee had arrived! I walked off but continued to watch. I concluded that they must have just come, for they seemed fatigued. Their plaintive note was not to be heard, their crests were not erect, and their usually vibrating tails were wanting in power. They glided down from their perches in a tree and back into the cave. I

* Appendix III lists the sources in order of presentation.

concluded that they must have reached this haven either during the night or at dawn.

Long before I reached the spot next morning my ears were saluted by their note. I saw them darting through the air and over the water after insects. Full of gaiety, they flew in and out of the cave, and to the tree near it, seemingly engaged in the most interesting conversation while fluttering their wings, jetting their tails, and erecting their crests in neat attitudes, no longer indicating fatigue. When I entered, the male flew violently towards the opening with the incredible swiftness of a shadow.

Before a week had elapsed, the Pewees and myself were quite on terms of intimacy. Redwings and Grackles were also about, here and there. The Pewees began working at their old nest. They relined it with a few large soft feathers of the Common Goose found along the edge of the creek. While the pair sat on the edge of the nest, there was a remarkable twittering, never to be heard on any other occasion . . . a soft tender expression of their pleasure. Their mutual caresses, simple as they might have seemed to another onlooker, excited sensations I can never forget.

One day the female seldom left her nest. Her mate, unusually despondent and uneasy, would alight by her for a moment, suddenly fly out, and return with an insect for her. About three in the afternoon she flew out, rose high, and circled with curious motions new to me, to be followed by her consort throughout her meanderings. Meanwhile I peeped into their nest and saw their first egg. The sight pleased me more than if I had seen a diamond of the size. In that frail covering life already existed. Before many weeks, a weak and delicate yet perfect creature would burst the shell and call for the most tender care. This knowledge filled my mind with the same wonder I feel when I search the heavens for the meaning of all I see.

Six eggs were deposited in six days. About an hour after laying the last egg, the female, having had a flight from the nest, arranged the eggs under her body, spread her wings a little, and began the arduous task of incubation.

I gave strict orders that no one should go near the cave, much less enter, or indeed destroy any nest on the plantation. Often I reached my hand out near the sitting bird. So gentle had they both become that neither moved. Now and then the female would shrink back into the nest; or the male would snap at my fingers, or leave the nest in great anger, fly round the cave a few times to querulous whining notes, then alight on the nest again.

A Pewee's nest was attached to a rafter in my mill. There was another under a shed in the cattle yard. Each pair, it seemed, had laid out the limits of its own domain and seldom trespassed on neighbors' grounds. All were descended of the same stock. I had ample proof of this the following spring when the young of the cave Pewees established themselves farther up the creek, and elsewhere.

On the thirteenth day the little ones hatched except for one egg which the hen very deliberately pushed out of the nest next day. In it I found the embryo of a bird, partly dried up and with its vertebrae attached to the shell, a condition that probably caused its death. The older birds no longer looked on me as an enemy and would often come in close by me. I now took it upon myself to handle the young frequently. I took the whole family out and blew the exuviae of the feathers from the nest. I attached light threads to the legs of the young, but these they or their parents invariably removed with their bills. At last, when they were about to leave the nest, I fixed a light silver thread to the leg of each, loose enough not to hurt the part, yet so fastened that the bird could not remove it.* After sixteen days the brood took to wing. The old birds began to arrange the nest anew. By the beginning of August a new brood made its appearance.

On October 8 not a Pewee could I find on the plantation. My little companions had all set off on their travels. For weeks afterward, however, I saw Pewees arriving from the North on their southward way.

In June, 1806, on my return from a visit to France, I observed them again, in and about the cave, but in a new nest . . . and in nests up the creek, under the bridge, in the meadows, and in the grain sheds. Several had the little banding ring on the leg, I was pleased to find. The old nest in the cave had been torn away. The male bird allowed me to approach within yards but his mate was very shy. On inquiring of the miller's son I found he had killed the old female and four young ones for fish bait. This was her successor. After I sold Mill Grove the cave was destroyed, along with nearly all the beautiful rocks beside the creek, to make a new dam across the Perkiomen.

Once in Virginia, while travelling on horseback, I went out of my way to visit the renowned Natural Bridge. My chance companion, the

* First "banding" of wild birds in America.—*Ed.*

merchant Vincent Nolte, who had been there before, wagered he could lead me across the rock bridge before I was aware we were on it. I trotted ahead, listened to the notes of different birds, and at last distinguished the Pewee [Phoebe]. I drew up to judge the distance the bird might be from me, then told my friend that the bridge was less than a hundred yards away. His surprise was great. "How do you know this?" he asked. "Simply because I hear the notes of the Pewee and know that a cave or a deep rocky creek must therefore be near," I answered. We moved on and pretty soon began to see the Pewees rise from under the Natural Bridge in numbers. I pointed to the spot and won the wager. This rule almost always works both ways. The nature of the place—whether high or low, moist or dry, whether sloping north or south, or bearing tall trees or low shrubs—generally gives a hint as to its inhabitants.[2]

I pursued my simple and agreeable studies in Pennsylvania with as little concern about the future as if the world had been made for me. My rambles invariably commenced at break of day. To return, wet with dew, bearing a feathered prize, was and ever will be the highest enjoyment. Hunting, fishing, drawing and music occupied my every moment. Cares I knew not, and I cared naught about them. My neighbor and future father-in-law, William Bakewell of Fatland Ford plantation, a recent arrival from England, an excellent man and a great shot, often hunted with me. I was pleased to believe that his daughter Lucy looked upon me with some favor. His son Thomas was skating with me one morning on the Perkiomen, that first winter. He challenged me to shoot at his hat as he tossed it in the air while I passed at full speed. Accepting with great pleasure I went off like lightning—up and down—until the trigger was pulled. Down on the ice came the hat, as completely perforated as a sieve. He repented (alas! too late) and was afterward severely reprimanded by Mr. Bakewell.

One day a party of us went on a duck-shooting excursion. The ice was fine except for a good many air-holes. On our return in the early dusk with our ducks I led the way, with a white handkerchief held high on a stick. When darkness came on we increased our speed. I approached a large air-hole so abruptly that I could not check my advance, and down it I went. I must have glided some thirty or forty yards when, as God would have it, up I popped at another air-hole and managed to crawl out. My companions gathered round after the narrowest escape of my life (not excepting later threats of murder, among other perils of existence), and shared their garments with me. In dry breeches from one, a shirt from another, I headed our line of march once more, this time with much more circumspection.[3]

When, as a little lad, I first represented birds on paper, I was under the impression that each sketch was a finished picture, because it possessed some sort of a head and tail and two sticks of legs. Oh! what bills and claws I did draw, to say nothing of a perfectly straight line for a back, and a tail stuck in, any way—like an unshipped rudder, and with never a thought of abutments to keep it from falling backward or forward. Many persons praised them to the skies. But my father constantly impressed upon me that nothing in the world possessing life and animation was easy to imitate, as I would gradually learn. I listened less to the others, and more to him; and his kind words and deep interest in my improvement became my law. My first collection of drawings— all stiff, unmeaning profiles—are such as one found in most such works. My next, begun in America, were from birds hung by a string tied to one foot, that I might show every portion as the wings lay loosely spread. In this manner I made some pretty fair signs for poulterers.

While watching the Pewees and their graceful attitudes a thought struck my mind like a flash of light. Nothing, after all, could ever answer my enthusiastic desire to represent Nature, alive and moving, except to copy her in her own way. I began again. On I went, forming, literally, hundreds of outlines of my favorites, the Pewees. How good or bad I cannot tell, but I fancied I had mounted a step on the high pinnacle before me. I continued for months, simply outlining birds as I observed them, either alighted or on the wing. But I could finish none of my sketches. I lay many different species on the tables or on the ground in attitudes for sketching. Alas! They were *dead*, to all intents and purposes, and neither wing, nor leg, nor tail could I place according to my wishes. Next I tried fastening threads to raise or lower a head, wing or tail, until I had something like life before me. Yet much was still wanting. When I saw the living birds I felt the blood rush to my temples. Almost in despair I spent about a month without drawing— deep in thought and daily in the company of the feathered inhabitants of Mill Grove.

I cogitated as to how far a manikin of a bird would answer. I labored with wood, cork and wires to form a figure, one so grotesque that when set up it was like a tolerable-looking Dodo. A friend roused my ire by laughing at it immoderately, assuring me that if I wished to represent a tame gander it might do. I gave it a kick, broke it to atoms, walked off, and thought again.

Young as I was, and impatient, I let my desire fill my brains with many plans. Not infrequently I dreamed I had made a new discovery. One morning long before day I leaped out of bed, ordered a horse to be saddled, mounted it, and went off at a gallop towards Norristown, about five miles away. Not a door was yet open. I went to the river, took a bath, returned to the town, entered the first open shop, bought wire of different sizes, leaped on my steed and was soon again at Mill Grove. I really believe my tenant's wife thought I was mad. On being offered my breakfast, I told her I only wanted my gun. I was off to the creek, shot the first Kingfisher I met, carried it home by the bill, sent for the miller, and had him bring me a piece of soft board. When he returned with it he found me filing sharp points on wire, ready to show him what I meant to do.

I pierced the body to fix it on the board, passed a second wire above the upper mandible to hold the head in a pretty fair attitude, and with finer wires arranged the feet according to my notions. Even common pins came to my assistance. The last wire delightfully elevated the tail, and at last—there stood before me the *real* Kingfisher. The lack of breakfast was not at all in my way. No, indeed! I outlined the bird with the aid of compasses, then colored and finished it without a thought of hunger. My honest miller stood by, delighted to see me so pleased. This was what I shall call my first drawing actually from Nature, for even the model's eye was still as if full of life when I pressed the lids aside with my finger.

To study Nature was, to me, to ramble through her domains late and early. If I observed all as I should, I knew that the memory of what I saw would be of service to me, even as La Fontaine imparted in his fable of *L'hirondelle et les petits oiseaux*. ("Whoever sees much will have much to retain.") The use of my wires was improved by constant practice. Whenever I improved upon one representation, I destroyed its predecessor. Gradually, the forms and habits of our birds impressed me with the idea that each part of a family must possess a certain degree of affinity. The fly-catching Pewees [Phoebe] led me to note that every bird truly of that genus was usually in a passive attitude when standing; that they sat erect, now and then glancing up or sideways toward insect prey; and that while in pursuit of prey they were the same—all their tribe—in their movements. I saw that gallinaceous birds had their peculiar movements and positions. Among the water-birds I found characteristic manners. The herons walked with elegance and stateliness. Every family had some mark by which it could be known.

The better I understood my subjects, the better I became able to represent them in what I hoped were natural positions. Once the bird was fixed with wires on squares, I studied—as its figure lay before me—its bill, nostrils, eyes, legs, claws, and the structure of wings and tail. The very tongue was of importance to me. I thought that the more I understood these, the better would be my collection of the birds of America. My first drawings, made entirely in water colors, wanted softness and finish. For a long time I was dispirited, particularly when vainly trying to imitate birds of soft and downy plumage, such as Owls, Pigeons, Hawks and Herons. A so-called accident came to my aid. After finishing a miniature portrait of the one dearest to me in all the world, Lucy my future wife, a portion of the face was injured by a drop of water that dried where it fell. After much labor to repair the damage I found that the blur still remained. I resorted to a piece of colored chalk, applied it, rubbed the spot with a cork stump, and at once caught the desired effect.[4]

II

To the Frontier

For a period of nearly twenty years my life was a succession of vicissitudes. I tried various branches of commerce, but all proved unprofitable, doubtless because my whole mind was ever filled with my passion for rambling.[5] William Bakewell, my father-in-law-to-be, advised me to study the mercantile business. My father approved of the idea. To make certain that I would be trained for it under the best possible auspices I went to New York City and entered on commerce as a clerk of Benjamin Bakewell, uncle of my fiancée Lucy.

My very first venture, on my own, was in an indigo speculation that cost me several hundred pounds, all of which I lost. My friend and future business partner, Ferdinand Rozier of Nantes, France, was no more fortunate than I. From the wine merchants and shippers' firm that hired him in Philadelphia, he sent off a cargo of hams to the West Indies, but collected not more than one-fifth of his investment. All the same, I suppose that we both obtained a smattering of business experience.

Rozier persuaded me to travel through the Western country with a view to settling. We thought well of it; in fact, we liked it exceedingly for its fertility and abundance, its hospitality and kindness. We marked Louisville as a spot fated to become a place of great importance. If we had been as wise, as to this, as we were both to become (but too late), I might never have quit commerce or published *The Birds of America*. If left to grow over with grass until 1825, land and also town lots would have been worth a fortune. But young heads are on young shoulders. It was not to be, and who cares?

I was married on April 5, 1808, at Fatland Ford, the Bakewell plantation. Lucy, Rozier, and I set out together three days later by stagecoach. On our way to Pittsburgh we met with a sad accident that might have cost the life of Lucy. The coach upset in the Allegheny Mountains, and she was severely but, fortunately, not fatally hurt. We floated down the Ohio in a flatboat in company with several other young families, and with many goods. We opened a large store at Louisville which went on prosperously when I attended to it. But birds were birds, then as now, and my thoughts were ever and anon turning towards them as to my greatest delight. I shot, I drew, I looked on Nature only . . . beyond this I really cared not.

Victor was born on June 12, 1809, at our temporary home, the Indian Queen hotel. The country was settled by planters and farmers, and all the sportsmen and hunters among them were fond of me. I seldom passed a day without drawing a bird or noting something respecting its habits, Rozier meantime attending the counter.[6]

I knew a gentleman who had a large mill by the Falls of the Ohio. On its rocky shelvings, thousands of wild Canada Geese rested at night, but they were by no means secure. Louis Tarascon, a native of Marseilles, used to kill them at a distance of about a quarter of a mile by means of a small cannon heavily charged with rifle bullets. At dawn, when the birds were busily trimming their plumage before flying off to their feeding grounds, he frequently obtained a dozen or more at a shot. Such a war of extermination could not last long. The Geese deserted the fatal rock, and the great gun of the mighty miller Tarascon was used only for a few weeks.[7]

I became acquainted with the amiable Major William Croghan, son of a veteran hero of the French and Indian Wars. He asked if I had seen the trees in which swallows [Chimney Swift] were supposed to winter, but where, he said, they only roosted. We were walking back to town when we came to a huge sycamore, nearly destitute of branches, and sixty or seventy feet high, seven or eight in diameter at the base. Swallows could enter the stump of a broken hollow branch about forty feet up. I found the tree hard, but hollow near the base. This was at about 4 P.M. in July, while the birds were still in the skies. I returned when the sun was going down behind the Silver Hills, that beautiful evening. Thousands of Swallows were flying above me. Three or four at a time were pitching into the hole like bees into a hive. I rested my head against the tree trunk, listening to the roaring noise within as the birds settled. I left at dark, convinced that many more had yet to enter. I had scarcely reached Louisville when a violent thunderstorm that passed suddenly over the town made me think the hurry of the Swallows was caused by their anxiety to avoid it. Almost the whole night I thought of them, so anxious had I become to ascertain their number (which was great). The birds had rushed into the tree so swiftly as to baffle the attempt.

I rose early to reach the place before the least sign of daylight. All was silent within the tree. I remained with my head against it for probably twenty minutes, when suddenly I thought the great tree was giving way and coming down upon me. Instinctively I sprang from it. The Swallows were now pouring out in a black, continual stream. I ran back to listen, in amazement, to the noise within—like a large wheel revolving under a powerful stream. I could hardly see the hour on my watch but estimated their time in getting out, with the quickness of thought, at more than thirty minutes.

To examine the interior, a friend and I succeeded in throwing a strong line across the broken branch. Fastening the rope to the line we drew it up and pulled it over until it reached the ground again. With a long cane ready, I mounted the tree by rope without accident and seated myself at ease on the broken branch. But my labor was fruitless. I could see nothing through the hole, and my fifteen-foot cane touched nothing within that could give any information. I came down fatigued and disappointed.

Next day I had a man cut a hole at the base of the eight- or nine-inch-thick shell. The axe exposed a matted mass of exuviae and rotten feathers, reduced to a kind of mould that held bits of insects and quills. To bore through nearly six feet for a passage took time; knowing that if the birds should notice the hole they would abandon the tree, I had it carefully closed. The Swallows came as usual that night. I did not disturb them for several days.

About nine one evening my companion and I went with a lantern to have a full view of the interior. We opened the hole with caution. I scrambled up the sides of the mass of exuviae and my friend followed. All was perfectly silent. Slowly and gradually I brought the light to play on the sides of the hole above us. Swallows, clinging side by side, covered the surface. Satisfied with the sight, I closed the lantern. Then with as much care as possible we caught and killed more than a hundred, stowing them away in our pockets and bosoms. As we slid down into the open air, not a bird dropped its dung upon us. Closing the entrance, we marched towards Louisville, perfectly elated. Among 115 we found only six females. Eighty-seven were adult males; I had no doubt the rest were the young of that year's first brood. We estimated the number of Swallows that roosted in this one tree at 9,000. I visited it on August 2 and found many more females and young than males. On August 13 not more than two or three hundred came to roost. On August 18 not one did I see near it, but only a few moving southward. In February I closed the entrance. About the beginning of June, after the birds had begun to resort to the tree again, I took it into my head to close the entrance above with a bundle of straw that I could draw off with a string. The result was curious enough. The birds passed and repassed with apparent discomfort. I noticed that many were flying away. I then removed the straw; they re-entered until I could no longer see them from the ground.

The ancient tenement was to give way and crash to earth some years later. General William Clark assured me at Locust Grove, plantation of his sister and brother-in-law the Croghans, that he saw this species all along his route to the Pacific with Meriwether Lewis [in 1804–05].[8]

Beargrass Creek, one of Kentucky's many beautiful streams, meanders through a deeply shaded growth of majestic beech woods, among which are walnut, oak, elm, ash and other trees. The spot where I saw an anniversary celebration of the glorious Independence Day is on its banks, near Louisville. The dense woods spread towards the Ohio shores on the west, and the gently rising grounds to the south and east. Every clearing holds a plantation that smiles luxuriance at the summer harvest. The farmer can admire both his orchards that seem to bow low to mother earth with fruit and his leisurely grazing flocks.

The free, single-hearted Kentuckians, bold, erect and proud of their Virginia heritage had, as usual, made their plans for the occasion. The whole neighborhood joined in, with no need of an invitation where everyone—from the Governor to the ploughmen—was welcome. All met with light hearts and merry faces. It was a beautiful day of blue heavens. Gentle breezes wafted the scent of gorgeous flowers. Little birds sang their sweetest in the woods, and the fluttering insects danced in the sunbeams. Columbia's sons and daughters seemed to have grown younger that morning.

The undergrowth had been cut away, and the low boughs of the trees lopped off. A carpet of green grass formed a clearing that was like a sylvan pavilion. Wagons moved slowly along, bearing provisions from the farms . . . hams, venison, an ox, and turkeys and other fowl. Flagons of every kind of beverage were to be seen. La Belle Rivière, the Ohio, had provided the finny tribe. There were melons, peaches, plums, and pears enough to have stocked a market. In a word, the land of abundance, Kentucky, had supplied a feast for her children.

Fifty or more cooks kept busy while columns of smoke rose above the trees beside a purling stream. The ladies set out dishes, glasses, punch bowls, and bottles of rich wine, not forgetting barrels of "Old Monongahela" for the crowd. Roast viands perfumed the air, and the word went round that this banquet—fit for the vigorous appetite of American woodsmen—would soon be ready. Every steward was at his post to receive the joyous celebrants already emerging from the woods.

Each pretty lass, in pure white, rode with her sturdy lover on a steed whose neighing proclaimed how proud the creature was of its burden. The couples leaped down, and after twisting the bridle around a branch, they joined the Barbecue. Soon the grounds were alive with humanity. A great wooden cannon bound with hoops and crammed with homemade powder boomed a salute, amid hearty huzzas. A good oration from the most learned gladdened every ear. Although it did not equal the eloquence of a Henry Clay, an Edward Everett, a Daniel Webster, or some others of note, it nonetheless reminded every Kentuckian present of the glorious name, patriotism, courage and virtue of our immortal George Washington. Fifes and drums sounded the march. The strains of "Yankee Doodle" brought an uproar.

The crowd thronged to the tables. The beaux seated their ladies. Then began the destruction of the feast; and it was followed by toasts, speeches and replies.

The ladies retired to booths erected at a little distance. Meanwhile their partners began a hearty round of toasts at the cleared tables. Before long the dance began, as double lines of a hundred of the fair sex were formed in the shade, ready for the first merry trill of the reels and cotillions. A burst of music from violins, clarionets and bugles was the signal for what seemed like the whole gathering to begin gracefully moving to the rhythms. The "hunting-shirts" led, their fringed shirts swinging as if keeping time with the whirling gowns of the ladies. The married couples and their children mingled with the dancers. No pride, no pomp, and no affection were to be seen, but only a joy that increased with the exhilarating, carefree exercise. Between times melon juice was passed to the ladies, and ample draughts of punch to the Kentucky hunters.

A visitor to this national *fête champêtre* would have overheard the ingenuous talk of the lovers. He would have sampled the wisdom of the elders on affairs of farm and state, and heard hopes of prosperity for the country and for Kentucky. He would have seen the men who did not join the dance shoot at marks with heavy rifles, or display their horsemanship on thoroughbred "old Virginia" horses, or recount their hunting exploits, while the woods rang with laughter. Thus it was that, for me, time sped by like an arrow.

Shades of evening crept over the scene. Large fires were lighted. Happy groups, loath to separate, formed columns that cast long shadows. The lamps of heaven began to sparkle in the still clear sky. After supper the departure began. The lover and his fair one, the hunter and his friend, and the families all returned in peace to happy homes.[9]

It may not be amiss to speak about Kentucky, before I attempt to give some idea of the pleasures experienced by its sportsmen. When it was attached to Virginia the Indians looked on its wilds as their own. They abandoned the district only when forced to move farther on into the unexplored forests. Its soil, and its handsome borders along one of the most beautiful rivers in the world, contributed as much to attract the Old Virginians as did the prevalent desire to bring its tracts under cultivation after unknown ages of only luxuriant, untamed wilderness.

The conquest was not without many difficulties. Warfare between the Redskins and the intruders was bloody and protracted, until the former drew off their shattered bands. The region was probably discovered by a daring hunter, the renowned Daniel Boone. Drawn by the richness of the soil, magnificent forests, numberless navigable streams, salt springs and licks, saltpetre caves, coal, and herds of buffalo and deer that still browsed on its hills and in its charming valleys, the Virginians thronged towards the Ohio with a spirit surpassing that of tribes who for ages were the sole possessors. An axe, a couple of horses, and a heavy rifle with a store of ammunition were equipment enough for a man and his family. They pushed through dark, tangled forests with only the sun for a guide; rested on the bare ground; crossed countless streams on rafts, often drifting a distance before effecting a landing. Again, their cattle strayed in the rice pastures, to be recovered only after days. There was the danger of being murdered, while asleep in encampments, by prowling and ruthless Indians. Before they could reach those rendezvous called *stations* hundreds of miles had to be traversed.

Some, of course, moved from the Atlantic seaboard to the shores of the Ohio River, and did so in more comfort and security. They had their wagons and their Negroes. They cut their way through woods by keeping their axemen a day ahead of them on the trail. The hunters among them came, to wherever camp was pitched, with the bounty of the forest . . . Buffalo, Bear, and Deer that soon hung in large delicious steaks before the embers underneath which cakes were baked. The wagons carried bedding. The horses were turned loose to graze near by, either hobbled with rope or wearing a bell about the neck. Such migrating bands were undaunted by the great difficulties, apart from the perils of forcing their way through pathless woods to the land of promise. Although the journey took months to accomplish, and was not always without the excitement of a skirmish between the Virginians and the Indians who sometimes crept into camp, the wagons kept on towards the Ohio. Struck by the beauty of that magnificent stream, the pioneers at once began to clear land for a permanent home near its shores.

Others, however, chose instead to descend the stream. They prepared arks, or flatboats, that were pierced with portholes. As the travellers glided down the river they were more annoyed by Indians who were on the lookout for them than were the parties that migrated overland. A boat thirty or forty feet by ten or twelve was considered stupendous. It carried men, women and children, all huddled together, and with horses, cattle, hogs and poultry for their companions, and with vegetables and packages of seeds. The roof or deck was not unlike a farmyard. Hay, ploughs, carts, wagons, implements, and spinning wheels were conspicuous. Even the sides of the floating mass were loaded with wheels. These boats moved through darkness, groping along without comfort of fire or light, lest Indians watching on shore surprise and then destroy them. Sometimes the boats became the first dwelling of these settlers at the end of the tedious voyage. I shall not describe the many massacres, because I have never been very fond of battles, and indeed have always wished that the world were more peaceably inclined. I shall merely add that, in one way or another, Kentucky was wrested from the original owners of the soil.

Let us turn to its sports. We have individuals in Kentucky who are considered wonderfully adept with the rifle. To *drive a nail* is a common feat, thought no more of than of cutting off a Wild Turkey's head at a distance of a hundred yards. Others will *bark* off Squirrels, one after another, until satisfied with their score. Some, less intent on destroying game, may be seen *snuffing a candle* after dark, at fifty yards—offhand —without extinguishing the flame. Some are so expert and cool as to take aim at the eye of a man who is their enemy, after a boast which, on examination of his target's head, proves to have been fully carried out.

Marksmen meet to display their skill, bet a trifling sum on it, nail up a target with a common nail about two-thirds of the way into the wood, then at forty paces or so they take their stand. After the man whose turn it is has wiped the inside of the gun barrel, he places a ball in the palm of his hand and pours from his powderhorn enough to cover the charge, for a one hundred yard shot. If he comes close to the nail his marksmanship is considered indifferent. If he bends the nail, this is, of course, better; but nothing less than hitting it right on the head is satisfactory. One out of three shots generally hits the nail. Two nails are frequently needed before each marksman can have a shot. Those who drive the nail receive another trial. The two best shots generally settle the affair.

Barking off Squirrels is delightful sport, and in my opinion requires a greater degree of accuracy than any other. I first witnessed this manner of procuring squirrels near Frankfort. The performer was the celebrated Daniel Boone. We walked out together along the Kentucky River until we reached flat land thickly covered with black walnuts, oaks and hickories. Because the nuts were generally good that year, Squirrels were gamboling on every tree around us. The stout, hale, athletic Boone, in homespun hunting skirt, moccasined but barelegged, carried a long heavy rifle. As he loaded it, he said he hoped it would prove as efficient as it had on other occasions, because he felt proud to show me his skill. He wiped it, measured powder, patched the ball with six-hundred-thread linen, and sent the charge home with a hickory rod. We moved not a step, for the Squirrels were so numerous that it was unnecessary to go after them. Boone pointed to one crouched on a branch about fifty paces off, watching us. He bade me mark the spot well, and gradually raised his rifle until the *bead* or sight was in line with the spot. A whip-like report reverberated through the woods and along the hills. Judge of my surprise when I saw that the ball had hit the piece of bark just beneath the Squirrel and shivered it into splinters. The concussion killed the animal and sent it whirling through the air as if it had been blown up by a powder-magazine explosion. Since that first interview with our veteran Boone, I have seen many others perform the feat.

The *snuffing of a candle* I first saw near the Green River banks, not far from a large Passenger Pigeon roost that I had previously visited. I heard many gun reports, early one dark night, and went to ascertain the cause. I was welcomed by a dozen tall stout men who told me they were practicing by torchlight, to be able to shoot at the light reflected from the eyes of Deer and Wolves by night. The smoke of a fire, blazing nearby, curled through the thick foliage. A burning candle, like an offering to the goddess of night, almost indistinguishable at fifty yards, was the target. One man stood near it to watch the effects of the shots as well as to relight the candle if it went out, or to replace it if the shot cut it in two. Each man had his turn. Some hit neither snuff nor candle and were congratulated with a loud laugh. Others actually snuffed it without putting it out and were recompensed by hurrahs. One, particularly expert at this, was very fortunate and snuffed the candle three times out of seven. His other shots either put out the candle or cut it immediately beneath the flame.

Kentuckians will cut off a piece of tree bark, make a target with powder wetted with water or saliva for the bull's eye, and shoot all the balls they have about them, picking them out of the wood again. The rifle is the source of their principal sports and pleasures.[10]

Daniel Boone and I once spent a night under the same roof, after he had displayed his extraordinary skill in managing a rifle. Anxious to know more of his exploits and adventures, I took the liberty of asking many questions of the broad-chested, muscular giant* of the Western forests. His countenance reflected his great courage, enterprise and perseverance. The very motion of his lips brought the impression that whatever he uttered could not be other than strictly true.

I undressed, but Boone merely took off his hunting shirt and arranged blankets on the floor rather than lie on any bed, even the softest. When we were both comfortably settled, each after his own fashion, he told me the following in this simple style:

"I was once on a hunting expedition on the banks of the Green River when the lower part of Kentucky was still in the hands of Nature, and none but the sons of the soil were looked upon as its lawful proprietors. We Virginians had for some time been waging a war of intrusion upon them. I, like the others, rambled through the woods in their pursuit as I now would follow the tracks of any ravenous animals. The Indians outwitted me one dark night and took me prisoner by a trick of great skill. I had put out my camp fire, laid me down to rest in, as I thought, full security, when an indistinguishable number of hands seized and

* Audubon exaggerated the height and brawn of Boone.—Ed.

pinioned me. Resistance would have been useless—dangerous to my life. I let myself be removed to their camp a few miles distant without a murmur, to prove myself born and bred as fearless of death as any.

"When we reached camp there was great rejoicing. Two squaws and a few papooses appeared particularly delighted. Very unequivocal gestures and words assured me that on the morrow the mortal enemy of the Redskins would cease to live. I never opened my lips but kept scheming how to give the rascals the slip before dawn. The women immediately fell to searching my hunting shirt for whatever they might think valuable. Fortunately for me, they soon found my flask of *Monongahela*—strong whiskey. Their murderous countenances took on a terrific grin while my own heart throbbed with joy at the prospect of their intoxication. The whole crew began to beat their bellies and sing, as they passed the bottle from mouth to mouth. How I wished the flask were ten times its size and filled with *aquafortes!* I noticed that the squaws drank more freely than the warriors, so that my spirits began to fall—until the distant report of a gun was heard. The Indians jumped to their feet, the singing and drinking came to a halt, and, to my inexpressible joy, the men walked off a little way to talk with the squaws about me. I foresaw that in moments the warriors would go to discover the cause of the firing, and that the squaws would be left to guard me.

"Well sir, it was just so. The men walked away with their guns. The squaws again sat down, and in less than five minutes had my bottle up to their dirty mouths, and were guzzling the remains.

"Much to my pleasure they became more and more drunk, until the liquor took such hold of them that they rumbled down, rolled about, and began to snore. Having no other chance of freeing myself from the cords around me, I rolled over and over towards the fire, to burn them asunder. Soon I rose, free, stretched my stiffened sinews, snatched up my rifle and, for once in my life, spared the Indians. I felt like laying open the skulls of the wretches with my tomahawk, but thought better of killing beings so unprepared and unable to defend themselves against needless murder.

"But I decided to mark the spot by cutting three large chips in a thrifty ash sapling before I ran off. I crossed the river, threw myself deep in the canebrake, and made Indian tracks with my feet back-tracked against the chance of recapture.

"It is now nearly twenty years since this happened; and it is more than five since I left there and the whites' settlements that I might never have visited again, had I not been called as a witness in a pending lawsuit over a certain boundary line. That is another tale:

"A Virginian received a Kentucky land grant near the very ash tree that bore my mark. He finished his survey of some thousands of acres, one of whose corner boundaries stood (as the deed expressed it) 'at an Ash marked by three distinct notches of the tomahawk of a white man.' The tree had grown much. Bark covered the marks; but somehow or other the Virginian heard all that I have just been telling you. He wrote for me to come and at least try to find the place or tree, all expenses paid. Not much caring to go back to Kentucky from Missouri, I nevertheless set off.

"On horseback I reached the Green River Bottoms with the Virginian. Great changes had taken place in those woods. But after some difficulty I at last found the spot where I had crossed the river. We waited for the moon to rise, then made for the place where I thought the ash tree grew. I began to feel as if I were again in the presence of the Indians and a prisoner among them. We camped near what I conceived to be the spot, to await the rising of the sun.

"At dawn I walked, after a good deal of musing, towards what I believed would turn out to be the very ash tree, while the Virginian went off to find witnesses.

"Meanwhile I rambled in search of Deer. What a wonderful difference thirty years makes in the country! When I was caught by the Indians you could not have walked more than a mile in any direction without shooting a buck or Bear. Thousands of Buffalo roamed the Kentucky hills and land that looked as if it never would become poor. But when I was left to myself on the banks of the Green River, I daresay for the last time in my life, a few *signs* only of Deer were to be seen. As to a Deer itself, I saw none.

"The Virginian returned with three gentlemen. They looked upon me as if I had been Washington himself, and they walked to 'my' ash tree as if in quest of long lost treasure. I took an axe and cut a few chips off the bark. No signs were to be seen. I cut again, with more caution, and scraped and worked away with my butcher knife, until I *did* come to where my tomahawk had left an impression in the wood. I scraped until three hacks, as plain as any three notches that ever were, could be seen. The gentlemen were astonished. I must admit I was as much surprised as pleased myself. The Virginian gained his cause by my affidavit, and I left Green River forever. . . . I wish you a good night."[11]

We lived for two years at Louisville, where we enjoyed many of the best pleasures life can afford. The beauty of its situation on the banks of *La Belle Rivière,* where the famed Falls of the Ohio begin, and its Silver Hills across the water, are such as to please even the eye of a Swiss. Fish and game are abundant. But it was the generous hospitality of the inhabitants, the urbanity of their manners, that induced me to settle there. Much of my time was spent at my ever favorite pursuits. I drew and noted the habits of everything I procured. My collection was daily augmented; every individual who carried a gun always sent me such birds and quadrupeds as he thought might prove useful. My portfolios already contained upwards of two hundred drawings. . . .

One March morning in 1810 I was surprised by the sudden entrance into our counting-room of Mr. Alexander Wilson, the celebrated author of the *American Ornithology,* a work of which I had never heard. How well do I remember him as he walked up to me, then! His long, rather hooked nose, keen eyes, and prominent cheekbones stamped his countenance with a peculiar character. His dress, too, was of a kind not usually seen in Kentucky: a short coat, trousers, and gray cloth waistcoat. His stature was not above middle size. He had his two volumes under his arm. I thought I discovered something like astonishment in his countenance as he approached the table at which I was working. The object of his visit was to procure subscriptions for his work. He opened his books, explained their nature, and requested my patronage.

Surprised and gratified, I turned a few of the plates over and had already taken a pen to write my name in his favor when my partner Rozier said, rather abruptly, in French: "My dear Audubon, what induces you to subscribe to this work? Your drawings are certainly far better, and again, you must know as much of the habits of American birds as this gentleman." Whether Mr. Wilson understood French or not, or if the suddenness with which I paused disappointed him, I cannot tell. But I clearly perceived that he was not pleased. Vanity and the encomiums of my friend prevented me from subscribing. Mr. Wilson asked me if I had many drawings of birds. I rose, took down a large portfolio, laid it on the table, and showed him, as I would any other person fond of such subjects, the contents, and with the same patience with which he had shown me his engraved drawings.

His surprise appeared great as he told me he never had the remotest idea that any other individual had been engaged in forming such a collection. He asked me if it was my intention to publish. When I answered in the negative his surprise seemed to increase. And, truly, such was not my intention; for, until long after, when I met Charles Bonaparte, Prince of Musignano, in Philadelphia, I had not the least idea of presenting the fruits of my labors to the world.* Mr. Wilson examined my drawings with care, then asked if I would have any objections to lending him a few during his stay. I replied I had none. He bade me good morning—but not until after I had made arrangements to explore the woods in the vicinity along with him, and had promised him some birds—in my collection—which he had never seen before.

It happened that he also lodged at the Indian Queen, where I was living. His retired habits exhibited either, I thought, a strong discontent or a decided melancholy. The Scotch airs he played sweetly on his flute made me melancholy too, and I felt for him. I presented him to my wife and friends; and, seeing that he was all enthusiasm, exerted myself as much as was in my power. To procure the specimens he wanted, we hunted together for birds he had never seen before. But I did not subscribe to his work; for, even at that time, my collection was greater than his. Thinking that perhaps he might be pleased to publish the result of my researches I offered them to him, merely on condition that what I had drawn, or might afterwards draw and send to him, should be mentioned in his work as having come from my pencil. At the same time I offered to open a correspondence with him that might, I thought, prove beneficial to us both. He made no reply to either proposal. Before many days had passed he left Louisville on his way to New Orleans, little knowing how much his talents were appreciated in our little town, at least by myself and my friends.

Some time elapsed during which I never heard of him, or of his work. At length, in Philadelphia [in 1812], I inquired for him and paid him a visit. He was drawing a White-headed [Bald] Eagle. He received me with civility, and took me to the Exhibitions Rooms of Rembrandt Peale, the artist, to see *Napoleon Crossing the Alps.* Mr. Wilson spoke not a word of birds or drawings. Feeling, as I was forced to, that my company was not agreeable, I parted from him; and after that I never saw him again. But judge of my astonishment when, some time after, on reading the thirty-ninth page of Volume Nine of his *American Ornithology,* I found the following: *"March 23d, 1810 . . . I bade adieu to Louisville, to which place I had four letters of recommendation,*

---

* Not quite true. Audubon's journal of 1820 and much else point to a decision earlier than 1824.—*Ed.*

and was taught to expect much of everything there; but neither re-
ceived one act of civility from those to whom I was recommended, one
subscriber, nor one new bird; though I delivered my letters, ransacked
the woods repeatedly and visited all the characters likely to subscribe.
Science or literature has not one friend in this place."[12]

III

Louisville Years

M ERCHANTS crowded to Louisville from all our Eastern cities. None were intent on the study of birds, as I was, but all were deeply impressed with the value of dollars. Louisville did not give us up, but we gave up Louisville. I could not bear to give the attention required by my business—and therefore my business abandoned me. Indeed I never thought of it beyond the ever-engaging journeys to Philadelphia or New York to purchase goods, journeys I greatly enjoyed inasmuch as they afforded me ample chance to study birds and their habits as I travelled through the beautiful—the darling—forests of Ohio, Kentucky and Pennsylvania.

Were I to tell you that once, when travelling, and driving several horses before me laden with goods and dollars, I lost sight of the pack saddles and the cash they bore, in order to watch the motions of a warbler, I should only be repeating what happened a hundred times, and more, in those days. Very odd, but it is as true as that I am now scratching this poor book of mine with a miserable iron pen. Rozier and I became discouraged at Louisville. I longed to have a wilder range. We moved to Henderson, the former Red Bank, one hundred and twenty-five miles down the Ohio. We took the remainder of our stock there but found the country so very new, and so thinly populated, that the commonest goods only were called for. I may say our guns and fishing lines were the principal means of our support as regards food.

Nathaniel Wells Pope, our clerk, was a good shot and an excellent fisherman. He and I attended to the game and fish while Rozier again stood behind the counter.[13]

Although we well knew that three species of Catfish existed in the Ohio, all good, we were not sure as to the best method of securing them. To work on a large scale we made a trotline, an "engine" that I shall describe. The line is long and thick, according to the water and the fish. The Ohio is rather more than half a mile in breadth at Henderson. Catfish weigh from one to a hundred pounds, so we made a line about two hundred yards long, as thick as the little finger of some fair one yet in her teens, and as white as the damsel's finger well could be—of Kentucky cotton which stands water better than hemp or flax do. Then we made a hundred smaller ones, about five feet in length, to hold a capital hook.

It was the month of May. Nature had brought abroad myriads of living beings that covered the earth, glided through the water, and swarmed through the air. The voracious Catfish, not at all nice in feeding, contents himself, like the vulture, with carrion when nothing better can be had. Of the dainties with which we tried to lure them they showed a decided preference for *live toads*. These abundant animals ramble or feed, by instinct or reason, at twilight more than any other time, especially after a shower. They cannot bear the sun's rays during the hours before and after noon. Many "fine ladies" would no doubt have swooned, or at least screamed and gone into hysterics, had they seen one of our baskets filled with the toads, all alive and plump. Fortunately, we had no tragedy queen or senti-mental spinster at Henderson. Our Kentucky ladies minded their own affairs and seldom meddled beyond doing all they could for the comfort of others.

Now that the night is over, just watch us from that high bank beside the stream while we try our trotline. Under the large cotton-wood you are in no danger of catching cold at this season. Nat follows me with a gaff hook while I carry a canoe paddle. A boy bears on his back a hundred toads as good as ever hopped. Our trotline was set the night before; you see the small ones on my arm. We fasten one to a sycamore. With the rest nicely coiled in the stern of our canoe we paddle across to the opposite bank. There I throw a "sinker" over the side to weight the line and thoroughly soak it and avoid kinks and snarls. We launch our canoe. I have the basket of toads next to my feet in the bow and the small lines with looped ends across my knees. Nat paddles to keep the stern directly downstream with the aid of the current. The boy David fixes the living bait to the hook by the skin of the back and hind parts. I hold the main line all the while, and, after attaching one small line to it, drop the small one over. Can you see the poor toad kicking and flouncing in the water? No? Well, I do. Gradually all the lines are fixed, baited and dropped, one after the other.

More than once have I heard some knowing angler exclaim, "What a delightful thing is fishing!" With the patience of Job he stands or slowly moves along some rivulet with a sham fly to lure a trout, which, when finally caught, weighs half a pound. I never had such patience. Although in this year when I am writing—1836—I have waited nearly ten years to see only three-fourths of *The Birds of America* engraved—including drawings made as long ago as 1805—and although I must patiently wait two years more to see the end of it—I never could hold a line or rod for many minutes. If I did, I had to have, not a "nibble" but a hearty bite, before taking a fish I could throw over my head onto the ground. No, no—if I fish for Trout I must soon give up or catch fifty or more in a couple of hours, as in Pennsylvania's Lehigh, or in Maine waters.

But the trotline is in the river and there it may patiently wait until toward night. Meanwhile I take my gun and notebook and accompany my dog through the woods. Who knows, I may shoot a Turkey or a Deer. . . .

Evening returns. The heavens have already opened their twinkling eyes, although the orb of day has scarcely withdrawn. How calm is the air! The nocturnal insects and quadrupeds are abroad. The Bear moves through the canebrake. The Crows fly toward their roosts, their water brethren toward the interior of the forests. The Squirrel barks his adieu. The Barred Owl glides silently and swiftly from his retreat to seize upon the gay and noisy animal. We push off. I seize the main line. It shakes as if some fish have been hooked. I proceed, hand over hand, to the first hook. Nothing there! I feel several jerks, stronger and more frequent than before. I pass several hooks, then spy a fine Catfish twisting round and round a little line to which he is held fast. I tell Nat to look to his gaff and hook him close to the tail until we have him. When we reach the end, many goodly fishes are lying in the bottom of our boat . . . enough for ourselves and our neighbors. New bait is put on before we turn home, for another day's catch.

In those days a trotline could be left for weeks at a time with perfect safety. Navigation was mostly by flat-bottomed boats that kept to the middle current on calm nights, so that people on board could not observe the fish that had been hooked. Not a single steamer, in those days, had yet gone down the Ohio. Now and then a barge or keelboat propelled by poles and oars passed, it is true. But there the boats had to keep near the Indiana shore when ascending, until they were above the village landing where they pulled across to Henderson. (I always fixed my lines below it.)

The Mud Cat is best, if, usually, smallest. The Blue Cat is coarsest but, if four to six pounds, tolerable eating. The White Cat is preferable but less common. The Yellow Mud Cat is best and rarest. Blue Cats, known to weigh a hundred pounds sometimes, are looked on as monsters when so large. The form of all inclines to the conical, with disproportionately large head; body tapering to the tail root; eyes small, far apart, and placed at the top of the forehead, laterally; mouth wide, teeth small and very sharp; spines which stand out at right angles, when the fish is in the agonies of death, and so firmly fixed as sometimes to break before they are loosened. Feelers of proportionate length, are apparently for guiding it over the bottom of streams while it watches objects passing above.

Trotlines go best in waters of middle depth, because, when they are low, they are too clearly visible for even the extremely voracious to risk its life for a toad. And if the waters rise rapidly the lines may be carried away by a floating branch. The "happy medium" is best. A single line, twenty or thirty feet long, is used when waters rise fast and become muddy. One fastens it to the supple branch of some willow several feet above the water. Wild Turkey entrails, or a piece of fresh venison, furnish good bait. If when you visit your line next morning the water has not risen too much, the swinging of the willow indicates the prize that you have only to haul ashore.

One evening I saw the river was rising at a great rate, though still within the banks. The White Perch were running . . . ascending from the sea. Anxious for a taste of that fine fish, I baited a line with a Crayfish and fastened it to a bough of a tree. Next morning the line felt as if caught at the bottom, but slowly it came as I drew it. A strong pull, and the line slipped through my fingers. A large Catfish leaped out of the water. I played it until it became exhausted. It had swallowed the hook, so that I had to cut the line close to its head before passing a stick through one of its gills. My servant and I tugged it home. There, to our surprise, we found a fine White Perch, still perfect, in its stomach. The Perch had been lightly hooked, and because the Catfish had swallowed it and become hooked in the stomach, the torture doubtless disabled the captor. We divided the Catfish among four neighbors and ate the Perch. My relative Nicholas Berthoud once caught a remarkably fine Catfish at the Falls of the Ohio, and in it he found the greater part of a suckling pig. (A Catfish appears in my portrait of the White-headed Eagle, Plate *XXXI, The Birds of America.*)[14]

No sooner had the freshets of spring subsided, and the air turned pleasant, and the trees of our woods budded and blossomed than the White Perch rushed back up from the ocean to haunts where it had deposited its spawn the year before. Vigorously, it ascended the turbulent Mississippi current, too muddy, however to suit it; and then it entered one of the countless, pure and delightful tributaries. Easily it progressed through shoals along the banks, and over many a pebbly or gravelly bar where Mussels were due to be crunched and devoured. The Perch darted to overtake minnows, with the speed of an arrow, or to catch Crayfish beside stones or under some rocky ledge. No impure food will the "Growler" touch.

Watch the fishermen, excellent anglers, on the shore of a stream that seldom exceeds a mile an hour. Silence reigns under clear skies and along the smooth waters. Each angler has a basket or calabash holding live Crayfish. Each line, as thick as a crow-quill, measures scarcely a furlong. Two hooks are fastened so as not to tangle. A few inches below the hook is a quarter-pound sinker, bored through its length and passed upon the line with knots to secure it. The other end of the line is fastened on shore. Notice the neat coil of tackle at the fisherman's feet. He fixes a Crayfish on each hook, piercing the shell beneath the tail, and up to the head, but leaving all legs free. Taking his line in hand a yard or so from the hooks he whirls it overhead then sends it off to its full length across the stream. The current rolls it over and over in its gravelly bed until it is nearly in the line of the water. After a bite, a short jerk hooks the fish and the line is hauled in, hand over hand. Poor Perch, useless for thee to flounce and splash in that manner . . . thou shalt be left to quiver in the sand.

I see some of the lines have been robbed by cunning inhabitants of the water. What beautiful Perches, these! . . . so silvery beneath, so deeply colored above! What a fine eye, too! In places above Louisville on the Ohio, fishermen prefer the trotline, for White Perch, placed on or just above the river bottom, with Mussels for bait because these are more plentiful. Many are caught in seines, especially during a rise. The preference of the fish for the edge of sandbars beside deep water limits pole fishing.

Like others of its tribe the White Perch deposits its spawn on gravelly or sandy beds in water four or five feet deep. The round beds have a curb formed of sand from their center. The fish remains over its treasure for some days but will start off at the least sign of danger. I have floated over their beds and noticed that the very sight of the boat's shadow drove them off. I think most return to the sea about the beginning of November but am not certain. Ohio's White Perch is called the "Growler" in New York. It may be fifteen to twenty inches, its weight from one and a half to six pounds. During the first six weeks of their arrival the flesh is white, firm and excellent to eat, but during summer they are seldom good. I have eaten them late in September when they were as tasty as in spring. When poised close to the bottom of a quiet boat it emits a rough, croaking groan, seldom heard except in fine calm weather. It takes the hook with care, and, very often, the bait without being caught. If not hooked at the first touch it is rarely caught. I have seen young hands at the game, catch no more than one or two of a morning, although they lost perhaps twenty Crays.

The Cray is certainly not a fish, but a handsome crustaceous animal, one whose tribe I consider as dainties of the first order, above all when stripped of its coat and blended in "gumbo." Boiled or roasted, too, they are excellent in my estimation, and mayhap in yours. I speak here of the Crayfish. (I shall not deprive it of its caudal appendage lest like a basha [military insignia] without his tail it seem of less consequence.) It swims or crawls in abundant numbers, or works at muddy burrows. The best inhabit rocky streamlets. It swims by means of rapid strokes of the tail which propels it backwards. They are absolutely, I regret to say, little aquatic Vultures, and feed on everything impure that comes their way when unable to obtain pure aliment. However that may be, Crays somehow fall in with this sort of food. A line baited with flesh and retrieved from the water with the aid of a hand-net is a good way to catch those that live in running waters. The lively, light olive, delicately formed species hide beneath shelf rock, stones or water plants. The larger, dark greenish-brown, less active ones, less truly amphibious, burrow in damp earth like welldiggers. You may note how they dispose of mud, by glancing at my portrait of the *White Ibis*. The kind of ground determines the depth of the burrows. Where the Cray can reach water after a few inches, it rests contented by day, but it crawls out to feed by night. Otherwise it may burrow down five or six inches, or even two or three feet or more. Those in shallow holes are easily taken. As for the others, a baited thread is dropped down for them to seize eagerly and be gently drawn up, and thrown a distance before being retrieved. I leave you to judge whether the White Ibis or man is the better fisher for Crays. They earn many maledictions from millers and planters, nay even from overseers of the Mississippi levees, for perforating embankments. Created no doubt for useful purposes, the curious creatures are worthy of your notice.[15]

Few of our smaller freshwater fishes surpass the American Sun Perch in beauty or delicacy of flavor. But you must expect to find it in pure waters either rapid or gentle, small or large, deep or shallow . . . such as a tree-shaded mill dam or reed-bordered lake. But it must be clear enough for the sun to glisten on the rich "mail" of the surface of the water.

Look at him as he lies poised under the lee of the rock beneath our feet! How steadily he maintains his position, yet with how many motions of his fins! Another, glowing with equal beauty, is now at his side and equally easy and graceful of movement. The little creatures rise to the surface to enjoy the bright rays which enhance their beauty. Their golden and emerald green blend with their coral lower parts and red sparkling eye, rendering themselves, our little favorites, a perfect gem of the waters.

The rushing stream boils, gurgles, forces its way over the craggy, stony bed and logs strewn along the bottom. Every obstacle proves a place of rest, safety and observation to the little things whose eyes are ever on the lookout for favorite prey. An unfortunate moth that is swept along by the current labors in vain to save itself. Its body rises a little but its broad wings, wet and heavy, bear it down again as the Sunfish darts towards it with twenty of his fellows, the swiftest of whom swallows it in a moment. All return to their lurking places where they fancy themselves secure. Alas, the Sunfish is no more without enemies than the moth or any other living creature. Nature has thus determined —to promote prudence and industry with which to reap life to the full.

On the dam of the miller the ardent fisherman stands boldly erect, up to the knees, regardless of the danger. He prepares his apparatus of destruction, a keen hook hidden within a worm or grasshopper at the end of his grass-line. Knowingly he eyes every surge below, then sends his hook towards a protruding rock with gentle assurance. The bait floats then sinks. He slowly reels out his line until he feels it tighten. He feels a fish at its end. The reel again whirls as the fish spends its strength at full speed until, panting and exhausted, it floats on the surface for a moment. It is brought to hand, and again the angler sends forth a treacherous morsel. After an hour or more a hundred "sunnies" are attached to the willow twig fastened to his waist. With a different hook and bait he might catch a fine Eel or two; but, seeing the suddenly overcast sky, he wades carefully to shore and plods his homeward way. A beautiful sight it is to see the ease and grace of such "scientific" anglers.

However, thousands of fishermen, like some boys I see on shore, catch as many "sunnies," without allowing them to play a moment. Their rods are hazel or hickory shoots, their lines simple twine, and their hooks none of the finest. One has a calabash filled with worms and grubs kept alive in damp earth, another a bottle of live grasshoppers. A third borrows from the others. The "three merry boys" whirl their rods to unroll their lines, on one of which a cork is fastened, while on another is a bit of wood, and on the third a grain or two of large shot to draw it down. They have already probed the depth to decide the best point. Bob, bob, goes the cork! The bit of wood disappears. The leaded line tightens. In a moment up swing the "sunnies." Unhooked, they soon struggle on the grass where they are tossed.

On such an October day dozens of the fish will dash at the same bait. The lads have rare sport. In an hour scarcely a fish remains in the hole. The happy children have caught perhaps some hundreds of delicious "pan fish" to feed their parents and delight their little sisters. Their pleasure is fully as great, surely, as that of the scientific angler.

For some reason better known to the miller than to myself, all the Sunfish betake themselves to one or two deep holes when the waters are let out, as if to keep to their favorite abode. I have seen them there in such multitudes that anyone with a pinhook and any sort of line or bait could catch as many as he pleased. All of a sudden, without apparent cause—and I am unable to account for it—they and the other fishes in the pool will cease to take any allurement whatever from the hook.

The species seldom bites during high freshets but may be taken with a cast-net or seine by those who know their haunts. But when the waters are low and clear every secluded hole, every eddy under the lee of a rock, every place sheltered by a raft of timber will afford amusement. In the South the Negroes wade in shallow ponds or bayous late in autumn with a barrel-shaped wicker apparatus open at both ends. This is pressed to the bottom of the stream for the catch. The fish may be six inches or so in length, and two or so wide. It is not bony, and at all seasons proves delicate fare. Its color varies in different parts of the United States, from olive-brown, to reddish, to coppery, or, sometimes, to the pale and sallow.

The Sun Perch, or Sunfish, prefers sandy, gravelly or rocky beds of clear streams, especially when depositing eggs. The little creature is then seen swimming rapidly over shallows. It hesitates, then sinks to the bottom. There it pushes aside the sand with its fin until it has formed a circular cavity of eight or ten inches, to hold the roe. A person may count forty, fifty or more such beds if he wades out with care . . . some apart, some within feet of each other. It does not abandon its spawn but keeps guard over it with all the care of a sitting bird, watching the environs from above the bed. Should a rotten leaf, piece of wood, or any other substance disturb the border, the Sunfish carefully removes the obnoxious matter with its mouth.

Having many times witnessed this act of prudence and cleanliness in the little "sunny," who will not seize bait at this period, I took it into my head one fair afternoon to experiment a bit. I wished to judge how far its instinct or reason might induce action if it were disturbed or harassed. I took a fine line and some insects to a sandbar covered by about a foot of water where I had seen deposits. Leaving the greatest part of a live earthworm to writhe from my hook I threw the line upstream over the border of the nest, then let it remain on the bottom. The fish, I noticed, had seen me, and it swam to the farther side of the nest. It poised there, then approached the worm that had intruded on its premises, and carried it in its mouth over the edge next to me with a care and gentleness so very remarkable as to amaze me. I repeated the experiment six or seven times—always with the same result. Next I tried floating a young grasshopper into the egg-bed. It was removed, as the worm had been. I now threw a bare hook. The "sunny," quite alarmed, swam rapidly to one side then another, evidently afraid that the removal of the suspicious object might prove extremely dangerous. Yet it gradually approached the hook, took it delicately up, and the next instant dropped it over the edge of the bed!

If, like me, you are one who has studied Nature with a desire to improve your mental faculties, and contemplate the wonderful phenomena to be seen at every step in her wide domain, you would have been struck by the action of this little fish, and with admiration for the

Being who gave such instincts to so humble an object. I gazed in amazement on the little creature endowed by Nature with such feelings and powers. The irrepressible desire for knowledge prompted me to continue the experiment. But not all the dexterity I could bring to the hooking of a fish, in those days, rendered my efforts other than abortive . . . not with this individual only, but many others which I subjected to the same trials. Satisfied that this Sunfish was more than a match for me, I rolled up my line, and with my rod rapped the water as nearly over the fish as I could. The "sunny" darted off several yards, poised steadily, and as soon as my rod left the water returned to its station. Busily it smoothed the bed again. Here my experiment ended.[16]

While collecting Crayfish on one of those flats that border and divide Green River near its junction with the Ohio, I observed some signs that I took for Owls on a range of high cliffs. But my companion stoutly maintained that Eagles and not Owls nested there, and that he had seen one of the old birds dive and catch a fish some days before.

In high expectation I seated myself about a hundred yards from the foot of the rock. Never did time pass more slowly. I could not help betraying the most impatient curiosity, for my hopes whispered that this was an Eagle's nest. Two long hours elapsed before the old bird's arrival was announced by the loud hissing of two young ones which crawled to the edge of the hole to receive a fine fish. I had a perfect view of the noble bird as he held himself to the edging rock, hanging like the Swallow, with tail spread and wings partly so. I trembled, lest a word escape my companion's lips. The slightest murmur would have been treason despite his own comparative disinterest. He only gazed towards me sympathetically.

In a few minutes the other parent joined her mate. The mother, larger than the male, had also brought a fish. But, more cautious than her mate, she glanced around with piercing eye and instantly perceived that her abode had been discovered. She dropped her prey with a loud shriek to the male, and together they hovered over our heads and kept up a growling cry to intimidate us and foil our suspected designs. This watchful solicitude I have ever found peculiar to the female. (*Must I be understood to speak, here, only of birds?*) The young had meanwhile concealed themselves.

We picked up the fish that the mother had let fall, a White Perch of about five and a half pounds, its head broken in, and its back torn by the talons of the Eagle which she had borne the way that the Fish Hawk does.

This day's sport being at an end we agreed to return next morning to obtain both the old and young Eagles. Tempestuous weather delayed the expedition until the third day. Some of the men posted themselves at the foot of the rock, others on it. We passed the entire day in readiness, but in vain, without either seeing or hearing an Eagle. No doubt having anticipated an invasion, the pair had removed their young to new quarters.

Two years went by, before the opportunity so often and so ardently desired. I was travelling from Henderson to my friend Dr. Rankin's Meadow Brook farm, near the village, when I saw an Eagle rise from a small enclosure not a hundred yards away, where the Doctor had slaughtered some hogs a few days before. It alighted on a low branch over the road. I prepared my double-barrelled piece that I constantly carried and cautiously approached. Quite fearlessly he watched me, undaunted. I fired and he fell, and before I reached him he was dead. With what delight did I survey the magnificent bird! Had the finest Salmon ever pleased him as he did me? Never. I ran to present him to my friend the Doctor, and with such pride as only those know who have devoted themselves from earliest childhood to such pursuits, and as those who ever derive their truest pleasures thus, can feel. (To all others I must seem to "prattle out of fashion.") The Doctor, an experienced hunter, examined the Eagle with much satisfaction and acknowledged that it was new to him.

The name I have chosen for this Eagle, "The Bird of Washington," may be considered preposterous and unfit by some.* But as it is indisputably the noblest of its genus that has yet been discovered in the United States, I trust I shall be allowed to honor it with the name of one yet nobler, the saviour of his country. . . . As the new world gave me birth and liberty, the great man who insured its independence is next to my heart. Such nobility of mind, generosity of soul, are seldom possessed. Like the Eagle he was brave . . . the terror of his foes. His fame, extending from pole to pole, resembles the majestic soarings of the mightiest of the feathered tribe. If America has reason to be proud of her Washington, so has she to be proud of her great Eagle.[17]

The Bald Eagle has the power to seize and lift any floating object

* It was; this was the immature Bald Eagle.—*Ed.*

not heavier than itself. Its audacity is quite remarkable. Once on the Upper Mississippi I saw one pursue a Green-winged Teal—so close to me that I could see the gleam in its eye. The Teal was saved when one of our guns winged the Eagle. We took it on board, tied it with string to the deck, and fed it Catfish pieces which it ate only after nearly three days of confinement. A very disagreeable and dangerous associate, it was forever trying to strike someone with its talons, and had to be killed and thrown overboard.

When surprised and approached suddenly, it exhibits great cowardice, and then flies off in zigzag lines, as it hisses with a sound that is not at all like its usual, disagreeable imitation laugh. It is very wary of persons with guns. Its sight, although probably as perfect as that of any bird, is much affected by snowfall. I grieve that it should have been selected as the emblem of my country, and agree with Franklin that it is a "bird of bad moral character." Besides it is a rank coward. The little King Bird attacks it boldly and drives it out of the district. The Bald Eagle is therefore not a proper emblem for the brave and honest Cincinnati of America, all officers of the Continental Army, who drove out all the British "King Birds" from our country although these are perfectly suited to represent those French knights called *Chevaliers d'Industrie*.[18]

Once, as I made my way through the magnificent woods of the undulating Green River country of Kentucky, night overtook me. A little doubtful as to my course, I proceeded slowly and cautiously by the friendly light of the moon. The air seemed unusually keen; and the wind in the treetops made me think of halting to camp for the night. The strange adventures of Daniel Boone in these very woods, and his extraordinary walk to save those at Fort Massacre from scalping, kept passing through my mind.

Now and then a Racoon or Opossum, rustling the fallen leaves, made me pause for a moment. In short, I was thinking of many things, both dismal and pleasing, until the glimmer of a distant fire broke upon my reveries. As I drew nearer I could see figures moving to and fro like spectres. Pretty soon I heard bursts of laughter, shouts, and songs of merrymaking. I thought I was stumbling across a camp meeting, at first, but soon saw that the mirth came from a band of sugar-makers.

Every man, woman and child stared as I passed them, but all

were friendly. Without much ceremony I walked up to the fire
where two or three old women and their husbands were attending
to the kettles. The plain dresses of Kentucky homespun were a far
more pleasing sight, to me, than ribboned turbans of the city dame
of the powdered wigs would be, to say nothing of the embroidered
waistcoats of antique beaux. I was heartily welcomed with a serving
of good pone bread, a plate of molasses and some sweet potatoes.

Fatigued by my long ramble, I lay down under the lee of the
smoke and fell sound asleep.

Frost lay heavy in the morning, but the campers, cheerful and
envigorated, prepared for work. The place was pleasing and had
been cleared of underbrush. Several brooklets meandered among the
tall straight maples that seemed as if planted in rows. The sun began
to melt the frozen dews. Some feathered songsters joined in the chorus
of the woodsmen's daughters. As often as a burst of laughter echoed
through the woods an Owl or Wild Turkey responded with a sound
that was very welcome to the young men of the party. With large
ladles, the sugar-makers began to stir the thickening juice of the
maple. They collected pails of sap from the trees. Some hacked cuts
in the trees then bored a hole with an auger, for a piece of hollow
cane to drain off the sap into the pails.

Half a dozen men felled a fine yellow poplar, sawed its big trunk
into many pieces, and split them to make troughs to go beneath the
cane-corks.

These maple grounds, in January or March, or those on the
broader Monongahela in April, are well worth a visit. Whether the
visitor be on foot or horseback (and thirsty) he can find no beverage
more agreeable or wholesome than the juice of the maple. A man
may drink molasses and water in the Floridas, or whatever he can
get in Labrador; and in New York and Philadelphia he drinks what he
chooses. But in the woods a draught from the sugar maple is delicious
and most refreshing. How often have I quenched my thirst with the
limpid juice of these troughs, then moved on with regret! Even my
horse, I have thought, would have preferred to linger.

The sugar is obtained in a certain way. The trees that yield it
are abundant in all parts of the Union from Maine to Louisiana.
They grow on high rich ground. The incision is made at a height
of from two to six feet. The pipe down which the juice trickles
need not be of cane. The juice is as limpid as the purest spring
water. When the tapping is over and the troughs are filled the sugar-

makers fill large vessels (iron boilers on stone or brick supports). Several families may join in the labor that goes on for several weeks. The troughs and kettles must be attended to from the moment they are placed on the fire until the sugar is produced. Men and boys perform the heavy tasks, but women and girls are no less busy.

Ten gallons of sap are needed to produce one pound of fine sugar. But an inferior, lumpy cake-sugar is obtained in greater quantity. Towards the close of the season the juice will no longer grain by boiling and only produces syrup. I have seen maple sugar so good that it resembled candy some months after it was manufactured. Well do I remember the time when it was an article of commerce through Kentucky. Around 1810 or so it brought from 6½¢ to 12½¢ per pound, according to quality, over my own counter.

Maples that have been bored rarely last many years. Their health is injured by the cuts and perforations. After some years of "weeping" they become sickly, exhibit growths near the ground, gradually decay and die. I have no doubt, however, that with proper care the same quantity of sap might be obtained with less damage to the trees. And it is high time the farmers and land owners looked to preserving their sugar maples.[19]

On a journey from Louisville to Henderson in Kentucky in very severe winter weather, my companion, a foreigner, spied a beautiful black and pale yellow animal with a bushy tail. "Mr. Audubon, is not that a beautiful Squirrel?" he exclaimed.

"Yes," I answered, "and of a kind that will let you approach and lay hold of it if you are well gloved."

Mr. D.T. dismounted, took up a dry stick and with his large cloak floating in the breeze advanced on the pretty animal, laid the stick gently across its body, and thought to catch it. I can still laugh almost as heartily as I did then when I recall his discomfiture. The Polecat, for such it was, raised its fine tail and let fire with a weapon of defense given him by Nature. My dismayed and infuriated friend began to belabor the poor animal, whose swiftness and good management spared its bones and sped it towards its hole, while at every step it ejected fluid. This fully convinced the gentleman that pursuit of such "Squirrels" was at best unprofitable employment.

This was not all, however. I could not stand to have him approach, nor could my horse. It was with difficulty that he mounted his own.

We had to continue our journey far apart—he much to leeward. Nor did the matter end there. We could not go much farther that night, because in the first place it was nearly dark when we saw the Polecat, and in the second, a heavy snowstorm began. We had to make for the first cabin we saw. After asking permission to rest there for the night, we dismounted and found ourselves in the midst of a *corn-shucking* gathering.

To explain, corn is gathered in the husk by breaking each large ear from the stem. These are heaped in the field, then carted to the barn, or, in Kentucky, to a shed made of dried corn leaves that are also used to feed livestock. The leaves of the husk protect the ear of corn from the weather. It is quite a chore to husk the leaves of thousands of bushels. Families take turns helping one another.

We found the good people at this hospitable house about to go to the barn to work until well towards midnight. When we had stood the staring that strangers must get used to, no matter where—even in a drawing room—we approached the fire. What a shock for the whole party! The cold evening air had almost stifled the Polecat scent of my companion's vestments. But now it recovered its primitive strength. Although the cloak was put out of the house, its owner could not very well be treated in such a way. Everybody took to their heels, leaving only the black servant who waited on us until supper was served.

I felt vexed with myself as I saw my friend's displeasure. But he was too well bred merely to dismiss the matter, and said he was sorry for his ignorance of zoology. The good gentleman was not only deficient in zoological lore but fresh from Europe and uneasy in this out-of-the-way place. He would have continued on his way to my own house had I not at last managed to persuade him that he need fear no further indignities.

As we were almost total strangers to each other he at first thought it a very awkward thing to be obliged to lie in the same bed with me, but then he spoke of it as a happy circumstance. He asked to sleep on the inside, next to the log wall, and presumably away from any more risk from Polecats.

We started away by daybreak, taking the frozen cloak along.

Some years later, in a distant land, I met my former companion once more. He assured me that whenever the sun shone on his cloak, or it was brought near a fire, the scent of the Polecat became so noticeable that finally he turned it over to a poor monk in Italy.

The Polecat, common in America, burrows among tree roots or in rocky places, feeds on birds, young hares, rats, mice and the like, and commits great depredations on poultry. Its most remarkable peculiarity is its power, as we have noted, of defense . . . even from a distance of several yards. Yet unless extremely harassed by its enemies it does not spray its own tail. If the glands are removed, the Polecat may become a great domestic favorite, and with great dexterity render the same services as the common cat.[20]

IV
Journeys of Adventure

M<small>Y</small> wife and I were as happy as could be. The people of the Henderson neighborhood loved us, and we loved them in return. Profits were enormous but sales small. My partner Rozier, who spoke English badly, suggested that we move on to the French community of Ste. Genevieve on the Mississippi. I agreed, but decided to leave my wife and our son Victor at Henderson, because I was not quite sure that our adventure would succeed as we hoped. I placed her and the child under the care of Dr. Adam Rankin and wife of Meadow Brook, a fine farm about three miles from town.[21]

My partner, young Pope the Clerk, the crewmen, and I left Henderson in a heavy, late December snowstorm in the year 1810. Our keelboat was open to the elements except for its covered stern that served as a cabin. It was about sixty feet long, guided by a steering oar, and propelled by four oars in the bow for a speed of about five miles an hour when going with the current. Except for some cane grasses and a few dingy grape leaves on dead vines, the Ohio's banks were barren and very dreary.

Our first night was indeed a dismal one. But the storm ceased by daylight. We found ourselves opposite the Cumberland's mouth, where the Ohio River widens and becomes a truly magnificent stream bordered by vast trees. Beyond the mouth of the Tennessee River, a severe and sudden frost had closed the neighboring lakes and lagoons. Thousands of water fowl were flying over, and whenever large flocks approached us we shot a great number.

About the third day out we entered Cash Creek, a very small stream. Here I met a French artist, Jules De Mun, also bound for Ste. Genevieve. We learned that the Mississippi was covered by thick ice and impossible to ascend. Cash Creek (now the flourishing town of Trinity), located about six miles above the confluence of the Ohio and Mississippi, flows from some hills (north of its mouth) which are covered with oak, sumac and locust. Between it and the junction are walnut, ash, and pecan in rich alluvial soil, along with some tangled cane and nettles. Now high, it abounded in fish and attracted innumerable Ducks driven south by winter from the Polar regions. The large sycamores contrasted with the cane beneath them. Thousands of Carolina Parrots* roosted in their trunks. About fifty Shawanee Indian families camped here to harvest the pecans, and hunt Deer, Bear, and Racoon. I knew a few words of their language and they spoke French passably. As soon as they learned of my anxiety for natural history curiosities after crowding round me, they all—even the squaws—set traps. They expressed gratitude for a knife, scissors, and the like as gracefully as the most educated female would have done.

All day my friend and partner Rozier—neither hunter nor naturalist —sat in the boat, brooding in gloomy silence over the delay. The Count hunted a great deal and was as unperturbed by the weather as I was. Here we were, in any case . . . forced to await the thaw. Next morning I noticed that half a dozen squaws and their braves were about to paddle across to the Tennessee side to hunt. A large lake to which immense flocks of Swans resorted each morning was their object. Incredible as it may seem, the Swans keep such lakes open by swimming night and day. I asked to go along, seated myself in the canoe, and was not much astonished to see the paddling done by the squaws while the hunters slept.

The squaws made the canoe fast and went off for pecans, while the *gentlemen* made off for the lake through the cottonwoods and thickets.

What a feast for the sportsman! There they lie, by the hundreds, the rich creamy white Swans, dipping their bills, arching their necks backward, resting with one leg outstretched, and floating and basking in the sunshine. At the sight of us they started up, but the Indians knew how to make every shot tell, from behind the trees, as the Swans flew off toward another little band of hunters waiting with rifles. At least fifty were brought down by the time the conch-shell horn was blown for the squaws to come and collect the game, bring it to the river's edge, and paddle us back to camp.

Pecans and Bear's fat were passed about beside the fire, before each brave stretched out, with his feet towards the embers for the

* Extinct.—*Ed.*

night. The squaws skinned the birds of their beautiful feathers intended for the ladies of Europe. Well satisfied with this Christmas Day, I watched them a while then retired to rest.

A squaw gave birth to beautiful twins in the night. I woke to see her tan a Deer skin, cut vines, form a bark cradle, and begin to swing the infants by a gentle push of the hand. From time to time she gave them the breast, and to all appearances seemed as unconcerned as if nothing had taken place. How different from the lady of fashion!

One tall robust Indian assured us that he would have some good sport that day with a Bear that he wished to combat alone. We went to watch. Half a mile from camp he saw tracks when I myself saw nothing. Beyond the canebrake we came to a decaying log of immense size in which he said the Bear was hiding. His eyes sparkled with joy as he threw his blanket from his shoulders. His brawny arms swelled and the veins dilated. He drew his knife with a fantastic gesture that plainly declared *la guerre à l'outrance*. (War to the death.) He ordered me to climb a tree too delicate to support the Bear if it chose to pursue me. The other Indians stood at the entrance of the hollow log which the hero entered with resolute determination. All was still for a few minutes. Then he emerged, said the Bear was slain, and that I could safely descend. With our united strength we all drew the Bear out by a long vine. In such confinement the Bear offers no resistance, but retires farther and farther back until killed. An Indian broke twigs along our way back, to guide the squaws to the animal; then they brought back its flesh and skin.

One morning, after the pecans were gathered and the game had grown scarce, the Indians put off in their canoes towards the Arkansas. Also anxious to move on, I set out with two others on foot and I found the ice much sunk in the Mississippi. Finally we reached Cape Girardeau. After loudly calling for a boat for some time we saw a canoe put off from the opposite shore. A stout swarthy man who said he was the son of Lorimié, the one-time Spanish governor of Louisiana, leaped ashore. He and his six men agreed to bring our boat up the stream. The pilot hauled his canoe into the woods, and back we went to Cash Creek in about a third of the time that it took to come, and ten times more comfortably.

We made tow ropes of bullock's hide, cut good oars, and by daylight left Cash Creek for wider waters. Going downstream was fine sport. My partner fancied himself near the end of the journey. But alas!—when we began to ascend the Mississippi we had to stem a current at three miles an hour through sunken ice. The pilot—or pa-troon—ordered all ashore to tow the boat by a rope fastened in the bow while one man steered. We advanced only seven miles up the Mississippi that day. At dusk we pitched camp on the bank, built a tremendous fire, ate and drank like men who had worked hard, and fell asleep. Two hours before daybreak we started, but we could make only about a mile an hour against the current. Contrary winds made our sail useless. After two more days of such camping and toil with little progress, the patroon declared the frost too severe for us to do other than put up at the bend of Tawapatee Bottom until the thaws.

What a place for winter quarters! Not a cabin within twenty miles on the far bank, and none within fifty or more on our own. We cut trees and built a cabin. Soon I knew all the Indian passes and lakes in the neighborhood. As quickly as vultures find a dead Deer the Osages and Shawanees, by some intuitive faculty, discovered our camp. Several Osage bands camped near us to hunt the few Elk and Buffalo remaining in the region; but they kept apart from the others. Un-fortunately, they spoke no French and only a little English, so that I could hardly get acquainted. They were delighted to see me draw, and when I made a tolerable portrait of one in red chalk, the others—to my astonishment—laughed to excess. They bore the cold better than the Shawanees and were abler with bow and arrow.

Nat Pope and I chased Wolves at night. The beasts prowled on the river ice, crossing to and fro, howling, and sneaking about the camp for bones.

I studied the habits of the Wild Turkey, Bear, Cougar, Racoon and many others. I drew, more or less, every day beside our fire. Our axemen tumbled down four or five towering ash trees three feet in diameter, cut them into ten-foot logs for a heap several feet high, kindled brushwood on top with flint and steel, and sent up a flame that would roast a man at five paces. Under the smoke of the fire the party slept in safety. One raw night Rozier also slept on shore, instead of in the cold cabin; unfortunately, he drew himself so near the fire that he had one of his sideburns singed away. We all laughed, but it was no joke to him; ruefully he shaved off what was left next morning.

After six weeks our stocks of bread ran low. We were soon tired of Wild Turkey for bread and of Bear oil instead of red meat, and also of Racoon and Opossum no matter how tender. Nat and I crossed the bend in search of Indians with cornmeal. We shot a Deer, hung it on a tree, marked the place well, and went on until nearly dark, but no river did we see. Suddenly we struck Indian tracks that would lead us, we hoped, to the Mississippi. Then *many foot-tracks* began to confuse us. At length we arrived—at our own camp! The boatmen laughed and the Indians joined in the chorus. We ate Racoon again for supper.

What had happened is no uncommon occurrence. Once I went hunting for Ducks in winter no great distance from Henderson. As I entered the woods again toward dusk, well laden with birds, it began to snow. To hurry, I left half my game beside a tree. I was no longer able to see my way through the snowfall but kept on, as I thought, in a straight line, until, after about two hours of smart walking, I came back to my Ducks, mistook them for another hunter's, and moved on. In about an hour, to my disagreeable surprise, I came upon the Ducks again, and finally saw that I had been circling back to them, as if by magic. It was useless to attempt reaching home by morning. I lighted a fire, scooped out the snow to form a very good nest, and spent the night comfortably beside my Ducks. With daylight I reached home in about half an hour, having been only three miles away.

Next time Nat and I set out we pushed straight on to Cape Girardeau. On reaching there around sunset we called in vain for a boat. None dared enter the swiftly running ice floes. We spent the night in a deserted hut and our meal was mostly pumpkin that had withstood the frost. Boards of the abandoned house fed our fire, along with some broken branches. I gained more information that night about the roosting of the Prairie Hen than I had ever done before. So frozen over were the branches by morning that the Wild Turkeys, quite dazzled by the glitter of the trees, preferred the ground. Some Indians paddled towards us and let us barter for a barrel of flour, several large loaves and a bag of cornmeal. We impaled the loaves on our gun barrels and left the rest in a tree, for our crewmen to fetch to camp by sled over the snow.

The river had now begun to subside. In order to keep our boat afloat we unloaded our cargo, and the squaws helped stash it away from the weather. We cut trees and framed a jetty a trifle higher than the stream to ward off the fast-accumulating ice.

Now fairly settled we spent our time very merrily, until the surrounding trees began to look like butcher stalls. The lakes abounded in fish. We would walk on the ice, deal it a blow of our axe and kill a Catfish beneath before drawing it out. Other times we cut fishing holes and shot at surfacing fish. The squaws tanned Deer hides, stretched those of Otter and Racoon, wove cane baskets. Nat and I played the fiddle, and I had a flute. The squaws laughed heartily at the dancers and our merriment. The Indian hunters sat on the outer ring and smoked their tomahawks with serenity such as no white man ever displayed at a social gathering.

After six weeks the river fell swiftly. A channel began to appear amid the ice. All was bustle as we prepared to depart for Cape Girardeau. We and the Indians parted like brethren. Navigation was most dangerous, as we propelled the boat against the ice with long poles, or against the bottom wherever we could touch it. With the ice higher than our heads our progress was extremely slow. Fortune was with us, and we reached the Cape.

The little village contained nothing remarkable or interesting except the father of our patroon, an original indeed, and a representative of a class of men fast disappearing from the earth. His portrait is so striking and well worth preserving that I shall try to draw it for you:

Imagine a man not more than four feet six, thin in proportion, looking as if just shot out of a pop-gun. His nose formed, decidedly, the most prominent feature of his spare, meager countenance. It was a true *nez à la Grand Frédéric*—a tremendous promontory fully three inches in length—hooked like a Hawk's beak and garnished with eyes like an Eagle's. His hair was plastered down close to his head with a quantity of pomatum; it ended in a long *queue* rolled up in a dirty ribbon that hung down below his waist. The upper part of his dress was European, once rich but now woefully patched and dilapidated, with shreds of gold and silver lace here and there. The fashion of his waistcoat, as antique as that of his nose, had immense pocket flaps that covered more than half his tight buckskin trousers that were ornamented with big, iron knee-buckles, to support Indian hunting gaiters long past their prime. His moccasins, to complete his costume, were really of the most beautiful workmanship. Though these articles of dress, along with his stature and singular features, made him the most ludicrous caricature imaginable, his manners were courteous and polished. He said he had been Louisiana governor when it was a Spanish possession.* Since his retirement to this little village he had come to be looked upon as a great General and was held in highest esteem.

We proceeded to Grand Tower, and round its immense rock against

* Actually, Spanish territorial agent.—*Ed.*

which the current crashed, without mishap. All night we heard the howling of Wolves from the hills of the Illinois shore. I thought them hunting Deer in packs, like dogs, but with more sagacity and cunning. They drive the game before them toward Wolves, posted in ambush, which overtake their prey. It is well known that a cry brings the pack, somewhat in the way a hunter's bugle sounds the death note.

We arrived safely at Ste. Genevieve, an old French town—small and dirty. I far preferred the time I had spent in Tawapatee Bottom. I waited only for a thaw to return home. The ice broke at last. Bidding Rozier good-by, I whistled to my dog, crossed the Mississippi, and was on the road on foot and alone, bound for Shawanee Town. But I found the prairies covered with seas of water. My desire to rejoin my family made me oblivious to all else. My moccasins constantly slipped, so that wading became irksome. Nevertheless I made forty-five miles and swam the Muddy River that first day out, and saw only two cabins. Deer stood ankle-deep in water. Thousands of Buffalo skulls lay about, just appearing above the water.

I made straight for a curl of smoke that promised a good dinner. The boys of the house examined my handsome double-barrelled gun while their mother and sister ground coffee, fried venison, and cooked eggs. The kind hostess was stirring at daybreak to get me a good breakfast and would take no recompense, so I gave each boy a horn of powder—a rare and valuable article to a squatter in those days. I left another forty-five miles behind me by nightfall, and camped that night with a party of Indians beside a canebrake. I awoke to find—to my surprise—that all the Indians had departed with their guns and left only two dogs to guard the camp from Wolves. I was now about forty miles from Shawanee. My dog knew very well that he was near home and seemed happy as I was. I met no one all day, and found no cabin on the road. At 4 o'clock I passed the first salt well. Half an hour later I was at the village inn, with friends who had come to purchase salt, forty-seven miles from home. The next day, to my great joy, brought me to my family, and to the end of this pleasant excursion.[22]

I had sold out to Rozier, who paid me a certain amount of cash and gave me bills for the rest.[23] In Henderson, not long afterward, I met a man just back from the Arkansas River headwaters country. His newly caught "wild horse" was one he had bought from the

Osages who had taken it captive and broken it for the saddle. It was a descendant of those horses (brought from Spain to the New World by the Conquistadores) that have roamed free on the vast plains of Mexico and the Rio Grande.

The animal was by no means handsome. His large head had a bulge in front, his thick, unkempt mane hung along his neck to the breast, and his tail that was too scanty to be called flowing almost reached the ground. But his chest was broad, his legs clean and sinewy, and his eyes and nostrils indicated spirit, vigor and endurance. Although he had been ridden hard and had performed a long journey, his black hoofs—never yet shod—had suffered no damage. His color inclined to bay, gradually darkening below to nearly black and with legs a deeper bay tint.

I asked what the value of such an animal might be among the Osages, and was told that the four-year-old had been surrendered with the tree and buffalo tug fastened to his head, for articles and trinkets worth about thirty-five dollars. The man added that he had never mounted a better horse. He had very little doubt that it could, if well fed, carry a man of ordinary weight thirty-five to forty miles a day for a month, his own rate. Until he crossed the Mississippi to Natchez and a ration of corn, the horse had had only the grass of the prairies and cane of the bottom lands. Anxious to sell him now that the journey was over, his owner thought he might prove a good hunting horse for me because of his easy gait and the ability to stand fire as well as any charger the man had ever seen. Needing such a horse, I asked to try him and was told I could keep him a month for his care and feeding, if I chose.

About two hours after I had had him stabled and fed, I took my gun, mounted the prairie nag, and went to the woods. I was not long in finding him very sensitive to the spur. He moved with great ease both for himself and rider. We jumped a log several feet in diameter to see how useful he might prove in a Deer or Bear hunt. I gave him the reins, pressed my legs to his belly without use of spurs, and we cleared the log as lightly as an Elk. I turned him round and made him leap it several times, which he did with equal ease and as if aware I wished to try his mettle . . . until I was satisfied he could clear any impediment in the woods.

To try his strength we entered a muddy and tough swamp and rode in different directions. He kept his nose close to the water as if to judge its depth, with a caution that pleased me. He was prompt, decided, and unflinching; but could he, I asked myself, swim well? There are horses which, though excellent, cannot swim at all but will now and then lie on their side as if content to float with the current, forcing their rider either to swim off, or to drag them to shore, or abandon them altogether. To the Ohio we went and rode into the water. He made off obliquely against the current, his head well above the surface, his nostrils expanded, his breathing free and without the grunting noise made by many horses. I turned him downstream, then directly against it, and finding him quite to my liking I returned to shore. He stopped of his own accord, spread his legs, shook off the water, and in the process nearly shook me off my seat.

I galloped him home toward Meadow Brook through the woods. After I shot a Turkey cock from the saddle on the way, the wild horse approached it as if trained for the sport and enabled me to pick it up without dismounting. From the Rankin farm, where I was staying with my wife and son while again setting up in business in town, I sent for the owner of the horse, paid him the fifty dollars in silver that he asked, took a bill of sale and became its master. Rankin, an excellent judge of horseflesh, offered to pay me the same for the "capital animal" if ever I tired of him.

I had to go to Philadelphia on business in ten days. I set off on Barro (he was so named after his former owner) at four miles an hour. The line of my journey was from Henderson to Russellville; Nashville; Knoxville; Abington (Virginia); the Natural Bridge; Harrisonburg; Winchester; Harpers Ferry; Fredericksburg (Maryland); Lancaster (Pennsylvania); and Philadelphia.

Four days after my arrival in the East I returned by way of Pittsburgh, Wheeling, Zanesville, Chillicothe, Lexington and Louisville. My business compelled me to leave the main post roads, so that the whole distance came to nearly two thousand miles instead; or four hundred more than it might have been. The horse, my friend Dr. Rankin said, was in as good condition on my return as when I set out. Such a journey on a single horse may, to European eyes, seem somewhat marvellous. In those days almost every merchant had to perform the like, even from St. Louis on the Missouri, although they often sold their horses in the East and returned by boat. My wife rode with me from Henderson to Philadelphia, once, also at forty miles a day, when the country was still comparatively new; then coaches were fewer and roads scarcely fit for carriages. About twenty days were considered necessary for a journey on horseback from Louisville to Philadelphia; now the distance is covered in six or seven, or even less, depending on the rise or fall of the Ohio.

I treated my horse well on these journeys, cleaned him each morning, pressed his back for signs of galling, arranged a double-folded blanket so that half the cloth turned over the saddle. The saddle bags were kept beneath the surcingle which held the blanket to the seat. My great coat or cloak I kept tightly rolled up on the pad behind me. The bridle had a snaffle bit. I buckled a breastplate to each skirt in front to hold the seat fast during climbs. My horse's shoulders, high and well-formed, required no crupper. I usually traveled fifteen to twenty miles before breakfast, and after the first hour allowed my horse to drink all he wanted. During the two-hour stop for breakfast I cleaned him and gave him his fill of corn blades. We kept on until half an hour before sunset. I then watered him well, poured a bucket of cold water over his back, had his hide well rubbed and his hoofs examined and cleaned. Corn blades, a good-sized pumpkin, or some hen eggs were thrown in the rack and trough—or oats instead of corn, if oats were to be had. (Corn is apt to heat some horses.) Empty trough and rack afforded sufficient evidence of the state of his health.

I had not ridden my wild horse many days before he had become so attached to me that I could let him graze at liberty when I had a mind to bathe in some limpid stream. He would not drink if told not to do so. Ever sure-footed, in continual good spirits, he needed only the sign of the bending of my body forward to bring him to a smart canter. This he would do if a Turkey happened to rise from its dusting place before me. He would canter until the bird left the road for the woods, then resume his usual trot.

On my homeward way I met, at the Juniata River crossings, a gentleman from New Orleans whose name was Vincent Nolte. He was mounted on a superb horse for which he had paid three hundred dollars. A servant on horseback led another as a change. I, an utter stranger to him, approached and praised his horse. He observed not very courteously that he wished I had as good a one. I asked when he would reach Bedford, his destination for the night.

"Just soon enough to have some Trout ready for our supper, if you will join me when you get there," he said.

I almost imagined that Barro understood our conversation. He pricked his ears and lengthened his pace. At this, Mr. Nolte caracoled his horse and put him into a quick trot—all in vain; for I reached the hotel nearly a quarter of an hour before him, ordered the Trout, had my good horse put away, and stood at the door ready to welcome my companion. Next morning we rode on together. In Kentucky, on parting, Vincent Nolte repeated that he had never seen so serviceable a creature as Barro. The importation of horses of this kind might improve our breeds generally. A few days after I reached Henderson, I parted with Barro, and not without regret, for a hundred and twenty dollars.[24]

[Nolte wrote his own colorful recollection of this meeting:]

". . . I resolved to cross the Allegheny mountains to Pittsburgh . . . and there purchase a couple of flatboats. . . . I managed to procure an excellent horse in Philadelphia. . . . I started in December. . . . Early one morning, I rode entirely alone over the loftiest summit of the Allegheny ridge, called Laurel Hill, and about 10 o'clock arrived at a small inn, close by the Falls of the Juniata river. Here I ordered a substantial breakfast. The landlady showed me into a room, and said I perhaps would not object to taking my meal at the same table with a strange gentleman who was already there.

"As I entered I found the latter personage, who, at once, struck me as being . . . an odd fish. He was sitting at a table before the fire, with a Madras handkerchief wound around his head, exactly in the style of the French mariners. . . . I stepped up to him, and suggested politely, 'I hope I don't discommode you, by coming to take breakfast with you.'

" 'Oh no, sir,' he replied with a strong French accent that made it sound like, 'No, sare.'

" 'Ah,' I continued, 'you are a Frenchman, sir?'

" 'No, sare,' he answered, 'hi emm an Hennglishman.'

" 'Why,' I asked in turn, 'how do you make that out? You look like a Frenchman, and you speak like one.'

" 'Hi emm an Eenglishman, becas hi got a Heenglish wife,' he answered.

"Without investigating the matter further, we made up our minds . . . to ride together to Pittsburgh. He showed himself to be an original throughout, but at least admitted that he was a Frenchman by birth and a native of La Rochelle. However, he had come in his early youth to Louisiana, had grown up in the sea-service, and had gradually become a thorough American . . . : 'When all is said

and done, I am somewhat cosmopolitan. I belong to every country,'
he said.

"This man who afterwards won for himself so great a name . . .
was by no means thinking, at that time, of occupying himself with
the study of natural history. He wanted to be a merchant . . . and
as he was a good companionable man and, moreover, an accomplished
sketcher, I invited him to take a berth [in one of my flatboats
at Pittsburgh]. He thankfully accepted, and we left Pittsburgh in very
cold weather, with the Monongahela and Ohio Rivers full of drifting
ice in the beginning of January, 1812. We had our horses taken
ashore at [Limestone, now Maysville, Kentucky]. I resolved to go with
him overland, first to visit the capital, Lexington, and ride from there
to Louisville. . . .

"We had scarcely finished our breakfast at Limestone when Audubon
all at once sprang to his feet and exclaimed in French, 'Now I am
going to lay the foundation of my establishment.' So saying, he took
a small packet of address cards and a hammer from his coat pocket,
some nails from his vest, and began to nail up one of the cards. . . .

" 'Oh! Oh!' thought I, 'there you have competition before you have
got to the place yourself.' "[25]

Later, travelling through the Barrens of Kentucky, I was jogging
along one afternoon on my way home to Henderson on Barro, when
a sudden, strange darkness rose from the western horizon. Used to
thunder and rain I took no more notice of it. I thought the speed
of my horse would enable me to reach shelter beneath the roof of
a friend not far distant. A mile further on I heard distant rumbling
as of a violent tornado. I spurred my steed into a gallop toward
shelter. The animal, however, knew better than I what was coming.
Instead of going faster he nearly stopped. He put one foot down
after another with such measured caution that he might have been
walking on ice, and seemed to founder. I spoke to him and was
about to dismount and to lead him. Then all of a sudden he began
a piteous groaning, hung his head, spread his four legs to brace himself, and stood stock still. I thought my horse was about to die,
and I would have sprung from his back the next minute, had not all
the trees and shrubs begun to sway from their roots. The ground rose
and fell in billows like ruffled waters of a lake. Bewildered, I none-

theless discerned that all this awful commotion in Nature was the result of an earthquake.

Never had I witnessed anything like this before, though I had heard of earthquakes. I found myself rocking on my horse and I moved to and fro with him like a child in a cradle, expecting the ground to open at any moment and reveal an abyss to engulf me and all around me. The fearful convulsion lasted only minutes, however. The heavens brightened as quickly as they had darkened. Barro drew up, raised his head, and galloped off, as if loose and frolicking without a rider.

Still many miles away from home, I was not without great apprehension for my family, lest I learn that the shock had caused greater havoc there. I slackened the bridle and was glad to see Barro was as anxious to get home as I. His pace accomplished this sooner than expected.

I was pleased to find that hardly any greater harm had been done to my family than their apprehension for my own safety had inflicted.

Almost every day or night for weeks shock succeeded shock, but gradually diminished into more vibrations of the earth. I for one became so accustomed to the feeling, strange to say, as rather to enjoy the fears shown by others. I never can forget the effects of one of the slighter shocks. The occasion was a wedding at Meadow Brook. After the supper was over, fiddles tuned for the dancing. The party retired at a late hour in the large log house. In a corner cabinet were Dr. Rankin's lancets, tourniquets, amputating knives, and other sanguinary apparatus, along with jars and phials of different sizes. These had narrowly escaped destruction some days before, and only because the doors of the cabinet happened to be closed. Morning was approaching as the rumbling noise that precedes an earthquake began . . . so loudly as to waken and alarm all, and to drive them out of their beds in great consternation. To do justice to the scene, it would take the humorous pencil of "Boz," the English artist [George Cruickshank, 1792–1878]. Young and old, in fear of instant destruction, rushed wildly out to the grass enclosure before the cabin. A full moon was descending but partly visible from behind rolling clouds. All huddled together in night clothes. The earth waved like a field of corn in the breeze, while birds left their perches and flew about they knew not whither. The Doctor thought of the danger to his gallipots [apothecary bottles], he ran to his shop room to prevent them from dancing off the shelves. But spreading his arms before the open case-front, he pushed back the falling jars with so little success that he lost nearly all before the shock was over.

The quake ceased, but not until after it had caused serious consequences in other neighboring places, rending the earth and sinking islands.[26]

The recollection of another awful phenomenon that I witnessed makes my blood congeal.

I was returning from Shawneetown on the Ohio, southwest of Henderson, in pleasant, seasonable weather. My horse jogged quietly along and for once in my life my thoughts were focused entirely on commercial speculations. I forded Highland Creek and turned toward a valley to one side of Canoe Creek beyond. Suddenly a thick haze spread over the country. My horse showed no inclination to stop and prepare for a possible earthquake. I drew up near a brook to quench an anxious thirst that had come upon me, got off, and knelt to drink. As I did so I heard an extraordinary rumbling from the southwest, then saw a yellowish oval spot quite new to me. A smart breeze began to shake the trees. Branches and twigs were falling. Within two minutes the whole forest was in wild tumult. The noblest trees creaked and bent, and branches broke with a startling crackle before the massive trunks snapped off. Many crashed to the ground on the instant.

Never shall I forget this hurricane; the strange motion of the trees in its central path; the snapping; the momentary resistance; the uprooting; and the mass of dust, foliage, branches and twigs that whirled through the air like a cloud of feathers, leaving in their wake fallen trees, naked stumps, and heaps of ruins. For a quarter of a mile the devastation resembled nothing so much as the dried bed of the Mississippi. The horrible noise resembled the roar of Niagara. The twigs and branches—masses of them—that had been "harvested," and brought from a great distance by the blast of wind, followed it as if drawn onward by some mysterious power. They even floated in the air for some time after, supported by the clouds of dust that rose high above the ground against the greenish lurid hue of the sky. The air was filled with an extremely disagreeable sulphurous odor.

Shocked, but uninjured bodily, I waited for the calm. Whether I ought to return to Morganfield or try to force my way onward

through the wreckage I did not know. Business drew me on over the
path of the tempest against innumerable odds. I had to lead my horse
by the bridle, in order to guide his leaps over fallen trees, while I myself scrambled over or under the best way I could, sometimes hemmed
in by broken treetops and tangled branches almost to the point of
desperation.

Surprisingly enough, I learned, at home, that there had been a
wind that only scattered some twigs and branches in streets and
gardens. Many and wondrous were the accounts of the devastation
elsewhere, however. Log houses had been overturned and their inhabitants destroyed. A cow was found lodged in the fork of a broken
tree. The valley where I saw the hurricane descending is still a
desolate place overgrown with briars, bushes, and fallen trees . . . a
resort of ravenous animals pursued by man after depredations on
farms. Later I crossed the path of the storm as far as four hundred
miles east into Ohio. I even saw traces of it long after, in the Great
Pine Forest of Pennsylvania three hundred miles from that same
valley. Yet nowhere did it appear to me to have exceeded a quarter of
a mile in breadth.[27]

V

In Field and Woodland

ONE morning at the break of day I lay hidden in a pile of drift logs, to wait for a shot at some wild Geese, beside the Falls of the Ohio. I saw a Snowy Owl lying, flat and lengthwise, towards a "pot" or hole in the rocks, with its head down near the water. One might have supposed the bird sound asleep. It would remain in that position until it had a good opportunity to seize a fish, one that it never missed. The instant a fish rose to the surface, near the edge, the Owl thrust out the claw that was next to the water, seized it, and then drew it out like lightning. It withdrew, a few yards, to devour its prey. If, after returning to the hole, it saw no more fish it flew to one of the many other "pots," spotted one, alighted, squatted down, moved slowly towards the edge, and lay flat, as before. Once it had hooked its fish with one claw it struck the other into it and flew off. Twice I saw the Snowy Owl carry its prey across the Indiana side of the Falls into the woods, as if to be out of harm's way. I never heard it utter a single note on such occasions. Often two Owls joined in the repast if the catch was a big one. At sunrise or soon after, the Owls flew to the woods and I saw them no more until next morning. I witnessed the same feats, watched for my opportunity, and killed two at one shot.

Years later, during a winter spent in Boston, a superb male Snowy Owl was brought to me. He stood upright, kept his feathers close, and would not suffer me to approach. His fine eyes watched my every move. If I attempted to walk round him his head instantly turned as far around as it could before he opened his wings, hopped to a corner, and again watched my approach. My gunner had caught him on one of the sea islands off Boston.[28]

In Kentucky the Golden-eye Duck is known by the name of the "Whistler." One day, near Canoe Creek ford, I saw several of them fishing and swimming about. They allowed me to come within yards of the shore before they swam close together. Then they shook their necks, and gave their rough croaking notes. I clapped my hands and they rose, passed and repassed the ford, then alighted on some large sycamore branches over the creek quite near me. This was the first time I had seen Golden-eyes in a tree. I waded across and stood gazing up at them, amazed, and was about to go my way, when with nearly closed wings one glided down upon the water, then dived —to be followed by the others, one after the other like Pigeons or Starlings, still apprehensive of danger.

A little further on I met a family of country people bound for Henderson. They asked me the depth of the ford. I replied that the water was low, but that they should take care lest some Ducks there frighten the horses of the women riders—at which they laughed, for we were all acquainted.

About 4 o'clock as I was returning with a fine Turkey cock slung across my back I met the party again. They said the Ducks were still at the ford and I would most likely have "a good crack at them." I forced the flock to fly off and was not more than fifty yards beyond before I heard them splash in again. Each time I passed that way, for a fortnight, I found these five Ducks still there. To learn the cause I undressed, and examined the bottom, a rather hard blue clay full of holes bored by Crayfish. To make quite sure that it was these creatures that attracted the Ducks, I shot two birds, examined them, and found that they had been feeding on Cray. I have never since seen such attachment to one spot.[29]

Travelling on horseback from Henderson to Vincennes in June I was struck by the sight of several Avocets hovering on the margins and islets of a large pond. Although it was late and I was fatigued and hungry, I could not resist the temptation to try and find the cause of their being so far from sea. As I walked toward them, having let my horse go free to graze, four of them convinced me—by their threats —that their mates were either sitting or attending their young. I made my way through some bulrushes in shallow water, but in mud to above my knees, toward an islet under the diving and noise of the four birds.

My desire to shoot them was restrained by my anxiety to study their habits. I found three nests of eggs, but disturbed none and rode on.

At sunrise I returned from Vincennes. Concealed among the rushes and with a view of the whole pond, I watched. The Avocets moved their heads to and fro sideways while passing their bills through the soft mud, sometimes immersing the entire head and part of the neck in the search for food. Or they ran with wings partly spread, to take insects. As the males flew together to the females their note was louder then usual. Pairs seemed to congratulate each other with odd gesticulations. Then the females took to the water, washed, shook their wings and tails as if heated or else tormented by insects, then searched for food as the males had done. Towards noon all rested, as if asleep, for about an hour before flying off towards the Wabash.

Slowly and silently I went to the nearest islet where I had broken weeds to mark the spot. (You will not, I am sure, think me prolix; some may say I am tediously so. I must tell them here and now that no student of Nature ever was, or ever can be, too particular about marking the precise situation of a bird's nest. . . .) Softly and on all fours I crawled, panting with heat and anxiety, within three feet of the sitting Avocet. Lovely bird, how innocent, how unsuspecting of thine enemy, who is an admirer of thy race, notwithstanding! Her head was almost mournfully sunk among her plumage, her eyes were half closed as if she were dreaming, and her legs hung neath her. I have seen and am content. Now she observes me, poor thing, and off she scrambles . . . running, tumbling, then rising on the wing to clicking notes of grief and anxiety that sound the alarm. She flounders hither and thither over the pool, now lying on the surface as if ready to die, now limping to induce me to pursue her and abandon her eggs. On that day I learned that gregarious birds can induce other incubating individuals to leave their eggs also, and help try to save the colony. Two other sitters rose and flew directly at me. One with four younglings took to the water. The brood of Avocets paddled along—to my astonishment—as well as do ducklings of the same size.

How far such cries can be heard by other Avocets I cannot tell. But this I know: Those that had gone toward the Wabash reappeared, minutes after I disturbed the nest, then hovered over me. I visited the islets twice the next day but not a single Avocet was to be seen.[30]

There seems to be a universal feeling of hostility for the Wolf, whose strength, agility and cunning—though scarcely less than that of his cousin Reynard the Fox—make him an object of hatred, especially to herdsmen. In America where this animal was formerly abundant, and where it is still found in considerable numbers in certain places, it is dealt with no more mercifully than in other parts of the world. Traps and snares are set for it. Hounds and horses are used for the Fox hunt. More powerful and perhaps longer-winded than the Fox, the Wolf is rarely pursued with hounds or dogs in open chase unless injured in some way. But great exertions to exterminate his race and its depredations, at times so extensive and highly injurious to the farmer, are made.

Only one instance of an attack on man has come to my own notice among a few that have occurred. Two young Negroes living near the Ohio in southern Kentucky often called on sweethearts living on a plantation ten miles distant, after the labors of the day were over. To the lover every moment is precious. To save time they took the shortest route and crossed a great canebrake. Winter had set in, cold, dark and forbidding. After sunset scarcely a glimpse of light or glow of warmth could be found in that dreary swamp . . . except in the eyes and bosoms of those ardent youths, or the hungry Wolves prowling about. Snow covered the earth and made it easier for the famished beasts to follow the scent and tracks of the men, unprotected except for the axes across their shoulders. The faint lights that the men now and then saw ahead were caused, they believed, by snow glittering on distant reeds. Suddenly a long, frightful howl burst upon them. They knew instantly that it came from a troop of hungry, perhaps desperate Wolves. They stopped and braced themselves for the attack.

Except for a few feet of white snow around them, all was dark, and the silence of the night dismal. There was nothing to do but walk on. No sooner had they again shouldered their axes and begun to move than the leader was set upon by several Wolves. His legs were as if clamped and held fast by a powerful screw while the fangs of the ravenous animal inflicted their torture. More Wolves leaped toward the breast of the other Negro and dragged him to the ground. Both men struggled manfully, but in no time one of them ceased to move. The other, weak and in despair of holding his ground —much less of helping his friend—managed to spring to a branch and climb speedily to the top.

By morning the pack had disappeared. Beside the mangled remains of his comrade, Scipio saw, on the blood-stained snow, three dead Wolves. He slid down, took up the axes, and made his way home, full of his sad adventure.

About two years after this occurrence, while travelling between Henderson and Vincennes, I stopped at a farmer's for the night. After putting up my horse and refreshing myself, I was asked whether I should like to visit the Wolf pits half a mile distant. Glad of the chance I went with the farmer across the fields to a deep wood and soon saw the engines of destruction: three pits, a few hundred yards apart, about eight feet deep, and broader at the bottom so as to make the escape of the most active Wolf impossible. The opening was covered with twigs caught together at the center. On either side of this platform of twigs was fastened a large piece of rotting venison and other tidbits not pleasing to the nostrils of any except Wolves.

That evening my host wanted to visit the pits to see that all was well. Wolves were very abundant that autumn and had killed nearly all his sheep and one of his colts. He was now "paying them off in full."

We went to bed early and were up at dawn. I had been promised some sport rarely seen in those parts.

"I think things have gone all right," said the farmer as he took up his gun, axe and a large knife, and noticed the howling and barking of the dogs. "I see the dogs are eager to be off to the pits, and though they're nothing but curs their noses are none the worse for that."

When we reached the first pit we found the bait all gone and the platform in bad condition. The animal had fallen through, tunneled his way from the bottom of the pit, and escaped. The farmer peeped into the next one and assured me that "three famous fellows were safe enough" in it. I saw the Wolves, two black and one brindle, all of a good size, sure enough. They lay flat on the earth, their ears close over their heads and their eyes more afraid than angry. "How are we to get them out?" I asked.

"Why," said the farmer "by going down and hamstringing them, to be sure."

Being a novice in these matters I begged to be merely an onlooker. The farmer left his rifle to my care and glided down. He took their hind legs and cut the principal tendon above the joint with as little fear of the cowardly Wolves as if he had been marking lambs.

He had to go back down again for his rope, returned out of breath, wiped his forehead with the back of his hand and exclaimed, "Now for it!" He asked me to keep the platform centered while he threw a noose over the neck of one Wolf with all the skill of an Indian. Together we hauled it up. Motionless with fright, it let its disabled legs swing to and fro and its jaws hang open as if it were quite dead. The gurgling in its throat alone indicated life. Letting it drop, the farmer loosened the rope around its neck by means of a stick, then left it to the dogs. They set upon the Wolf with great fury and soon worried it to death.

The second was dealt with in the same manner. But the third, probably the oldest because it was the blackest, showed some spirit the moment it was left to the mercy of the curs. This female scuffled along on her forelegs at a surprising rate. She snapped at the nearest dogs and sent one of them—a mouthful of skin torn from its side— howling dismally off. So well did the furious beast defend herself that the farmer, apprehensive of her escape, levelled his rifle and shot her through the heart, whereupon the curs made a rush to seek vengeance on the destroyer of their master's flock.[31]

Once on returning from the Upper Mississippi I had to cross one of the wide prairies. The weather was as fine, fresh and blooming as if just from the bosom of nature. I had only my knapsack, my gun and my dog. Attracted by the brilliance of the flowers, and by the fawns gamboling around their dams, I moved slowly along in well-moccasined feet on the long march.

Before I saw anything resembling even woodland or man on the old Indian trace that day, darkness began to overshadow the prairie. The Nighthawks skimmed over and around me after their food, the buzzing beetles. Distant howling of Wolves gave me some hope that soon I should arrive at some copse or the edge of woods. I did so, and instantly firelight caught my eye and drew me confidently toward what I supposed would prove a camp of wandering Indians. But I discovered the glare was from the hearth of a small log cabin, in front of it a tall figure moving about at household tasks. I asked the woman if I might take shelter under her roof for the night. Gruffly she answered yes. I walked in to a wooden stool by the fire and sat quietly. The next thing I saw was a finely formed young Indian who sat with his head in his hands and his elbows on his knees. His long bow was against the log wall near him. He moved not . . . apparently breathed not. Used to Indians and their studied indifference to civilized strangers, I addressed him in French. He raised his head, pointed to one of his eyes, glanced at me significantly with the other. His face was covered with blood. The fact was that only an hour before he had drawn his bow at a Racoon in the treetops. The arrow split the cord then sprang back and destroyed his right eye.

Such a thing as a bed was not to be seen, but many bear and buffalo hides lay piled in a corner, ready for tanning. I drew out my fine timepiece and told the disheveled woman that it was late and that I was fatigued. She spied my watch covetously, with electric quickness. In reply to my question as to what sort of fare I might expect she said there was plenty of venison and jerked buffalo meat, and to remove the ashes to find a cake there. My watch had struck her fancy. To gratify her curiosity I took it and its gold chain from around my neck and passed it to her. She was all ecstasy, praised its beauty, asked its value and put the chain round her brawny neck with frank longing for it. Fancying myself secure in so retired a place I paid little attention to her talk. I helped my dog to a good supper of venison and was not long in satisfying my own appetite.

The Indian rose as if suffering extremely, passed me several times, and once pinched me so violently on the side that I almost exclaimed in my anger. When his eye met mine its look was so forbidding that it struck a chill within me. He sat down again, drew his butcher knife from its greasy scabbard, examined the edge as I would that of a razor, replaced it, and again taking out his tomahawk he filled its pipe with tobacco. All the while, or as often as our hostess had her back to us, he glanced expressively at me. At last aware of the danger about me, I returned glance for glance which managed to assure me that whatever enemies I might have in this place the Indian was not one.

I asked for my watch and wound it up, then on the pretext of seeing how the weather might point for the morrow I took up my gun and walked outside. I slipped a ball into each barrel, scraped the edges of my flints, renewed the primings, returned to the hut, and spoke favorably of the weather. I took some Bearskins to make a pallet for myself and my dog, drew my gun close to my body and—to all outward appearances—fell fast asleep.

In a little while I heard voices. Two athletic youths entered with a dead stag on a pole between them. They helped themselves freely to whiskey, asked their mother who I was, and why the devil that rascal the Indian was in the house. She tried to hush them, but I heard her mention my watch before she drew them into a corner to connive. I tapped my dog gently. With indescribable pleasure I noticed the wag of his tail and the way he gazed, knowingly, from me to the trio in the corner as if aware of danger. The Indian and I also exchanged glances.

Before long the lads had eaten and drunk themselves into such a state as to be *hors de combat* as I saw it. The frequent trips of the bottle to the ugly mouth of their dam would, I hoped, soon reduce her to a like state. Judge of my astonishment when I saw her take a large carving knife and, like the incarnate fiend she was, whet its edge at the grindstone. She poured water on the turning machine until sweat covered my body. I watched her test the dangerous instrument. Turning to her reeling sons she said "There, that'll soon settle him! Boys, kill yon————and then for the watch."

I turned, cocked my gun-locks silently, touched my faithful dog, and lay ready to start up and shoot the first comer. The infernal hag was apparently contemplating how best to despatch me as she slowly advanced. The Indian she was leaving for her sons to dispose of.

That night might have been my last in this world had Providence not staged a rescue. The door opened just as I was about to rise and shoot the woman. Two stout travellers walked in, each with a long rifle on his shoulder. I bounced to my feet, gave them a hearty welcome, then explained how fortunate for me was their arrival at this moment. In a minute the tale was told. We tied up the drunken sons, along with their mother in spite of her vociferations. The Indian danced for joy. He gave us to understand, by his signs, that he could not sleep because of his pain and would keep the watch. We slept far less than we talked. The strangers told of having been, themselves, in a similar situation, once.

At daylight we unbound the feet of our captives who by now were quite sober. We marched them into the woods off the road. In the way of the Regulators with such miscreants we set fire to the cabin, gave their skins and implements to the young Indian warrior, and went upon our way.

Not far from the scene of this adventure large roads are now laid out. Those woods are fertile fields. Taverns have been erected. Much of what we Americans call comfort is to be found, so fast does improvement occur in our free, abundant country.[32]

Much of the American population comes from the unwanted of other countries. Even in this we have reason to feel a certain pride, for often we see our worst citizens turn from the error of their ways and become useful, respectable citizens. The most objectionable are forced to withdraw more and more from decent society and its rules that prove too much for their unbridled habits. On the fringes of civilization, however, their evil ways find free reign. The dread of punishment alone helps to reform them.

No sooner is an outlaw discovered in the more remote places than a band of honest citizens is formed to investigate his behavior. These Regulators, as they are called, are vested with the power to keep peace on the frontier. They arrest the accused, his conduct is considered, and if he is found guilty of a first crime he is warned to leave the district not later than the appointed time. Woe unto the offender so callous as to disregard the sentence and remain, and to commit new crimes! If his second sentence is not life itself, it is sure to be one he will never forget . . . a severe whipping, and the destruction of his cabin by fire. For repeated murder or thieving, death is sometimes deemed necessary, after which the head of the desperate criminal is stuck on a pole as an example to others.

I will give you an account of one desperado, told to me by a person who helped bring him to justice.

The name of Mason is still familiar to navigators of the lower Ohio and Mississippi. So industrious a horse thief did he become that his notoriety helped establish a worthless following from eastern Virginia to New Orleans. From their Wolf Island lair, not far from the meeting of the Mississippi and Ohio, they used to stop all flatboats and rob them of whatever provisions they needed. Mason's depredations became the talk of the Western countryside. To pass Wolf Island was dreaded as much as anchoring under an Algerian sea wall, until at last some Regulators undertook to bring the villain to book for the sake of the country.

Mason was as cunning and watchful as he was active and daring. Many of his haunts were found out and searched, but each time his spies helped him escape seizure. One day, however, he was riding a beautiful horse in the woods—across the path of a Regulator who immediately recognized him but let him pass for a stranger. While Mason rode on at a leisurely gait, as if he had seen no one, the Regulator dogged his path. At dusk, deep in a ravine no doubt well known to him, Mason tied the forelegs of his stolen horse to let him feed without straying far. He then concealed himself in a hollow log for the night.

The Regulator knew every hill and hollow of those woods. With a hunter's eye he marked the location of the log that held the well-armed Mason before galloping off to the nearest house for help.

Mason defended himself with desperate valor. When it became clear that he could not be taken alive, a rifle dropped him. The Regulators cut off his head and stuck it on the end of a broken branch which they set up by the road nearby. Their leader lost, the gang of outlaws soon dispersed. His punishment helped deter others from following a similar career.

Punishment by whipping is handled in a certain way. The convicted man is led to a remote corner of the woods by an escort of forty or fifty Regulators, tied to a tree while the forest is cleared of other observers, then surrounded by a wide ring of armed horsemen. Another circle on foot surrounds the culprit. At the "ready" signal he receives whatever number of lashes from young hickory twigs his sentence calls for. The men untie him and order him to leave the region at once.

One such whipping took place in my time down that way. The fellow was neither thief nor murderer but guilty of a crime bad enough so that he was taken to a place overgrown with nettles, and stripped and lashed with them so hard he took the hint, left the country, and was never heard of again.

But those were the early laws of our frontier people. Few if any parties of Regulators, probably, exist any longer among settlers, with such terrible examples of justice to keep them from committing flagrant crimes.[33]

After the birth of my second son, John Woodhouse, in November, 1812, we left Meadow Brook farm for Henderson and a lot of four acres and a meadow of four more with a log cabin, barns and sheds, and an excellent orchard. The pleasures known to us under that roof can never be effaced in life. The little stock of goods brought from Louisville answered so perfectly that in less than a twelve-month I had again risen in the world.[34]

In Pennsylvania, where we found ourselves the previous June, a pair of House Wrens built in a hole in the wall, within inches of my drawing room at Fatland Ford. The male caroled within a few feet of my wife and myself while I drew various birds. Now and then the male would dive into the garden after food for his mate, creep into the hole then be off again in a moment. I threw him some flies and spiders that he seized with alacrity and carried to his mate after eating some. In this way we became acquainted. After a few days he would enter the room, and once or twice he sang while there. One morning I took him in to draw his portrait, quickly closed the window, easily caught and held him in my hand. He was more cautious after that. Never again did he venture inside, although he sang as before and continued to keep an eye on us.[35]

My brother-in-law William Bakewell spied a nest—whether a Crow's or a Hawk's we were not sure. He climbed the tree to bring down the sitting bird beneath a kerchief. I looked at it with indescribable pleasure. It was new to me. But I felt vexed that it was not of a more spirited nature; it had defended neither its eggs nor itself. It lay quietly in the handkerchief. I put it on a stick that I fastened to my drawing table. It merely moved its feet to grasp the stick, stood erect, drew its neck low on its shoulders and raised its feathers. I smoothed its feathers with my hand. It moved not, but its feathers remained as I wished. I took measurements, outlined the figure and finished the drawings without the bird's ever once moving. I raised the window, laid hold of the poor bird, and launched her into the air. She sailed off out of my sight without swerving from her course and without uttering a single cry.[36]

While at Henderson I had a fine male Turkey that I caught when it was no more than two or three days old. A favorite of our little village, it would follow any person who called it, but would never roost with the tame Turkeys. Each night it roosted on our roof till dawn. At the age of two it began to fly to the woods for most of the day. The following spring I saw it fly over to Ohio several times, to roost at the top of a tall cottonwood to rest before sailing across the half-mile-wide river. One morning I saw it fly off very early to the woods, in another direction. Several days went by without a sign of it.

I was going towards some lakes near Green River to shoot. My dog was with me. (Good dogs scent large Turkey flocks from extraordinary distances—say half a mile. The dog sets off at full speed in silence, barks the moment he sees the birds, which scatter in all directions, enabling the hunter to shoot at pleasure rather than if they had gone one way together.) I saw a fine gobbler cross the path ahead of me and move leisurely along. I ordered my dog to chase it. He loped off but as he neared the Turkey I saw (to my great surprise) that it paid little attention to him. Juno was about to seize the bird when it turned its head toward me. My own favorite Turkey had recognized the dog and would not fly from him as it would from a strange retriever. A friend who happened to be searching for a wounded Deer agreed to take my pet home for me. The following spring it was accidentally shot, for a wild bird, and brought to me because of the red ribbon around its neck. Was the Turkey's recognition of Juno the result of instinct or reason . . . an unconsciously revived impression or the working of intelligence?[37]

In passing over the Kentucky Barrens about twelve miles from Henderson, during autumn, I saw Passenger Pigeons flying southwest in greater numbers than, I thought, I had ever seen before. I dismounted, sat on a knoll, and began to count the flocks that might pass within reach of my eye in one hour. But the birds poured onward in such multitudes that I rose, discouraged, after having recorded 163 flocks in twenty-one minutes. The farther I proceeded the more I met. The air was literally filled with Pigeons that obscured the light of noonday like an eclipse. Dung fell, here and there, like melting snowflakes. The buzzing of wings had a curiously lulling effect on my senses.

While waiting for my dinner at Young's Inn, where the Ohio and the Salt River meet, I saw immense legions still going by, with a front that reached far beyond the Ohio on the west and the beechwood forest just east. Not one alighted, for not a nut or acorn was to be seen. Consequently they flew so high that not even a capital rifle could reach them or disturb their flight in the least.

I cannot describe to you the extreme beauty of their aerial evolutions when a Hawk happened to press upon the rear of a flock. All at once —like a torrent—and with a noise like thunder—they rushed together to form a compact mass. These almost solid masses of Pigeons darted forward in undulating and angular lines, descended and swept close over the earth with inconceivable velocity, mounted perpendicularly in such a way as to resemble a vast column, and, when high, wheeled and twisted within their unbroken lines that presently resembled the coils of a gigantic serpent.

That night at Louisville, fifty-five miles from where I had been watching, I found the Pigeons still passing, undiminished. They did so for three days in succession. Men and boys crowded along the banks of the Ohio to shoot incessantly at the pilgrims that flew lower as they passed the river. Multitudes were destroyed. For a week or more the population fed on no flesh other than Pigeons, and talked of nothing but Pigeons.[38]

At Henderson I thought of taming a number of Wood Ducks. Juno helped me capture as many as I had a mind for. I kept them covered in empty flour barrels for several hours to tame them the sooner. These I placed in my farmyard. I looked in later and found all the little ones hooked by their sharp claws to the very edge of their prison, ready to tumble out and off in all directions. They had moved from the bottom to the brim of the cask, a few inches at a time, small hooked claw after claw that bore points almost as fine as needles. They thrived on corn-meal soaked in water, and they collected flies expertly, or, when they were half grown, locusts unable to fly from tree trunks or wild hemp where the insects gather. I would throw the locusts on an artificial pond in my garden, for the Ducks to scramble after and fight for. When they were grown I pinioned them all. They bred in boxes over the water, in which they arranged nests of proper materials placed there for them.

When March returns and the Dogwood spreads its pure blossoms to the sun, the Wood Duck, unlike the Crane and other water fowl that are in migration, remains on the pool of its choice. Its great beauty and neatness affords its observer pleasure during this love season. The fine drake chases his rivals away from some coquetting female, raises his head, curves his neck, bows before her, and, his silken crest high, lets a guttural note emerge from his swollen throat. To the female it is as the song of the Wood Thrush. She swims by his side, now and then bills his feathers, shows displeasure if another of her sex comes near. They separate from the rest, mate, then fly to the woods in search of a Woodpecker's hole or the hollow of a tree. While she deposits her eggs he flies swiftly past the hole where she is hidden. Erecting his crest he sounds his love notes which she never fails to answer. Once, when I noticed a hole forty or more yards from the water, I saw the mother let the young ones fall onto grasses or dried leaves below; then lead them to the edge of the creek. Other times she would carry them one by one in her bill from their birthplace to the water.[39]

I kept a male Trumpeter Swan alive for more than two years in Henderson. I caught it after long pursuit on a pond from which, because I had winged it a little, it could not escape. Its size, weight and strength made carrying it nearly two miles by no means easy. But because it was sure to please my wife and my then very young children I persevered. I cut off the wounded wing-tip and turned the Swan loose in the garden. Extremely shy at first, it gradually became used to the servants, who fed it abundantly. At length it came gently to my wife's call to receive bread from her hand. Indeed it laid its timidity aside to become so bold as to chase my favorite Wild Turkey cock, my dogs, children and servants. Whenever the gates of our yard happened to be open, he would make swiftly for the Ohio and permit himself to be driven home again only with much difficulty. Once he was out a whole night. I thought he had left us for good and all, until word came that he had been sighted on a pond not far distant.

My miller, six or seven servants, and I went to the pond and there saw our Swan swimming buoyantly about as if in defiance of us all. We had a great deal of trouble in driving him ashore.

Pet birds seldom pass their lives in accordance with the wishes of their owners. On a dark and rainy night a servant left the gate open. Trumpeter made his escape, and was never heard of again.[40]

An accident to two hundred of my original drawings nearly put a stop to my researches in ornithology. . . . Once, before proceeding to Philadelphia on business, I looked to the welfare of all my drawings, placed them carefully in a wooden box and left them to the care of a relative for several months. On my return I asked for my box and what I was pleased to call my treasure. It was produced and opened. But reader, feel for me . . . a pair of Norway Rats had taken possession, and reared a young family among the gnawed bits of paper which, a few months before, had represented nearly a thousand inhabitants of the air!

The burning heat that rushed through my brain was too great to be endured, affecting the whole of my nervous system. I slept not for several nights, and the days passed like days of oblivion . . . until the animal powers were recalled into action through the strength of my constitution. I took up my gun, my notebook, and my pencil, and went forth into the woods as gaily as if nothing had happened. I felt pleased that I might now make much better drawings than before. Ere three years had elapsed I had filled my portfolio again.[41]

By your leave I shall take you on a "Coon Hunt," to capture that cunning and crafty animal found in all our woods, where it feasts on all kinds of birds in its nightly prowlings.

Let us suppose that a few hours ago the sun went down, that the woodland choristers are silent. The babe is in its cradle, its mother beside her spinning-wheel. The menfolk chat before the fire. Autumn, sallow and sad, prepares to bow to nearing blasts of winter. The corn has lost its blades. The wood pile stands as high as the cabin. The nights are chill; the morning dews change to a glittering white that coats the withered herbage.

A thousand twinkling stars in the cloudless sky are reflected in tranquil waters. The forest is calm except for its nocturnal prowlers. A Kentuckian gets to his feet, takes down his horn, opens the wooden door of the cabin and blows a blast to send the Racoons scampering out of the cornfields and into the woods. He fetches his axe from the wood pile in anticipation of some rare sport. He blows through his rifle to clear it, examines his flint, and thrusts a feather into the touchhole. At his side swings his powder horn. His knife is in its sheath. He takes out a bullet, pulls the horn's stopper with his teeth, and covers the ball with powder, which he places in the barrel before springing its box. He greases a patch of homespun linen with melted tallow or damps it before placing it on the honeycombed muzzle. He puts the bullet on the patch above the bore, presses it with the handle of his knife, then trims the edges of the linen. With his elastic hickory rod in both hands he pushes the ball to its bed. He draws the feather away and closes the powder-filled pan.

The dogs are barking. Out we go behind a servant, Toby, whose torch lights the way, over ground covered with logs, past grape vines hanging everywhere. Already the dogs have surprised a Racoon. I rub my knee painfully against a log—jam my foot between two roots and, while the hunter laughs at my shackled state and while Toby holds the light near the ground, a hatchet sets me free. Off we start again. We see the dogs baying a Racoon in a small puddle. It is all but swimming, yet holds to the bottom with its claws. Distressed by the glare of the light, the animal watches the dogs with eyes that shine like emeralds, its coat standing on end, its rounded tail appearing thrice its ordinary fullness. It is ready to seize the first dog that comes near by the snout. They keep it busy until the water thickens into mud. The coat of the Racoon hangs dripping; its bedraggled tail floats on the surface. Its growls, far from intimidating its assailants, only excite them the more. The curs, without the breeding of gentle dogs, close in, seize it by the rump, and tug until forced to let go, except for two that hang on. One receives a bite in the muzzle that sends him off yelping. The rest of the dogs come up to seize the Racoon and worry him into letting go of the one luckless captive. The hunter steps in and with his axe puts an end to the contest. A good scene for a skilful painter!

The cur soon trees another. When we come up we find them seated on their haunches, looking up and barking. The hunters chip away with their axes at such a rate as to send a chip towards my cheek, so that for a week friends will ask where in the name of wonder I got that black eye. The tree cracks, leans, falls to earth with a crash. One coon leaps off craftily in time; two more stick to the hollow of a branch. Two dogs go after the cunning old fugitive. The hunter's son attacks the coons on the tree while the other dogs drive them forth.

Onward we go beneath the full moon that rises in the sky. Overhead, all around, our eyes search for something round, a coiled up Racoon. Between me and the moon I spy one of the cunning fellows crouched in silence. Down he falls . . . another and another, until finally towards the cabin we trudge. We find a cheerful fire, leaving to Toby the stretching of the skins on a frame of cane. The table is already set with cake, and sweet potatoes beneath the hot embers are now well done. Four bowls of buttermilk are ranged in order. The hunters fall to.

The Racoon makes a pleasant pet. Monkey-like, he is quite dextrous with his fore paws. He will amble after his master like a bear. He is fond of eggs, especially a dozen in the nest of a game bird. He knows the habits of Mussels better than most conchologists. An expert climber, he will ascend to a woodpecker's hole and devour the young. He knows, too, how to watch the soft-shelled Turtle crawl off the nest, and better still how to dig up her eggs. By the edge of the pond he will lie, Grimalkin-like, as if asleep, until the Wood Duck comes within reach. No Negro knows better when the corn is juicy and pleasant to eat. Although Squirrels and Woodpeckers know too, the Racoon is found in the cornfield later in the season than any. The havoc he commits there amounts to a tithe. His fur is good in winter; many think his flesh good also. For my part, I prefer a living Racoon to a dead one, and find more pleasure in hunting than in eating this quadruped.[42]

PART TWO

I

Visit of Rafinesque

Thomas Bakewell, the brother of my wife, joined me in commerce. We prospered at a round rate for a while. But, unfortunately for me, he took it into his brain to persuade me to erect a steam mill at Henderson. Up went the mill at an enormous expense in a country then as unfit for such a thing as it would be now for me to attempt to settle on the moon.[43]

We erected the infernal mill on the Ohio shore. I was amused and vexed by the pertinacity of the little winged laborers—the Bank Swallows or Sand Martins—who continued to bore holes day after day while the pickaxes and shovels demolished them. The birds seemed to have formed a strong attachment to the place, perhaps on account of the fine texture of the soil. Those forced to abandon their holes joined others a few yards off in work on newly opened excavations.

We added partners and "petty officers" to our concern . . . ; I was gulled by all. Of all the follies of man, the building of that accursed mill was one of the greatest. . . . Thomas Bakewell, who possessed more brains than I, moved to Louisville, then Cincinnati, where he made [and lost] a large fortune. I had heavy bills to pay which I could not meet. But I started again with new partners, my brother-in-law Nicholas Berthoud of Shippingport among them.[44]

One day while walking by the river I noticed a man landing with what I took to be a bundle of dried clover on his back. "What an odd-looking fellow, how the boatmen stare at him! Surely he must be an original!" said I to myself. He ascended the banks with rapid step, then asked if I could point out the house where Mr. Audubon lived. "Why, I am the man and will gladly lead you to my dwelling," I replied.

The traveller rubbed his hand with delight while I broke the seal of a letter of introduction that he handed me. It read: "My dear Audubon, I send you an odd fish, which you may prove to be undescribed, and

hope you will do so in your next letter. Believe me always your friend."
With all the simplicity of a woodsman I asked the bearer where the
"odd fish" was. Again he rubbed his hands and with the utmost good
humor said, "I am that odd fish I presume, Mr. Audubon." I felt
confounded and blushed, but managed to stammer an apology to that
renowned naturalist, Constantine Rafinesque himself.

I presented him to my family, and was about to send a servant back
to the landing for his luggage when he told me he had none but what
he brought on his back—a pack of weeds that he proceeded to loosen,
to the surprise of the ladies, whose critical glances I discouraged. He
pulled off his shoes, drew his stocking so as to cover the holes about the
heels, telling us, all the while, in the gayest imaginable mood, that he had
walked a great distance. He had taken passage on an ark for Henderson;
hence the sorry state of his apparel that had suffered on the journey.
He refused clean clothes. With evident reluctance he performed the
usual ablutions before he sat down to dinner.

His agreeable conversation at table made us forget his singular appearance. Indeed it was only during a stroll in the garden that his attire
struck me as exceedingly remarkable. A long loose coat of yellow nankeen cloth—much the worse for the rubs of time and stained all over
with the juice of plants—hung loosely like a sack. His nankeen waistcoat that buttoned to the chin reached, below, over a pair of tight panta-
loons that buttoned around the ankles. His beard was as long as I have
known my own to be during some of my peregrinations. His lank black
hair hung loosely over his shoulders. His forehead was so broad and
prominent that any tyro in phrenology would instantly have pronounced
it the residence of a mind of strong powers. His words afforded a sense
of rigid truth as he directed the conversation to the study of the natural
sciences. I listened with as much delight as Telemachus could have done
to Mentor.

Rafinesque had come to visit me for the express purpose of seeing my
drawings, having been told that my representations of birds were accompanied with drawings of shrubs and plants. He wished to know
whether I might chance to have in my collection any with which he was
unacquainted. I observed a degree of impatience in his request to be
allowed, at once, to see what I had.

We returned to the house. I laid my portfolios open before him. He
turned to the drawing of a plant quite new to him, inspected it closely,
shook his head, and told me no such plant existed in nature. For
Rafinesque, although a highly scientific man, was suspicious to a fault.

He believed that only such plants as he himself had seen existed, or only those with a "venerable beard" discovered of old. I told my guest the plant was common in the immediate neighborhood, as he should see on the morrow. "And why tomorrow, Mr. Audubon?" he importuned. "Let us go now."

We reached the riverbank and I pointed to the plant. I turned to Rafinesque and thought he had gone mad. He began plucking the plants, one after the other, danced, hugged me, told me exultingly that he now had not merely a new species but a new genus.

On our return he opened his bundle to take out a journal in a water-proof leather case and note down a description. The examination of my drawings was resumed. His criticisms were of the greatest advantage to me, for he was well acquainted with books as well as with Nature and qualified to advise.

It was summertime, and the heat so great that the windows were all open. The light of the candles attracted many insects, including the large scarab beetle. I caught one, and, aware of my guest's inclination to believe only what he saw for himself, I showed him the insect with the assurance that it would crawl on the table for us with a candlestick on its back. He asked to see the experiment. The insect moved about, dragging its burden in such a way as to change the position of the candle-stick as if by magic. It escaped after it reached the edge of the table and dropped to the floor.

I led Rafinesque to the room he would occupy during his stay, and I tried to make him comfortable. Heartily glad to have a naturalist under my roof, I left him a good supply of writing materials. The household was soon fast asleep. But upon a great uproar from the naturalist's room I got up, opened his door, and, to my astonishment, saw him running about naked in pursuit of Bats. He had my favorite violin by the handle and proceeded to bash it against the wall in an at-tempt to kill the winged animals that the insects flying round his candle had probably attracted. I stood amazed while he continued to jump and run round and round until fairly exhausted. Then he begged me to procure a Bat for him—"a new species," he felt convinced. Convinced to the contrary, I took the bow of my battered Cremona violin, administered a smart tap to each Bat as it came up, and soon got specimens enough. The war over, I bade him goodnight again. I could not help noticing the state of the room. Plants that he had evidently arranged in groups were strewn about in confusion. "Never mind, Mr.

Audubon, never mind, I'll soon arrange them again. I have the Bats and that's enough," quoth the eccentric naturalist.

Rafinesque searched for plants, I for birds. He also followed the Ohio margins to gather the many shells that he afterward extolled. When told that, among us, the shells were ground into lime, he exclaimed, "Lime! Mr. Audubon—why, they are worth a guinea a piece in any part of Europe."

One day he saw me return, wet and mud spattered, from a hunt in a canebrake. He asked to be shown one of those thickets or brakes of the district, in which the cane grows from twelve to thirty feet in height, to an inch or two around, and so close together that hunters often cut little paths through the thickets to pass through. The hunter then pushes himself backward to wedge his way between the stems. To follow a Bear or a Cougar pursued by dogs through these brakes is a task so difficult and so dangerous that it must be left to the imagination. I cannot describe it. Of course farmers sometimes clear part of the brake. They cut the fistular, knotted stems. The burning heaps cause a sound like musketry as the moisture between the joints turns to bursting steam. Travellers floating down the rivers have been known to pull on their oars with redoubled energy, at the sound, in dread of attack by savages ready to scalp them.

Determined that my companion should view a canebrake in all its perfection I led him off, after an early breakfast, across the Ohio. After several miles we entered as fine a sample as any I knew, at first proceeding without much difficulty as I cut away the cane most likely to discommode him. But farther on we had to turn our backs to the "foe" and push through the best way we could. Rafinesque paused here and there to pick up a plant and examine it. A fallen tree obstructed our passage. We were about to go round it when from out of its bed, in the center of the tangled mass of branches, sprang a Bear— with such force, and snuffing the air in so frightful a way, that Rafinesque was terrified. In his haste to escape he fell and was pinioned—jammed —between the stalks. Despite his thorough fright I could not refrain from laughing at the ridiculous exhibition he made. Not very pleased at my gaiety the savant called out for aid and at once received it. He would have been glad enough to retrace his steps, but I wished him to be able to describe a canebrake. The Bear was out of the way. Our worst difficulties were nearly over, I assured him as I enticed him to follow me.

The way became more and more tangled. I was delighted to see a heavy cloud, portentous of thunder and wind, approaching. My companion, in constant difficulty, panted, perspired, and seemed almost overcome by fatigue. The thunder began to rumble. A dash of heavy rain drenched us in minutes. Withered leaves and cane bark stuck to our clothes. Briars had scratched us, nettles stung us. Seriously, Rafinesque enquired if we should ever get out of our horrible situation alive. I urged courage and patience, mentioned that we would soon be reaching the edge of the brake, which, however, I knew to be two miles distant. I made him rest and gave him a mouthful of brandy from my flask, before we continued on our slow, painful march. He threw away all his plants, emptied his pockets of fungi, lichens, and mosses, and finding himself much lighter he went ahead for a little way with a better grace. But enough—I led him first one way then another until I myself, though well acquainted with the brake, was all but lost in it. I kept him stumbling, and crawling on hands and knees, until long after midday. At length we reached the edge of the river. I blew my horn to bring a boat to our rescue. We were ferried over the river, then I went to work to replenish my empty coffers, and left Rafinesque to his own devices.

The naturalist remained with us for three weeks. He collected multitudes of plants, shells, Bats and fishes, but never did he express a desire to revisit a canebrake. We were perfectly reconciled to his oddities, found him a most agreeable and intelligent companion, and hoped that his sojourn might be of long duration. But, one evening when tea was prepared, and we expected him to join us as usual he was nowhere to be found. His grasses and other valuables were all removed from his room. We spent the night in search of him. No eccentric naturalist could be discovered. Whether he had perished in a swamp, or been devoured by a Bear or a Garfish, or taken to his heels, were matters for conjecture. Nor did a letter, thanking us for our attention and assuring me of his safety, come to hand until some weeks after.

[*Audubon sent the unsuspecting Rafinesque off with copies of drawings of supposedly real but actually horrendous, nonexistent fishes of the Ohio, as well as some Herons from imagination. Well pleased with himself and these species which he claimed as his own discoveries, Rafinesque later wrote concerning "Species 91, the Devil-Jack Diamond Fish,* Litholepis adamantinus":]

This may be reckoned the wonder of the Ohio. It is only found as far up as the falls, and probably lives also in the Mississippi. I have seen it, but only at a distance, and have been shown some of its singular scales. Wonderful stories are related concerning this fish, but I have principally relied upon the description and figure given me by Mr. Audubon. Its length is 4 to 10 feet. One was caught which weighed 400 pounds. It lies sometimes asleep . . . on the surface . . . and may be mistaken for a log or snag. It is impossible to take it in any other way than with the seine or a very strong hook, the prongs of the gig cannot pierce the scales which are hard as flint, and even proof against lead balls! Its flesh is not good to eat. . . . The whole body is covered with large stone scales . . . in oblique rows . . . conical, pentagonal, and pentahedral . . . half an inch to one inch in diameter, brown at first, but becoming the color of turtle shell when dry: they strike fire with steel! and are ball proof![45]

II

On to Cincinnati

For nearly twenty years my life was a succession of vicissitudes . . . doubtless because my whole mind was ever filled with my passion for rambling. I had to struggle against the will of all, except my wife and children, who in that period called themselves my friends. Anyone unacquainted with the extraordinary desire I then felt to see and judge for myself would doubtless have pronounced me callous to every sense of duty. I was to undertake long and tedious journeys, ransack the woods, the lakes, the prairies, and the shores of the Atlantic.[46] Henderson, and the world around me, assailed me with its invective. The once-wealthy man was now nothing. I parted with every particle of property to my creditors and kept only the clothes I wore, my original drawings, and my gun. I paid every bill before I left Henderson forever without a dollar in my pocket, and with nothing left to me but my humble talents.

That I was a good draughtsman was to me a blessing in those days. To any other man, be it a thousand years hence, it will be a blessing also. I began to take black chalk portraits of the human "head divine" in Louisville.

In a few weeks I had as much work as I could possibly wish. I rented a house for the family whom Senator Isham Talbot sent up in his carriage from Henderson without a cent of expense to me. Sometimes I was sent for, from four miles away, to take likenesses of country people on their death-beds. A clergyman of Louisville had his dead child disinterred that I, the best delineator of heads in that vicinity, might make a facsimile of his face which, by the way, I "gave" to the parents as faithfully as if he were still alive, to their intense satisfaction.

My drawings of birds were not neglected. A mania seemed to hover over me. I would even give up doing a head—the profits of which ($5.00) would have supplied our wants for a week or more—to represent a little citizen of the feathered tribe. I thought that I now drew birds better than I had drawn them before misfortunes intensified, or at least that I had developed my abilities. I received an invitation to go to Cincinnati, a flourishing place above, on the Ohio, and stuff birds for the Western Museum, at $125 per month until the collection was mounted. My wife and sons soon followed.[47]*

One morning while I was at the Western Museum in Cincinnati a woman came in, holding in her apron one of those delicate birds called the Least Bittern. It had fallen down her chimney during the night. She had wakened at daybreak and the first object she saw was the young bird perched on one of her bed posts. I placed it on the table before me. It stood perfectly still for two hours while I drew its portrait. But at a touch from my pencil it flew off to the window cornice. I took two books, set them upright an inch and a half apart on the table, for the Bittern to pass between them. This it did with ease. I brought the books still closer together to reduce the passage to an inch. I tried the Bittern again, and again it made its way between, not moving either book.[48]

The curator of the Museum, Robert Best, led me across the Ohio to Newport, Kentucky, to see a settlement of Swallows nesting on the garrison walls. No sooner had we landed than I heard the chirruping of my long-lost little strangers, the Republican or Cliff Swallows. They were busily repairing the damage done to their nests by the storms of the preceding winter. The garrison commandant informed us that since 1815 they had been coming—first, to nests beneath the eaves and cornice of the arsenal, then, by the hundreds, to about fifty nests against its walls, with new ones now progressing in a regular, peaceable manner. I took the precaution of visiting their nests at sunset. The energy with which they defended them was truly astonishing. I supposed they would all have been at rest in the sycamores on the banks of the Licking. But a single female gave the alarm and called out the whole tribe. They snapped at my hat, body and legs, passed between me and the nests, and within an inch of my face, while twittering their rage and sorrow. They continued their attacks as I descended, and accompanied me for some distance. Their note may be perfectly imitated by rubbing a cork damped with spirit against the neck of a bottle.[49]

I established a drawing school in Cincinnati. My twenty-five pupils met thrice weekly at a good tuition. I hunted whenever I had an

* Two daughters, Lucy and Rose, had died in infancy.—Ed.

opportunity, drew every specimen I could find, and dared steal time
from my business until I had a tolerably large number of drawings.
So industrious were Best and I that in about six months we had finished
all that we could do for the Museum. I returned to my chalk portraits
and made a great number of them. Without this we would have been
once more on the starving list, for Best and I found, sadly too late, that
the Museum members were splendid promisers and very bad paymasters.

I concluded that perhaps I could not do better than to travel and
finish my collection, or so nearly finish it that it would be a valuable
acquisition. My wife hoped it might do well. I left her once more with
the intention of returning in seven or eight months. I left Cincinnati on
October 12, 1820, on board Mr. Jacob Aumack's flatboat . . . bound
for New Orleans. I took with me Joseph Mason, a young man of
thirteen, of good family and naturally amiable, to be a companion and
friend. Without money, I had my talents for my support, as well as my
enthusiasm for my guide in my difficulties.[50]

Although every European traveller who has glided down the Mississippi
at the rate of ten miles an hour has told his tale of the Squatters, none
has given any account of them other than that they are "sallow, sickly-
looking, miserable beings" living in swamps and subsisting on pignuts,
Indian corn and Bear's flesh. It is obvious, however, that only a person
acquainted with their history, manners and conditions can give any
real information respecting them.

Squatters choose that sort of life of their own free will, after coming
from various parts of the United States westward, away from land too
high in price, towards the country extending along the great streams
of the West. They have it on good authority that of all parts of the
Union this soil is richest, its timberlands the best, its game most
abundant. They have heard that the Mississippi is the great road to and
from all markets of the world; and that every vessel on its waters
affords settlers the chance of selling their commodities or bartering for
others. Of even greater weight with persons called Squatters is the
prospect of the chance to settle on land they may hold for years without
purchase, rent or tax of any kind. How many thousands in all parts of
the globe would gladly try their luck with such prospects!

I am not disposed to color the following picture too highly. Instead of
pitching on those who have removed—in numbers—from the East, I
shall introduce a family from Virginia where for a hundred years their

fathers and forefathers farmed until their land of red clay—cut by deep ravines and much eroded—has been completely worn out. Strenuous efforts to restore its productivity have failed. Except for a few horses, a servant or two, some farm implements and cooking utensils, they dispose, finally, of cumbersome possessions. They hitch their wagons that are filled with bedding, provisions, and the younger children. They even fasten spinning-wheels and looms to the sides. A bucket filled with tar and tallow swings between the hind wheels. Axes are fixed to the bolster. The feeding trough holds pots, kettles and pans. A servant drives on horseback. The father of the family shoulders his gun. His sons, in homespun, drive the cattle ahead of the procession, followed by the hounds and other dogs. Behind her husband rides a woman on her own horse.

The day's journey does not bring them far, nor is their lot an agreeable one. The stubborn or else unruly cattle often leave the road for the woods and are no end of trouble. Harnesses break and must be repaired. A basket, accidentally dropped, must be gone after, for nothing can be spared. Bad roads sometimes require all hands to push, or to prevent upsetting. Perhaps twenty miles have been travelled by sunset. Supper is prepared, by a campfire, where the fatigued wayfarers pass the night.

Days and weeks, or even months of unremitting toil, pass before the journey over the Carolinas, Georgia and Alabama ends. Perhaps the family has been coming since early May, to find, by the beginning of September, that they are at last traversing the state of Mississippi. They gaze in amazement on the dark deep woods by the Mississippi River banks. They see boats of various kinds gliding with the current or slowly ascending against it. They make inquiries at a nearby cabin whose inmates help them, with boats and canoes, to cross the stream and select a spot in which to settle.

The vapors of surrounding swamps and morasses have a powerful effect on the arrivals while they prepare for winter. They nevertheless clear a patch of ground and put up a temporary cabin. They tie cowbells to their cattle before turning them loose in the canebrake. From the first trading boat to stop at their landing they buy flour, fish hooks, ammunition, other commodities. Their spinning-wheels are soon supplying yarn to replace ragged clothes with new ones suited to the climate. The menfolk sow turnips and other vegetables. A Kentucky flatboat supplies live poultry.

October tinges the leaves of the forest. Morning dews are heavy, and the days are as hot as the nights are chilly. Ague soon attacks the family that is not yet acclimated, and the illness hangs on until the time of the hoar frosts. Little by little each individual recovers his strength that is to be needed for felling ash trees, then for cutting, splitting, and cording the wood that will be sold to passing steamers that need it for fuel. These boats stop by, attracted by the firelight. New courage returns for the strength of countless exertions.

With the return of spring the place has a cheerful look. Venison, Bear's flesh, Wild Turkeys, Ducks and Geese, with now and then some fish, have been the fare. Corn, potatoes and pumpkins are planted in new clearing. The cattle have increased. A passing steamer may stop to buy a calf or pig along with wood. The future looks hopeful.

Industry rewards the settler on the Mississippi. When another autumn returns, the family is better prepared to meet the ague season. Besides stores of food and supplies of clothing they have a knowledge of the district around them. A swamp with excellent timber inspires the sons to try their luck at a little enterprise. They have seen many rafts of saw logs floating by on the way to New Orleans mills. They buy cross-saws and make some broad-wheeled "carry logs," then begin the hauling to the riverbank where they make their first raft, to load it with cord wood. With the next freshet it is launched by means of cable or grape-vine. Father and sons float down the mighty stream, dispose of their stock in New Orleans, then with light hearts take passage on the upper deck of a steamer for a trifling sum.

Mother and daughters stand joyfully watching the approaching vessel. As the steamer stops, three broad straw hats wave from the upper deck to their womenfolk, around whom stand a tub of fresh milk, and vegetables in heaps. These supplies the boat will take on, along with rolls of butter on plates ready to be handed over. Embraces are exchanged. A bag of dollars is surrendered to the wife. Presents are brought out of baggage. Such moments repay the Squatters for all their labors.

Every year their savings and goods increase, along with domestic comfort of every kind. The daughters marry sons of neighboring Squat-ters and gain sisters by the marriage of their brothers. The government grants them the land after twenty years, during which time larger buildings, safer from inundations, have replaced the first one that did not stand on piles. Where one cabin once stood, a neat village springs up with its warehouses, stores and workshops to dignify the place. The Squatters live respected and, in due time, die regretted by all who knew them.

Thus are the vast frontiers of our country peopled, and cultivation gradually extended over the Western wilds. No doubt the time will come when the great valley of the Mississippi, still covered with primeval forests and dotted with swamps, will smile with cornfields and orchards. Crowded cities will rise along its banks, for all the world to marvel at Providence and its bounty.[51]

III

Down the Mississippi

ON the frosty December morning of my arrival in Natchez the shores were crowded with boats of produce from the Western country. The bustle was like that of a fair. Yet this market scene was far from pleasing until the flatboat moved on out from "under the hill" and the lower town, towards an open view of the city on the cliffs. Vultures unnumbered flew close along the ground in search of food. Large pines and superb magnolias were to be seen on one side of the water. On the opposite shore of the Mississippi vast alluvial beds stretched along towards dense forest beyond. Steamers were moving rapidly up and down stream. The way the sunbeams fell on distant objects was peculiarly pleasing. I watched the motion of the White-headed [Bald] Eagle in pursuit of the Fish Hawk, my mind filled with the wonderful ways of that Power to whom I too owe my existence.

Before we touched land I noticed several saw-mills on ditchlike canals of waters from inland swamps, rushing toward the river, and bearing timber along. One such temporary establishment was said to enjoy a net profit of upwards of six thousand dollars in a season.

There is much romantic scenery around Natchez. The lower town is made up of abandoned flatboats placed in rows, as if to form a street of dwellings for a medley of inhabitants impossible to describe. Hundreds of laden carts and vehicles jogged along the declivity between the two towns. I took a very rude causeway in order to reach the summit, and was relieved to come upon an avenue of those beautiful trees called, here, the Pride of China.

The streets of the upper town lay at right angles and were quite well lined with buildings of painted brick or board. Heaps of cotton bales and produce that congested the streets were a reminder of the agricultural richness of the country. I was thinking how little the churches pleased my taste—but just then I came across my relative, Nicholas

Berthoud, unexpectedly. The letters he carried from my wife and sons put me in high spirits. We moved on towards the best hotel in the place, that of Mr. John Garnier who was to prove an excellent friend to me as you will find a bit further on. The establishment was on the Spanish plan, very large and surrounded by wide verandahs overlooking a fine garden with plenty of space in all directions.

The Natchez population did not exceed three thousand at this time, but gave promise of greatly increasing. At its one bank mail arrived thrice weekly from all parts of the Union. The stranger is struck by the mildness of the temperature; and by the sight of fine vegetables, seldom available in our eastern markets before May. The Peewee Flycatcher [Phoebe] winters in the environs. Our deservedly famed Mockingbird sings and dances gratis for every passerby. I was surprised to see the immense number of Vultures that strode along the streets or slumbered on the roofs. For many miles inland the country undulates gently under many fields of cotton that bring wealth and happiness to most of the planters. Under plantation roofs the weary traveller may rest. Game is abundant. Indians used to bring ample supplies of venison and Wild Turkey to the city markets. At the foot of the hill where Natchez stands flows the Mississippi. Although the fish in the river are plentiful, the water is not fit to drink, and it must be brought on wheels or by sledges.

Orange trees which until late years bore well in the open air no longer do so, owing to the severe though passing frosts that have changed the temperature of Natchez.

The remains of an old Spanish Fort are still to be seen a short distance from the city. Two years before my visit a landslide of the hundred-foot hill occurred. The part that fell carried many houses of the lower town into the river. Quicksand springs, beneath pebbles and clay of which the hill is composed, were the cause. What remained of that part took on the appearance of a basin or bowl; this has become a refuse depot for the town, and the resort of Vultures when nothing better can be found. There I saw an Eagle chase one of those filthy birds, knock it down, and feast on the entrails of a horse that the scavenger had partly swallowed.

I met few people fond of ornithological pursuits, but am not likely to forget the hospitality—that of Charles Carré above all. This son of a French nobleman acquainted me with the history of the city, from Spanish to French, and up to present possession. He had the best religious principles; his heart was ever open to the poor; he spoke French with the greatest purity. He was a religious poet, and also well versed in the Indian languages. Many a pleasant hour did I spend in his company. But alas, he has gone the way of all earth![52]

My brother-in-law Nicholas Berthoud proposed that I accompany him in his keelboat to New Orleans. On the last day of December the steamboat *Columbus* took us in tow, leaving us with little to think about, as it plowed along at full speed, besides our arrival at the commercial emporium of Mississippi. Towards evening, however, we began to look over our luggage in which were drawings of birds, among them species which I was the first to sketch. These I had drawn while gliding down the rivers from Cincinnati to Natchez, work all the more valuable for being of birds perhaps entirely undescribed before.

The portfolio was nowhere to be found. I recalled bringing it under my arm to the river's edge, then leaving it to the care of one of my friend's servants. In the haste of departure he had neglected to take it on board. In addition to the drawings of the birds it held a black chalk of her to whom I owe so much of the happiness I have enjoyed; though her features were engraved in my heart it was no less dear to me than the other portraits. When, that night, I thought of this loss that I had suffered through my own negligence, I imagined the possible fate of the portfolio if it had fallen into the hands of some boatman lounging on shore, and saw the drawings pasted to a cabin wall, or nailed to the steering oars of the fellow's flatboat, or distributed among his cronies. Altogether I felt hardly less vexed than I had with the Rats which, you will recall, devoured a much larger collection.*

It was useless to fret. Instead I tried to scheme for the recovery of the drawings. I wrote to Mr. Garnier and my venerable friend Charles Carré, and had Berthoud write to a merchant. These letters we put off for Natchez at our first stop.

In due time we reached the eddy that runs beside that artificial embankment at New Orleans called the Levee, but not until after such adventures on the Mississippi as I mean to recount.

Twenty hours from the long file of beautiful bluffs beyond Natchez we reached Bayou Sara, where the *Columbus* left us to shift for ourselves in the keelboat. We floated and rowed along shores that gradually became lower, flatter and brighter in a country of orange groves and wealthy plantations. The air was mild. Butterflies fluttered among the

* Fortunately, Audubon had left the bulk of his work with Lucy in Ohio.—*Ed.*

flowers. We would not have been surprised to see Alligators floating sleepily among the drifting logs. Wood Ducks, among others, flocked on the eddies.

Baton Rouge, our next stop, was put behind us. Levees began appearing. We saw Negroes catching Shrimps and Catfish with scooping-nets.

As the river widened and deepened, the logs or sawyers decreased in number. The countryside became so level and destitute of trees along the water's edge that we could see the points far ahead of us upstream. Plantations became numerous on either side of the great river visible for miles beyond. Within the levees the land became lower than the surface at places where the waters ran high. At such stages we could see only the upper windows of planters' houses or treetops about them. The Spanish beard moss that covered the cypresses lent the scene a note of melancholy. Riders sped along the levees. Pelicans, Gulls, Vultures and Carrion Crows sailed overhead, above brilliant orange trees that deliciously, perfumed the breezes.

After we passed Bayou Lafourche a violent wind blew us off course. We landed, then made our way to the swamps for some hunting. The Mockingbirds on the fence stakes saluted us with such delightful strains that we could not think of injuring them, though we saw no harm in shooting a whole covey of Partridges.[53]

It is in Louisiana that you should listen to the love song of the Mockingbird. Light as a butterfly he flies round his mate. He ascends a short way, his tail spread wide, and describes a circle, then he returns to his loved one delightedly, raises his wings, and bows to her before bouncing up into the air again to pour forth his melodious exultation over his conquest of her. His are not the soft sounds of flute or hautboy but Nature's own, sweeter music—mellow, varied in its modulations and swells, of unrivalled brilliance in execution. Probably no bird in the world possesses all the musical qualifications of this king of song. When the courtship is over and the contract sealed he dances through the air in the promise of more love, and in imitation of all the other delightful songsters in the grove. After a fortnight has elapsed, the young brood in the nest of the pair demand all care and attention. No cat, no vile Snake, no dreaded Hawk is likely to visit their habitation.[54]

In the swamps we met with many kinds of lively and beautiful warblers that were waiting to leave their winter retreats on gentle south winds that would waft them toward their breeding places in the north. Thousands of Swallows flew about us. The Catbirds mewed in answer to their chatterings. The Cardinal elevated his glowing crest as he stood perched on the magnolia branch. Soft notes of the Doves echoed through the woods. Nature smiled.

On January 4 we stopped at Bonne Carré. The planter, a relation of my friend Carré of Natchez, received me, delighted that I was a student of nature anxious to ask him some questions about birds. A dozen young boys and girls appeared. The boys at once surrounded me, to answer my queries, and quite satisfactorily. They were never allowed to rob a bird of her eggs or young; but, Carré added with a smile, they were "welcome to peep at them and love them."

January 6 was so cold, at 30°, that our keelboat's running boards were iced until towards midday. All nature was again in full play. Peas, artichokes and other vegetables were unharmed by the frost.

Early next day tall masts loomed in the distance. They flew flags of many nations. We reached the Levee of New Orleans.

More than two months were to pass without word of my lost portfolio. Then on March 16 came word that it had been found and left at the office of *The Mississippi Republican* journal. Through the kindness of Monsieur John Garnier I received it on April 5. So very generous had the finder been that I found only one drawing missing, probably kept by way of a commission.[55]

At New Orleans hundreds of Fish Crows hovered about the boats. Uttering a cry like the young Buzzard when first out of the nest, they dashed down towards the water, like Gulls, for food. We dined at the house of Monsieur Arnauld. We had a good dinner and a great deal of mirth that I call *French gayety* that really sickened me. I thought myself in Bedlam. Everybody talked loud, and at once, and the topics and jokes were dry. A Monkey amused us all a good deal by his gambols and pranks. Formerly I would have been able as well as anxious to go to the theatre; instead I retired to the keelboat with a bad headache caused by drinking some wine.

The grand French fête for the anniversary of the memorable Battle of New Orleans was celebrated next day. At daybreak I went to market . . . found many Mallards, some Teal, Widgeons, Canada Geese, Snow Geese, Mergansers, Robins, Bluebirds, Redwings, Tell-tale Godwits . . . extremely high: $1.25 for one pair of Ducks, $1.50 for a Goose. Much surprised and diverted was I on finding a Barred Owl, cleaned and exposed, for sale at twenty-five cents. I went to the review and will remember it and the eighth day of January forever. My pocket was rifled of my pocketbook with a letter to the Governor. Nicholas called me a greenhorn. (I do not know the color of my horns but know well those of some neighbors of mine.) I do not blame fortune but peaceably keep the whole matter to myself and will try to grow wiser if possible. I think the knave a good deal disappointed. The parade was only tolerable. I had a good view of the Governor—all I may now expect. He looked about sixty. A French face of good countenance. This evening one of our boatmen fell overboard, drunk, and would have drowned if Providence had not interfered.[56]

One fair, very warm morning on the Levee the dress and mannerisms of a gentleman greatly attracted my attention. I wheeled about and followed him long enough to judge him a true original. His head was covered with a straw hat that had a brim as wide as those worn by the fair sex when in vogue. His neck was exposed to the weather. His fashionably, full-frilled shirt flapped about his breast. An extraordinary, carefully arranged collar fell upon his coat of a light green that harmonized with his flowing yellow nankeen trousers. From the bosom of his pink waistcoat and from the center of a large bunch of magnolias a young Alligator peered out, evidently more anxious to glide through the muddy waters of some remote swamp than to spend its life swinging to and fro among the folds of finest lawn.

The gentleman, John Wesley Jarvis, painter, held in one hand a cage full of richly plumed Nonpareils. In the other he sported a silk umbrella on which I read: *"Stolen from I,"* painted in large white letters. He walked as if conscious of his importance; that is, with a good deal of pomposity, singing, "My love is but a lassie yet," with such a good imitation of the Scotch burr that had his physiognomy not denied he was "within a mile of Edinburgh," I should have put him down in my journal for a true Scotsman. But no—his *tournure,* nay the very shape of his visage pronounced him an American from New England.

All curiosity, I accosted him. "Pray, Sir, will you allow me to examine the birds you have in that cage?"

He drew himself up, almost closed his left eye, spread his legs and answered with a quizzical look, "Birds, Sir, did you say birds?"

I nodded. He continued, "What the devil do you know about birds, Sir?"

So forcible was the question that I blushed as if caught in a trap (not at all an unusual kind of response in these United States). ("Sure enough," thought I, "little or perhaps nothing do I know about those beautiful denizens of the air.") But vanity gave me a pinch that urged me to suggest that perhaps I knew at least as much about them as this august personage.

"Sir," I replied, "I am a student of Nature and admire her works— from the noblest figure of man to the crawling reptile in your bosom."

"Ah, a-a-a naturalist, I presume!" he said. He handed me the cage. Out of the corner of my eye I saw him cunningly inspecting my face. After I examined the pretty Finches, I bowed low, and was about to continue on my walk. But the odd sort of being asked a question quite in accordance with my desire to know more of him: "Will you come with me, Sir? If you will, you shall see some curious birds, some from different parts of the world. I keep quite a collection."

At his lodgings I entered a long room. A full length, unfinished portrait stood upon an easel. Pictures lined the walls. Bird-filled cages hung near the windows. I saw two young men busily copying some finished portraits. Each picture in the room spoke for itself: the drawing, the coloring, the handling, and the composition all proved that this man possessed superior talents. Up to this moment I had not known who he was or what he did, and merely paid him the compliments I thought he deserved. He agreed that "the world" was well pleased with his work, but added that he wished *he* were, too. "Time and industry are required, as well as talent, to make a good artist," he assured me, taking up his pallet and turning to look for a rest-stick to support his hand while I began to examine the birds.

Not finding the rest-stick he drew the rod of a gun, to use in that way instead. He was about to sit down again when suddenly he threw down his pallet and brush, took up his gun, and asked if I had ever seen a percussion lock. I had not; that improvement was not yet in vogue. He undertook to prove it capable of action under water. After immersing the lock in a basin, he caused a report that so terrified the birds that they beat against their gilded prison bars. To my remark that they were disturbed, Jarvis said only, "Devil take the birds!—more of them in the market. . . . I wish to show you that I am a marksman as well as a painter."

He rolled the easel ten paces away, against the wall, before taking aim at one of its supporting pins. The bullet splintered the head of the pin but Jarvis complained that he meant to drive it deeper into its hole. His second shot not only gained its objective but passed through the hole and hit the wall behind. He told one of his copyists to have the studio windows closed, that he might show me the *ne plus ultra* of shooting. A servant brought a lighted candle. Jarvis put out the light with a bullet. I mentioned the uneasiness of the poor little Alligator that strove to escape the artist's waistcoat. He admitted that he had forgotten all about the reptile. "He shall have a dram," he said, unbuttoning his vest and unclasping a small chain. With that he placed the Alligator in the basin of water on the table.

I wished to withdraw but my time had not yet come. Jarvis bade me sit down. He paid no more attention to his pupils than if they had been a couple of cabbages. He offered to show me how he painted and to relate a sad incident proving the hard lot of the artist.

Adroitly he transferred the colors from his glistening pallet to the canvas. Before I could compliment him on his skill he began:

". . . This will be the portrait of one of our best Navy officers, a man as brave as Caesar and as good a sailor as ever walked the deck of a seventy-four." He interrupted himself to ask if I painted, to which I replied that I did not intend to try until my drawing improved. He agreed that "to draw was the first object," but that if ever I painted portraits to expect certain difficulties. "For instance," he said, "the brave Commodore of the portrait before me, though an excellent man at everything else is the worst sitter I ever saw. . . . The first morning that he came to sit he was in full uniform, with his sword at his side. After a few moments I bade him ascend the *throne,* pose in a certain way that I contemplated, and assume an air becoming an officer of the Navy. He did as I said, but merely looked at me as if I had been a block of stone. I waited—saw no change on his placid countenance, ran the chalk over the canvas to form a rough outline, looked up again, and opened a conversation calculated to warm his warlike mien. But in vain. I waited and waited, talked and talked. My patience about gone, I rose, threw my pallet and brushes on the floor, stamped, walked to and fro, and so roundly cursed our Navy that I startled the good Commodore. As placid as ever, he thought I had lost my senses. I colored my oaths still more, until I fell just barely short of insulting him as one of that Navy's men. Steering clear of personal insult I played off my batteries against the craft of his placidity. He walked up to me, his hand on the hilt of his sword, and told me resolutely that if I intended to insult the Navy he would cut my ears off. His features took on the spirit and animation of his noble nature that I had at last succeeded in arousing. I judged it time to retreat from the lion. Changing my tone I begged his pardon. He laughed and returned to his seat when assured that he now looked precisely as I wished to portray him. Now, see his bold countenance!"

No doubt Jarvis looked on me, as I did on him, as an "original," and a cracked man.[57]

On February 21 I met with one of those slightly discouraging incidents connected with the life of artists.[58] At the corner of a certain street that I take daily, so as not to be seen tugging my portfolio so much on Levee Street to the astonishment of many, I was accosted by a female of fine form, her face so heavily veiled that I could not distinguish her features. She addressed me in animated French—"Pray, Monsieur, are you the one sent by the French Academy to draw the Birds of America?"

I answered that I drew them for my pleasure.

"It's you who draws likenesses, so remarkably strong, in black chalk?"

I granted that I took likenesses in that medium.

"Then call in thirty minutes at Number ——— in ——— Street and walk upstairs. I will wait for you."

I bowed.

"Do not follow me now."

I bowed again, and taking out my pencil wrote down the street and number. Astonished beyond description, I waited in a book store a while, then started my walk.

"I am glad you have come—step right in," she said at the top of stairs where, apparently, she had been waiting.

I began to tremble like a leaf. She noticed this. After double-locking the door, she threw back her veil to show me one of the most beautiful faces I ever saw.

"Have you been married . . . are you married?" she asked.

I told her yes, for twelve years.

"Is your wife in the city?"

"No," I told her. I confirmed that my name was Audubon.

"Sit down—be at ease—I will not hurt you," I blushed to hear her say with the smile of an angel. A numbness stole through me so that I could not answer, whereupon she handed me a glass of cordial. I drank it for I needed it. Awkwardly I handed back the empty glass.

Seated exactly opposite me she looked me steadily in the eye and asked if I thought I could draw her face.

"Indeed I fear not," I answered.

"I am sure you can if you will, but first, what is your price?" she pursued the question.

"Generally twenty-five dollars."

Again, most sweetly she smiled. "Will you keep my name—if you discover it—and my address secret? . . . Do you promise to keep this sacred? I care not about anything else."

I promised.

"Have you ever drawn a full figure . . . naked?"

Had I been shot with a forty-eight pounder through the heart my power of speech could not have been more suddenly cut off.

To her impatient "Why don't you answer," I said yes, after which she rose, walked around the room, and sat down again.

"I want you to draw my likeness and the whole of my form, but I doubt you can work just now. Leave your portfolio and return in an hour. Do not try to speak."

The lady had judged my feelings precisely. I took my hat. She opened the door. I felt like a bird escaping from a cage filled with sweetmeats. Had a stranger met me on the stairs he would have taken me for a thief.

I walked off rapidly without looking back, beginning to reflect on her conduct. She seemed perfect mistress of herself; yet, as *I then thought,* too young for that. Mistakenly, I supposed her no more than sixteen, but apparently not at all afraid to reveal her sacred charms. I tried to talk myself into the challenge. In due time I was back again at the foot of the stairs.

Again she was waiting, again she beckoned to be quick. She locked the door as before, with, "Well how do you feel now? Still trembling a little? What a man you are. Come, come—I am anxious to see the outline you will make. Take your time and be sure not to embellish any of the details with your brilliant imagination. Have you paper sufficiently large? I have some beautiful paper and good chalks." She took some elephant-folio paper out of an armoire and handed it to me. The die was cast.

All at once I felt at ease, ready, pleased. I told her I was only awaiting her convenience. She repeated the urgency of secrecy as she drew the curtain to undress.

I noticed that the couch was superbly decorated, before it became hidden to my view. I heard her say she would take the position she thought best unless it proved not to my taste, in which case I was only to say so. With that she told me to draw aside the curtain and decide as to the light.

In the company of twenty other artists sketching a live model I had never, in the past, cared but for a good outline. But now, locked up with a beautiful young woman who was as much a stranger to me as I was to her, I could not easily master my feelings for the task without a mixture of some of a very different nature.

Nevertheless, I drew the curtain and beheld the beauty.

"Will I do, so?" she asked.

I eyed her, but only dropped my black lead pencil.

"I'm glad you're so timid—but tell me, will I do, so?"

Obviously, she herself had carefully considered the position, light, and the rest beforehand. I said I feared she looked only too well for my talents.

She smiled, and I began.

Fifty-five minutes later I pulled out my watch. She then asked that I close the curtain. In an instant she was dressed and looking at what I had done.

"Is it like me? Will it be like me? I hope it will. I am a bit chilled —can you work any more without me today?"

I said I could correct my sketch a little. She urged me to work as long as I could. "I wish it were done," she said. "It is a folly but all our sex is more or less vain." Very rightly, she discerned an error and made me correct it. Then she called for a servant to bring cakes and wine; insisted I rest; made me drink; asked a thousand questions about my family, my home, the birds, the reason for my travels, for my existence, and the like.

"Certainly this is a well-informed female," thought I to myself. "She employs the best expressions, demands respect and wonder by her manners."

After two hours the outline was cast. It pleased the lady very much. Finally she admitted to having had, herself, good instruction in art. I begged to know her name.

"Not today," she cautioned, "and if you are not careful and close-mouthed you never will see me again. I have thought well of you from hearsay and hope not to be mistaken."

She received my assurance. My thoughts were rather different, now, from those I had had while she was behind the curtain. I asked when to return.

"Every day at the same hour until you are done——but never again with your portfolio. I shall interfere, this once, with your drawing of birds."

For ten days (except a Sunday she spent in the country) I had the pleasure of this beautiful woman's company, undraped, during one hour of drawing, and for two of talking on various subjects after the sketching. She admired my work more each day, or at least was pleased to say so. On the fifth she sat down and worked at the study herself, and in a style much superior to mine.

I had told her that I would be satisfied with whatever she chose to pay me. On the second meeting she had said, "I take you at your word. It will be *un souvenir*. One who hunts so much needs a good gun or two. See if there is one in the city, and give this, on account, if you wish to please me to the last." She handed me five dollars. "I must see it, and if I do not like it you are not to have it." My assurance that it probably would be a costly piece did not deter her as she told me to do her bidding.

The note in my hand left me feeling very undecided. Nevertheless I found a good gun and left it at the store. She was much pleased. At the mention of the price, one hundred and twenty dollars, she suggested we say no more about it until I had turned out a deserving sketch.

I worked away, not only drawing the equivalent of a twenty-five dollar likeness, daily, in terms of labor, but at expense to my eyes at night on my other tasks. Still, many artists would have been delighted. How could I complain?

I finished my drawing—or rather she did. Every day I found the work much advanced on account of her touches to it—made, she said, not because she was fatigued of my daily company but because she liked mingling her talents with mine. She mentioned having intended to own such a picture ever since leaving the country she came from. (Italy or France, I suppose, but never could ascertain.) With my pencil she composed some lines that she wished engraved on the barrel of my gun beside some of my own. I declined to add any to those she said I must absolutely have put on for her sake—and soon.

On our last morning she had a beautiful frame ready to show me. She put her name at the lower edge of the drawing as if the work were *her own;* mine she wrote in a dark, shaded bit of drapery. I sealed the frame, put it in a favorable light, for her to gaze at its effect. She assured me her wish was gratified. Taking me by the hand she gave me a delightful kiss.

"Had you acted otherwise than you have, you would have received a very different reward. Go, take this the price of your gun, and think of me sometimes as you rest upon it. Keep my name forever secret," she said. I begged leave to kiss her hand. She extended it freely. We parted, probably forever.

I ought to add that she had first heard of me as well as of my collection, which she somehow understood to be by order of the Academy of Paris, after I had made a chalk likeness of a certain person. My way of living soon assured her to the contrary. To make sure of my veracity she had a servant shadow me for several nights, to see if I ever remained away from Aumack's flatboat on which I was once more living. In fact she knew every step I had taken since the day she resolved to employ me. I recalled seeing a mulatto near the gates of this Madame André, but never supposed anyone watched my steps. From the first day, she praised my drawings of birds and had no doubt I would be well recompensed for such a collection.

She did not ask me to call again. I tried several times, in vain. Always the servant said, "Madame is absent." I felt a great desire to see the drawing . . . because I can always judge better after some time has passed. Often, since, I have wished I might have shown it to Vanderlyn in New Orleans.

The lady was kind. The gun is good. Here is its inscription: *"Ne refuse pas ce don d'une amie qui t'est reconnaissante, puisse qu'il t'égaler en bonté."* (Do not refuse this gift of a friend who is grateful to you—may it equal yourself in goodness.) [59]

IV

At Oakley Plantation

I HAD been attending a Miss Eliza Pirrie to enhance her natural talent for drawing. Her mother asked me to think of spending the summer and fall at their farm, Oakley, near Bayou Sara. Though I would have preferred that she lived in the Floridas I was glad of her overtures. The bargain we made promised sixty dollars per month to teach Miss Eliza all I could—half time—in the way of drawing, music, dancing and so forth. I and my artist assistant Joseph Mason would have our room and board. We left our abode in Quartier Street and old Miss Louise, my servant, without the least regret. (The filthiness of her manners was not to our taste. We had fully discovered that a clean, sweet housekeeper is quite necessary to a naturalist.)

We reached the mouth of Bayou Sara landing on a hot sultry day of June, without mishap. I wished myself still on board the *Columbus* and bound for my beloved Lucy and my dear boys. We mounted the hill to St. Francisville, rested a few moments, then followed servants sent from the Pirrie place to manage our light baggage. The aspect of the country, entirely new to us, amazed me that it should be almost miraculously different, in so short a space, from New Orleans. The thousands of warblers and Thrushes, the richly blossoming magnolias, the holly, beech, tall yellow poplar, red clay earth and hilly ground delighted my eye. The long wished-for Mississippi Kite and Swallow-tailed Kite hovered over us. But our guns were packed and we could only anticipate the pleasure of hunting. The five miles seemed short. We were received kindly by Mr. James Pirrie at Oakley.

Our many excursions into the woods afforded countless observations. I found seventeen nests with eggs or young of the Orchard Oriole in two days of searching. The young of many were already flying. I was deceived one day by an Oriole's imitating the cry of the Logger-head Shrike and followed it a great distance before I discovered my mistake. It kept to the tops of high trees in the forest, a very unusual circumstance for this Oriole. (I may say, here, that Alexander Wilson's drawing of the bird shows the bill larger and longer than Nature, and the egg also larger.) I soon gave liberty to one captive, seeing that the departure of his tribe turned him extremely melancholy.

The Hummingbird was plentiful, and easily caught by pouring sweetened wine into the calixes of flowers—they fell, intoxicated. Wilson erroneously says this sweet bird does not sing. I have many times listened to its low-toned melody and can assure you that if its voice were as sonorous as it is varied and musical, it would be considered as surpassed by few if any other species.

The very few [Ferruginous] Thrushes that I saw had the appearance more of lost strangers than of happy residents. Rarely did I see more than one at a time.

On July 25 an Indian of the Choctaw Nation who hunts for James Pirrie brought me a female Chuck-will's-widow in full, handsome plumage. It was one foot long and had a wingspread of twenty-five inches. In its craw were many "pinch bugs," including a curious one with two pairs of pincers. Many planters think that if the eggs of this bird are discovered, it has the power and judgment to remove them a distance of several hundred yards. The bird is said to move the eggs and place them on the bare earth under a small bush or beside a log. A few weeks later I saw one while I was watching the arrival of some Wood Ibises. This Chuck-will's-widow flew as lightly as a Nighthawk, but kept close to the cotton plants. Like the Mockingbird, the Chuck-will catches insects while enchanting them with their melodies.

During a walk in the pine woods I had the pleasure of coming upon several Red-cockaded Woodpeckers. Their cry can be heard from a considerable distance on a still day. They watched my every move, peeping out from their hiding place around the tree trunk where they kept to the bark. One that I winged defended itself so powerfully by pecking at my fingers that I was forced to let him go. Some others that I confined in my hat remained still and stubborn. They tried to hide their heads, as if ashamed of their plight. Each time my gun went off they uttered a plaintive cry. One of the captive pair died on the way. The other I put in a cage which it immediately inspected— for a way out—while using its chisel bill with great adroitness. Sorry am I to say that Wilson's drawing of this species could not have been made from a *fresh-killed bird*. He put its small streak of red feathers immediately over the eye instead of a white line. The red should be placed far back of the ear. The wing is not at all marked as he has it, and the sides of the breast are also badly represented. In Nature the lines are longitudinal only. When I had finished my drawing of the Woodpecker and felt satisfied after a close comparison with the living original, I gave it its liberty. I was glad to think that it most likely would do well, because it flew forty to fifty yards at a time and seemed much refreshed by its return to liberty.

I spent one night, or nearly, in pursuit of the Wood Ibis. I killed one but could not find it in the morning. Some Fox or Racoon no doubt had a good repast. After a long search, begun with the dawn of day, I had to return to Oakley, fatigued and disappointed. The Negroes pronounced this bird excellent food.

I had seen several flocks of the White Ibis while waiting for a Wood Ibis flight—also Blue Herons, moving from the lake to their rendezvous, a large sandbar at the mouth of a creek that empties a few miles below Bayou Sara. The White Ibises flew in single waving lines, the Blue Herons at acute angles, passing the word of the march from first to last with a simple "*qua.*" Their passage takes place each evening for about an hour before sunset until dark. The noise of the Herons, the pure whiteness of the Ibises, identify the stragglers still going over as night falls.

I drew a very fine specimen of a Rattlesnake. It measured well over five feet; weighed six and a quarter pounds; and had ten rattles. Anxious to give it a position likely to interest naturalists, I put it in one it generally takes when about to inflict a wound. . . . My amiable pupil Miss Eliza Pirrie also drew this snake.

One day at the swamp I saw a beautiful Mourning Warbler. It was within a few feet of me, but I was knee-deep in mud, and so, rather than alarm it, I preferred to gaze at it quite as innocently as it gazed at me. What I hoped was that it would fly only a short distance. But with a *tweet* it was out of sight in an instant. Much disappointed was I to have lost the only opportunity I had ever had to procure this rare bird.

Alligators were as numerous as ever on that day. They basked in the sun which was hotter than usual. A little Flycatcher whose wing I touched spread its tail, opened its wings, and snapped its bill when I went to pick it up. Seldom have I seen a bird so small with eyes so large and beautiful. I took it home to the plantation and had the pleasure of drawing it alive and full of spirit. Often it flew from my fingers, suddenly and unexpectedly, to hop around the room. All the while it uttered its *tweet, tweet, tweet*. Every time I took it up it snapped.

Nero, a tame Sparrow Hawk, flew at liberty about the place, and returned every night to his roost, a window sash in Mr. Pirrie's room. He caught grasshoppers with ease. Often he sailed with the wild birds of his species. When still too young to sound the note of the old birds, he uttered his *cree, cree, cree*. When he was captured he looked like nothing more than a bit of moving cotton, but he grew into a handsome bird. It was on the first day of August, however, that he became too rash, too *téméraire*, and a hen who wished to guard her brood against his approach was his undoing.

On August 12, we left early for the rich magnolia woods and a famous lake about five and a half miles away. We saw two Wood Ducks, that we shot, carried off suddenly by two Red-shouldered Hawks before our very eyes. We watched a spider, rich in color, move towards a horsefly when it was caught in her web, and cover it instantly with the silk of her bag that she shot out towards it in a stream, then roll her captive into what looked like a small oblong ball of white silk. Then the spider returned to the center of its web. This is its way, no doubt, of preserving flies when not hungry.

Beyond the ridges that day we came upon a different kind of countryside, with tall white and red cypresses. To see the lake we forced our way through deep, heavy mud and water. When we reached it we saw several large Alligators sluggishly moving on the surface of the lake, and not in the least disturbed by our approach. I saw a White Ibis on a log . . . a great number of Prothonotary Warblers . . . Yellow-throated Warblers . . . and others . . . the Wood Pewee and the Mississippi Kite.

On October 20, 1821, we left the Pirrie plantation for New Orleans. Three months out of the four spent there were tranquil. Daily I gave Miss Pirrie lessons in drawing, music, dancing, arithmetic, and such trifling acquirements as working hair for jewelry and the like. I hunted and drew my cherished birds of America. I was seldom troublesome of disposition, and neither mixed nor cared to mix with the constant flow of guests and visitors at the house. Joseph and I were called *good men*, and now and then received a cheering look from the mistress of the house, and *sometimes*, also, one approving glance from the more circumspect Miss Eliza. Governor Robertson, a visitor, I consider a really true philosopher of the age. John Clay, brother of Henry, whom Lucy and I knew in Kentucky, I found to be a good agreeable man, and, to all appearances, a rather singular character.

Miss Pirrie had no particular admirers of her beauty but several very anxious for her fortune, a young lawyer among them. Mr. Pirrie was a man of strong mind, but extremely weak of habit that sometimes led to intoxication, and on such occasions he exhibited the paroxysms of a madman. But when sober he was generous and entertaining like a good *Free Mason*. His wife, an extraordinary woman, raised to opulence by dint of industry, was generous, I believe; but through lack of understanding she gave way at times, full force, to her violent temper. She was fond of quizzing her husband and of making an idol of her daughter, fifteen, a girl well formed but not handsome of features, proud of her wealth, and unable to stand much praise on account of vanity. God knows how hard I tried to please her, but in vain. God knows also that I have vowed never to try as much again for any pupil of mine. As usual, I had to do two-thirds of all her work, so that her rapid progress was truly astonishing to some observers. God forgive her sister Mrs. Smith for the injuries she did me [by her tongue]; she was a lady of a temper much like that of her mother Mrs. Pirrie's, but with a husband whom I admired. A good little woman from England, Mrs. Harwood, was very kind in mending our linen and clothing.

About a month before we left, Miss Pirrie was taken ill. She was the only remaining unmarried child, and the second of seven; five had died within a very few years of each other. So much fear was consequently entertained for her that too much care was taken. Long after her convalescence she would be kept in bed, it seemed, until she was sure to become thin and crabbed of speech. Her physician, Dr. Ira Smith, the *man she loved,* would not permit her to resume her lessons with me. He allowed her to eat so plentifully of everything that she had several relapses of fever. As if I were an ambassador to some distant court, I saw her at appointed hours during this illness, and had to keep the utmost decorum. I believe I never laughed once with her the whole four months I was there.

On October 10 Mrs. Pirrie dismissed me. I begged to remain eight or ten days longer, merely as a visitor. I continued my close application to my ornithology, writing all day, correcting my notes, rearranging them, and painting land birds.* The great many errors I found in the work of Alexander Wilson astonished me. I tried to speak of them

---

* The journal of 1820–21, printed in a limited edition in 1929, is of exceptional interest, belonging as it does to the beginning of Audubon's actual virtuosity as a painter of birds. At Oakley, a closeup of which we see here—in his words—he painted his *Mockingbird* plates, rattlesnake, and several other masterpieces, despite the handicaps imposed by his employers.—*Ed.*

1 MIERS FISHER of Philadelphia, first friend and host of Audubon in America.
Oil by James Sharples.   —City Art Gallery, Bristol, England

2 PHILADELPHIA, Third and Market Streets, 1799. Audubon spent his first weeks in America in the Quaker City. Copperplate engraving by W. Birch & Son.
—U. S. Library of Congress

3   MILL GROVE. First home of Audubon in America.
       —Audubon Shrine and Wildlife Sanctuary, Audubon, Pennsylvania

4   PHOEBE. Audubon used the "pewee" in the first banding experiment in America. (Plate 120, *The Birds of America*.)
—The American Museum of Natural History

5 BELTED KINGFISHER. Audubon used this species to test his new "method of drawing birds." (Plate 77, *The Birds of America*.) —U. S. Library of Congress

6   AUDUBON, THE AMERICAN WOODSMAN. Self-portrait, Liverpool, 1826.
Fate of sketch unknown.   —Reproduced by courtesy of Charles Scribner's Sons

7 RED-SHOULDERED HAWK. Pencil and crayon: "Falls of the Ohio, 29th
November, 1809."   —Princeton University Library

8 MAJOR WILLIAM CROGHAN. Kentucky hunting companion of Audubon.
Oil by John Wesley Jarvis.

—Mrs. Christopher B. Wyatt, Photo: Frick Art Reference Library

9 GEORGE ROGERS CLARK. The exploits of the general and his brother
William left their mark on Audubon the woodsman. Oil by Joseph H. Bush, 1818.
—The Filson Club, Louisville

10 WILD TURKEY. The initial and most-celebrated plate in *The Birds of America*.   —The American Museum of Natural History

11 RACOON. Water color by Audubon. "Young...Sep.r 10th—1841."
—The American Museum of Natural History

12 ALEXANDER WILSON. The "father of American ornithology" was for Audubon the rival of rivals. Oil by Rembrandt Peale.

—American Philosophical Society

13   AUDUBON. Self-portrait. Oil. 1823. Painted at Oakley with a mirror.
—Mrs. Harvey Breit

14   CONSTANTINE RAFINESQUE was the inspiration for Audubon's "The Eccentric Naturalist."   —Historical Society of Wisconsin and Transylvania College

N.G. Dinectus truncatus 14. Ich. Ohi: 82

Long. 2 p. Brun foncé dessus, beau blanc
... dessous, peau coriace épaisse. 2 Nag.
dus 3 rangs d'écailles. Jully 3 times int

Ich. ohi. 81.
... 14? N.G. Platirus
... clavisoides
Long 4 p. dessus brun foncé, dessous blanc
jaunes dessous 1 opercule Nag. abd
nulles ainsi qu'aux pieces Edula

Ich. ohi 76.

Devil fish
Diamond fish . 15.3

Jack fish N.G. Litholepis écaille belles
... couv. de tortue
Museau large c... dessus bouche à
grosses dents égues ... tout couvert d'...
pierreuses fais feu preuve ... balle
... coniques . Long 4 p. ... 400 #
Presque noir vorace non edule

15 DEVIL FISH, DIAMOND FISH. Rafinesque's copy of one of several fantastic
fishes drawn for him by the practical joker Audubon.—The Smithsonian Institution

16 DR. JAMES
MEASE introduced
Audubon to the
Philadelphia savants in
1824. Oil by Thomas
Sully.   —University of
Pennsylvania

17 GIDEON
FAIRMAN engraved
the "grous" drawn for a
bank note by Audubon.
Audubon recalled it as
his first artistic
commission. Oil by
Thomas Sully.
—Pennsylvania Academy
of the Fine Arts

with care and as seldom as possible in my ledger, not unmindful of his intentions and the hurry he was in, and his dependence on hearsay at times.*

We began to perceive a remarkable coolness, on the part of the ladies, towards us. We seldom saw them except at table. Then their looks were so far from cheering that my spirits were, unfortunately, low during my whole stay there. One day while I was finishing a portrait of Mrs. Pirrie, begun by Miss Eliza her daughter, another daughter Mrs. Smith spoke of me and of the work in the most grossly insulting terms. Never, after that, did Mrs. Pirrie look directly at me. Once when her husband told her she ought to make amends for her conduct, she burst into a ridiculous laugh at table. Unwilling to hear any more, I excused myself and left. A few days later a money settlement was necessary. I charged for ten days during which Miss Eliza was ill. My total bill was $204. In a perfect fit of rage Mrs. Pirrie told me I had cheated her out of $20. Coolly I let all her vociferations flow, then simply reminded her of our prior mutual understanding. I figured the bill which I sent to Mr. Pirrie who was laboring under one of his unfortunate spells of intoxication. He came to see me, apologized for his lady's conduct in the kindest manner, and ordered Mr. Smith to pay me. What with Mr. Smith's congratulations for my firmness, all went on pretty well that day.

Expecting that we would be gone on their return from a day in St. Francisville, the ladies bade us adieu. But Mr. Pirrie requested us to stay until next morning. Mrs. Pirrie sent for Joseph on her return, to present him with a full suit of fine clothes of her deceased son. I positively refused to allow him to accept, for I knew only too well how far some gifts are talked of. I did not intend that my companion Joseph should lose self-respect, so necessary to a man, no matter how poor, particularly one whose *talents,* health and industry were sufficient to his necessities.

After supper we left the table, to be joined in our room by Mr. Pirrie and Mr. Smith before bidding farewell to the other members of the family. Unfortunately, there was much company that evening. My entrance into the circle lacked my ordinary liveliness and spirit because I dreaded the fatiguing ceremonies. As simply as ever an honest Quaker might have, I bade Mrs. Pirrie good-by. I bowed to Mrs. Smith as I touched her hand lightly. My pupil rose from the sofa. I pressed her

* Although Wilson died in 1813, Audubon never ceased to regard him as a rival. Wilson has been called "the father of American ornithology."—*Ed.*

hand but did not offer the expected kiss. Then saluting the other women with one sweeping gesture I made my retreat, doubtless much to the surprise of those who now scarcely deigned to look at me, but who at first had spoken so respectfully of me. Joseph followed me. A volley of farewells from the three ladies of the house trailed after him in a ridiculous attempt to hurt me; the effect was lost on me, and merely raised a smile to my lips. We rejoined the gentlemen in my chamber. They remained until bedtime.

On Sunday, at daylight, we unloaded our trunks and drawing table, vaulted into the saddles, and left this abode of unfortunate opulence without a single sigh of regret. Not so with the sweet woods around us. To leave them was painful. I tried to fill my lungs with their pure air. We left Bayou Sara on the steamboat *Ramaso*.

Next day, in New Orleans, my long, flowing buckled hair was being stared at much as it had been by passengers on the boat. I had my long *chevelure* cut, separated from my head. My large loose dress of whitened yellow nankeen, and the unfortunate "cut" of my features, made me decide to dress like other folks as soon as possible. My clothes were extremely shabby. I bought some new ones and began to wait, very impatiently, for the gentlemen's tailor, that I might go in search of some pupils with a better grace.

I took a cottage in Dauphine Street suitable for my little family. I had forty-two dollars, health, and as much anxiety as ever to pursue my plans—the completion of my collection—along with hope that God would grant me the continuation of the same powers. Dressed all new, my hair cut, my appearance altered beyond my expectations—fully as much as a handsome bird robbed of his feathers and, poor thing, looking bashful and neglected to the point of contempt—this was my situation. Good God, that forty dollars should thus be *enough* to make a *gentleman!* Ah, my beloved country, when will thy sons value each brother's worth more intrinsically? Never!! At Mrs. Clay's I passed for a German for a while.

Fruitlessly, I spent some time in search of employment. Of several public institutions, one or two notable ones invited me to walk in but then out again in very quick order. I decided to exhibit some of my drawings at public places. *"A l'oeuvre on connait l'Artisan,"*[*] runs the fable of La Fontaine, as I recollected well. Like many others who appeared to be adventurers, here, I was eyed with suspicion. So moves

* "By his work is an artist known."—*Ed.*

the world, and doubtless it is right that this should be so. I began to give some drawing lessons to private pupils—but nothing was very certain.

An artist, Basterop, wished me to join him in painting a panorama of New Orleans. But my Birds, my beloved Birds of America filled all my time and, nearly, my thoughts. I did not wish to see any other *perspective* than the last specimen of them drawn. The high tuition rate I charged drew the ill-will of every artist in the city. One day I called on a "Bastard of Apollon" to see his *labors*. I also heard his *barkings*. I was unknown to him and the other daubers who came in. One of them began criticizing artists they considered intruders on the scene, myself among them. I held my tongue while he gave the unvarnished characterization of me as a "man that came no one knows from whence, and who goes through the streets like the Devil—has as many pupils as he wishes, and makes a wonderful quantity of what he calls portraits, assuring the good folks who employ him that in a few months of his method they will become able painters, while having, himself, bought his handsome drawings of beasts, birds and flowers that he shows and says are his own; and while the rest of us may be without a pupil or a portrait." At that point I seized my hat, told the gentleman my address, and said that I should be happy to see him. From this eloquent member of the "*sans culottes* of the trade" I moved away pretty briskly toward Basterop's rooms.

I met my lovely Miss Pirrie of Oakley but she passed me by, with never a thought of how beautiful I had once rendered her face in pastels at her request. She knew not the man who had danced attention on her wishes with the utmost patience. But thanks to my humble talents I knew I could run the gauntlet through this world without her help.

On December 18 my wife and two sons at last arrived, all in good health after our fourteen months apart. I thanked my Maker for this mark of mercy.[60]

V

Alligator and Rattlesnake

ONE of the most remarkable sights at the mouth of the mighty, sealike Mississippi is the Alligator. It may be seen basking and asleep, stretched full length on large floating logs, or along the muddy shores, or crossing the stream to and fro in search of food with only its head out of the water. It is neither wild nor shy, nor is it the very dangerous animal that travellers would have the world believe.

All the lagoons, bayous, creeks, ponds, lakes and rivers are well stocked with them; they are found wherever there is water enough to hide them and furnish food. I have seen them as far north as the mouth of the Arkansas, east to North Carolina, and as far west as I have travelled. Before the Red River was open to steam navigation they could be seen along its shores by the hundreds, or on immense rafts of floating or stranded timber, the smaller on the backs of the larger, all groaning and bellowing like thousands of irritated bulls about to fight. All were so oblivious of man that unless shot at or otherwise disturbed, they remained motionless. Boats or canoes could pass within yards of them, unnoticed. On the Red River in particular, thousands were killed during the mania for shoes, boots and saddles of Alligator. Many Squatters and wandering Indians followed no other business. The discovery that the skins are not sufficiently firm and close-grained to protect from water or dampness put a stop to the wholesale destruction.

If the Alligator spots an enemy while on shore, he will lower himself onto the ground. Then he will keep his head and jaws down, but, without moving either, watch with eyes that can roll far while he lies motionless. Particular strength and power in the water are his greatest defense. His large tail is his chief weapon. Woe unto him who ventures within reach of that tremendous, thrashing instrument. When Alligators fish, the lashing of their tails in the water may be heard for half a mile.

Near Bayou Sara, Louisiana, in autumn, the Squatter, planter and hunter go in search of sport among the shallow lakes and morasses. Here are myriads of fishes, and plenty of Alligators in the high waters. The grassy margins of the lake, then about two feet deep, are the resort of water fowl. These areas are overgrown with cypress that is heavy with Spanish moss which hangs down and tangles with vines and creeping plants and cane, a mass so dense that it almost turns daylight into dusk. Here and there are small islands whose clusters of cypresses attract flocks of Anhingas, Wood Ducks, and various species of Herons at nesting time. One hears the "honk" of the lesser Ibis as flocks rise from puddles filled with Crayfish. On reaching the open lake one must move along through deep mud, and also through brushy growth, with head down and with gunlock ready. The party launches its long, narrow, Indian canoe and sits in the bottom while the crew paddles or poles the craft along in the search for game.

Hundreds of Alligators are to be seen, floating like logs. Huge flocks, seemingly of the large Wood Ibis, muddy the waters as they wade about and strike the fishes with their bills. Here are the Blue Herons, the hoarsely crying Sand Hill Cranes, the Anhingas or Snakebirds perched on dead branches, and the fishing Cormorants. Buzzards wait patiently, like a mourning train, for the banks to dry and leave food for them. Against the horizon a Bald Eagle overtakes a Wood Duck, singled out from clouds of them that had been bred in the district. Then it is that you see and hear the Alligator at his work, in a deep spot which the hunter calls the Alligators' Hole, where they lie close together, stir about, splash, and, on missing a catch, throw the fish up into the air by a lash of their tails. So truly gentle are they at this season that I have waded through such lakes with no more than a stick in one hand to drive them off if they attempted to attack. The first time I tried moving along up to my waist in this way I felt, I admit, great uneasiness in the midst of, sometimes, hundreds of these animals. But the companion and experienced hunter who led the way banished my fears. After a few days I thought nothing of it. There is no danger, if one goes toward the head of the Alligator which, before it will attack the fearless man, swims instead after a dog, Deer or horse.

My good friend Dr. Richard Harlan of Philadelphia wished to have an Alligator's heart to study. I went out one afternoon, about a half mile from Beech Woods plantation a few miles from Bayou Sara, saw one basking on a log, shot it on the skull bone, and watched it tumble over into the water. Two Negroes helped drag it, supposedly dead, to the plantation, handling it without the least fear. Some young ladies asked to have its jaws propped open with a stick, that they might look inside. The instant an attempt was made, the animal began to recover from the stunning effect of my shot and to thrash and snap its jaws. I had the rope around its neck thrown over a branch toward which the Alligator was hoisted. Next morning we lowered it into a hogshead of spirits. A cooper sealed it for the journey to Philadelphia.

Alligators seek winter quarters away from the lakes about the time autumn colors the foliage of our woods. They burrow under tree roots or cover themselves with earth along their sides. They become so torpid and inactive that one can sit or ride on them as easily as a child on a wooden rocking-horse. I have thrown a blown bladder on the water towards an Alligator and been amused to watch it flap it toward its mouth or try to seize it in its jaws—but all in vain. The light bladder slides off. Presently many of the Alligators make for it like a crowd of boys after a football.

There is a season, however, when they are dreadfully dangerous—spring, the love season. The low country is under water. Fish are scarce. Quadrupeds are in the higher districts. The ferocious males have dreadful fights both on land and in the water, and wrestle like colossuses. No man swims or wades among them at this much more active season.

Along towards the first of June the female prepares a nest forty or fifty yards from the water in thick bramble or cane. She takes sticks, leaves and rubbish of all kinds between her jaws and forms a bed for her eggs. She lays about ten, the size of goose eggs, in a bladder rather than a shell, then she covers them up. But she goes on depositing more eggs in succeeding layers until fifty or sixty have been laid. She covers them in such a way that it is very difficult for Turtlers to break up the nest. Wary now, very ferocious, she seldom leaves it for the water except to feed. Her heavy body that always takes the same route forms a path. It is the heat of the nest, not the sun, that hatches her eggs.

The little Alligators all break through within a few hours from first to last. Beautiful, lively, as brisk as Lizards, they follow the female who leads them to the lake or, preferably, into the small, detached, and safer bayous. For now the males devour the little ones by the hundreds if they can get at them. The Wood Ibis and the Sand Hill Cranes also feast on them.

I believe the growth of Alligators is slow and that a twelve-foot monster will probably be fifty or more years old. A friend of mine, anxious to send some young ones to New York, had a bag of Alligators, quite small, brought to his house. They were put on the floor, to show the ladies how beautiful Alligators are when young. One of them made its way out into a servant's room and lodged itself, snug from notice, in an old shoe. It was not missed. More than a year later it was found in the house, full of life but scarcely any bigger. One of its brothers that had been kept in a tub was fed plentifully and yet had grown only a few inches during the same period.[61]

"My dear Sir," wrote Audubon to Dr. James E. De Kay of the Lyceum of New York City, on May 24, 1825, from Bayou Sara, Louisiana: "I this day forward directed to your name and for the Lyceum a Barrel containing a keg and several jars with a couple of Small Boxes with a few insects." [De Kay had recently edited and published Audubon's paper on Vieillot's swallow in the *Annals* of the Lyceum.]

"My object in forwarding this now is the hope I have that the Rattle Snake in the key is a new species or at all events one remarkable variety. You will soon perceive that its fangs lay in paired parallels, a thing that among the great number of Rattle Snakes that I have killed and examined has occurred only once." [Today herpetologists know that the snakes without fangs were what experts of Audubon's day called *Coluber constrictor*, the blacksnake.]

"I gave a drawing of the first to Dr. Harlan—that was killed about 5 years ago in this neighbourhood and as well as this in the *Low Lands:* all the Rattle Snakes that *I call* common reside in our most hilly regions and are less active than this as they are also generally much larger. The double fanged one now on its way to the Lyceum was in my possession alive for half a day, fastened around the neck with a fine piece of strong twine, during which time it made violent efforts of escape by coiling itself and throwing its body full length in a straight direction, elevating about two thirds of the Body nearly a foot from the ground. When coiling itself for the purpose, its rattles were silenced but the instant the effort had been made and whilst laying extended, it was renewed as if with new force. I put it whilst alive in a tub of whiskey where it laid a few moments motionless, then feeling the spirit it spring out and [lancing?] its head all around attempted to bite every object near him, even the hearth. I immersed it several times, covered the tub with a loaded board. The next morning it was dead and so stiff and firm that it felt more like petrified than anything else.

"The earthen jar contains a snake commonly called here the *Rattle-snake Pilot*. It vibrates its tail in the manner of the Rattle Snake, although deprived of Rattles, but this I have remarked in several other species. This is considered here very venomous. It resides in our hills that are covered with young cane, feeds mostly on small rabbits and squirrels." [The pilot or blacksnake is known to be a constrictor with a stinging, nonpoisonous bite.]

"There are in the keg two *Water Moccasins* that I consider also as different from those that live in the pine woods. They are found in our Cypress Swamps and are most of the time in the water. They lived for upwards of one hour completely in whiskey.

"You will please have the contents of the keg carefully examined as there are some minute reptiles in it.

"The few Insects in the Little Boxes and jars please to present to Captain John Le Conte with my respects and assure him that I will exert myself at procuring him a large parcel by next opportunity.

"I have wrote you much at length by a Captain Barclay of Philadelphia about the Publication of my work in the United States. I hope it has reached you ere this. Do let me have the pleasure of hearing from you often. I will prepare for the Lyceum a memoir that I will try to forward next month. With sincere regards to you and all our mutual friends, believe me for ever yours, John J. Audubon. Thermometer 90° at 2 o'clock P.M. P. S. I have just this instant received a Beautiful new species of Ibis of a large size."*[62]

On account of the slow growth granted Snakes, their periodical torpidity has been wisely ordained. Like Alligators they grow very slowly and are consequently long-lived.

One winter day my son, a friend, and I were hunting Ducks in West Feliciana, Louisiana. We struck up a fire to cook our game for dinner. While he ran about for wood my son discovered a Rattlesnake coiled up beside a log. It was in a torpid state, and so large that my son called us to come and look at it. It was stiff as a bone. I told him to put it in my game bag that I was wearing on my back. While our game was roasting on a wooden fork in front of our cheerful fire I felt something moving behind me. The time it took me to unstrap and throw off the bag was brief, I assure you—very. The Snake, quite alive, issued from the bag and began rattling with its head raised up and its body closely coiled to defend itself from all attacks. But it was a fair distance away from the fire, so it stopped its alarum and was bent on finding a place

* Historical Society of Pennsylvania (Gratz Collection), Philadelphia.—*Ed.*

of refuge and on becoming torpid again, even before our ducks were roasted. After we had finished our meal my son who had watched all its movements with the eagerness of youth brought it back again, saying with a smile, "Papa, look at Hercules and the serpent!"

We took the Snake home. It became torpid; or it revived at our pleasure as often as we brought it near the fire. Eventually we put it in a jar of spirits, and sent it to the New York Lyceum of Natural History.

One of the most wonderful faculties possessed by this and many other kinds of Snakes is its ability to live without any food whatever for years. Quite as remarkable is their failure to exhibit any signs of privation without it. And their movements, power of rattling and of inflicting mortal wounds, are perfectly kept up. One that I kept in a cage for three years never touched the Rats, young Rabbits and birds put in with it, sometimes alive. Not a move would it make in their direction. After the first spring of its confinement it abandoned the operation of shedding its skin. During the whole term of imprisonment it did not grow in the least. I have thought this power of abstinence might go a long way toward proving that it lacked that of fascination. It would be very unnatural for an animal thus gifted to lie and suffer while one glance of its magnetic eye could bring down a bird at once, from the top of any tree, into its mouth.

Now and then I turned it out of its cage. It sped about the room in all directions, looking for the chance to escape. Because I was armed with a stick it never made towards me, but if I put myself in its way it would stop, prepare for action, and rattle until I moved and afforded free passage.

Rattlesnakes are easily disabled, then killed. A single smart blow, even of a slender twig, will disjoint any of the vertebrae and leave the reptile at your mercy.

Allow me to remind you that birds of all kinds are full of courage. Have we not all seen the little Robin chase a cat? An Eagle will keep a man away from her nest. A cock will attack even a Lion. Can we, for a moment, imagine that the Creator has exposed the feathered race to such dangers as the power of fascination would imply? We may rest assured that Snakes destroy birds and animals by the quickness of their motion and the acuteness of their sight, seconded by cunning and strength but never by fascination.[63]

Some persons have attributed a mysterious power of *fascination,* or *charm*—more especially to the Rattlesnake and Blacksnake. The Basilisk of the ancients killed by a look. The eye of the Rattlesnake is supposed to paralyze and at the same time attract its intended prey. Slowly the bird approaches, advancing and retreating until finally it falls powerless into the open jaws of its devourer.

As long as we are able to explain the singular maneuvers of birds and squirrels when "fascinated" by a snake, it would be absurd to imagine that there is anything mysterious or supernatural about it. Fear and surprise cause an instinctive horror, when we find ourselves, unexpectedly, within a foot or two of a Rattlesnake. The shrill, startling noise from the rattles as its tail vibrates rapidly, and its hideous aspect, no doubt produce a much sharper effect on birds and small quadrupeds. It is said that the distant roar of the African Lion causes Oxen in the fields to tremble. Baron Alexander von Humboldt (1769–1859) relates that in the forests of South America the mingled cries of Monkeys and other animals resound through the whole night; but as soon as the Jaguar roars, terror seizes and silences all other animals. Birds and quadrupeds are curiously drawn to strange objects and to certain sounds. By waving a stick with a red cloth attached, Indians attract the Reindeer and Antelope. Or they throw themselves on the ground on their backs and kick their heels in the air to draw them. If any strange object is thrown into the poultry yard, all the fowls will crowd near to scrutinize it for a long time. Almost everybody has at some time watched birds collect by the dozens around a cat in shrubbery, or a Tortoise, or particularly a Snake.

The Squirrel is remarkable for its fondness for "sights." Sometimes it will come down from the highest branch of a tree to within a few feet of the ground to view a small Scarlet Snake not much larger than a pipestem, one without poisonous fangs and scarcely big enough to master a Grasshopper—a case decidedly in favor of theories of the fascinating powers of Snakes. But they will find it difficult to explain a thing that once happened to me.

After I observed a Squirrel come down to inspect just such a little Scarlet Snake, I captured the reptile, of a rare species, and put it in a box. I later realized that I had left a box of botanical specimens in the same spot. On my return there I saw the Squirrel darting back and forth, skipping around the root of the tree, then eyeing the box with the same curiosity. I could not help reflecting that if the little Snake had "charmed" the Squirrel, the tin box had the same "fascination."

Quadrupeds and birds have, like all mankind, certain antipathies —feelings. Susceptible of passion, sometimes spiteful and revengeful, they prove themselves wise to their "natural enemies" without any formal introduction. Often the Blue Jay, Thrush, White-eyed Fly-catcher [Vireo?] and other small birds may be heard scolding some animal concealed in a thicket about which they flutter. A Wild Cat or Fox may spring from the covert. Everyone must have seen the Owl or Buzzard chased by small birds that unite to drive off a common enemy. The birds may draw too near and be seized by the Owl. I once watched some Nighthawks darting round a tree in which an Owl perched. The Owl moved suddenly, to catch a Hawk in his sharp claws, and, paying no heed to the menaces and cries of the others instantly devoured it. Birds dart in the same manner at Snakes, and are often caught by passing too near. Shall we, therefore, conclude that they are fascinated?*

One of the most powerful "attractions" to be considered is the love of offspring—so deeply rooted in Nature as to be a rule, with almost no exceptions, among birds and quadrupeds. Snakes are among the most dreaded destroyers of eggs and young birds, and of young animals. Is it not likely that many supposed cases of fascination may be explained by the bold defense of eggs or young?

In *The Birds of America* I represented a Mockingbird's nest attacked by a Rattlesnake; also the nest of a Thrush invaded by a Blacksnake. The birds courageously advance even to the jaws of their enemy. These pictures were drawn after I had seen these incidents before my very eyes. Persons unacquainted with natural history might readily fancy that some of these birds were fascinated. I have more to say of the Rattlesnake in this connection. I have seen one in a very large cage use every means in its power and exert its cunning for a whole month before capturing a [Ferruginous] Thrush imprisoned with it. At night the bird roosted out of reach of the Snake. By day it was too cautious and too agile, even while snatching up its food, in flying back to its perch while the unwieldly serpent tried to strike it. This experiment offered a fair opportunity for the Rattlesnake to exert its powers of fascination, had it possessed any . . . but it was entirely destitute of any faculty of the kind. At length it seized the Thrush by stationing itself for three days beside the water cup.

If, notwithstanding these facts, it should be argued that snakes possess the mysterious, inexplicable power of fascination because birds have been seen to approach them with open wings and plaintive voice, seeming to wait upon their appetite, we must admit that the

* Scientists are at variance with Audubon, and with theorists before him, as to this.—*Ed.*

same faculty is possessed by other animals. I once saw a Mockingbird
approach a hog (in the way birds are said to behave when under such
influence) which was munching something at the foot of a cedar.
The bird fluttered before the grunter with open wings, uttered a low,
plaintive note, alighted on his back, and began to peck at his snout—
only because she had a nest in the tree. Several of her young had
fallen out. A friend told me of a similar scene enacted by a Catbird
and a dog which had disturbed the brood. The movements of the
bird were like those associated with the effects of fascination.[64]

VI

Red-tailed Hawk

REGARDLESS of certain acts of retribution between man and the
Hawk, it would be difficult to visit a Louisiana plantation, especially during winter, without observing a pair of Red-tails. Early in
February they begin to build their nest in some triple-forked branch
of one of the tallest and largest trees. Their depredations for the
feeding of their young is astonishing . . . among the Rabbits, Gray
Squirrels, tame Pigeons—and woe to the cock or hen that strays far
from home. The Red-tailed Hawk visits the farm houses to pay his
regards to the poultry, and without much caution. He sails over the
chickens, ducklings and young turkeys then plunges from on high upon
one of them, to sweep it off to the nearest wood. If still hungry he now
and then will manage to elude the vigilance of the Martins, Swallows
and little Kingbirds, and seize an old fowl. The farmer hears the clamor
and swears vengeance on the robber. He remembers having seen the
Hawk's nest. He angrily resolves to put a stop to this series of depredations. With his axe and rifle he strides toward the tree in which nestle the
hopes of the Red-tailed Hawk among the tall branches. He eyes the
trunk. He will not be outsmarted by a Buzzard, even if the victory costs
him much labor. He throws aside his hat, rolls up his sleeves. Brawny
arms fall to with the axe that sends large chips flying on all sides.
Well aware of the outcome, the poor mother-bird sails sorrowfully
over and around. She would fain beg mercy for her young. She alights
on the edge of the nest to urge her offspring to take flight. The farmer
sees her, sticks his axe in the core of the tree, raises his rifle to his
shoulder. A whizzing ball pierces her heart. The farmer changes sides
to renew his work with the axe. For an hour his blows to the tree
trunk keep falling. Looking upwards he judges which way the giant
of the forest will fall. Under his redoubled blows the huge oak begins
to tremble. Were it permitted to speak, it might ask why it should
suffer for the deeds of another. But it slowly inclines and its broad arms
sound an awful rustling, before the noble tree crashes to earth like
lightning. The work of revenge has been accomplished.[65]

VII

Shadow of Destiny

I N October, 1823, my son Victor and I sailed on the Mississippi from Bayou Sara for Louisville on the steamer *Magnet*. The very sight of that beautiful river the Ohio, above, would fill me with joy, I knew. But at Trinity village low water compelled us to land and continue by some other means to Kentucky. There were no horses to be had. Anxious to continue my journey without delay, I consigned my effects to the tavernkeeper, to have them forwarded when the waters rose, then questioned my son—newly fourteen—whether he thought he could go the rest of the way on foot. He was not many months over a nearly fatal bout of yellow fever, but with the ardor of youth considered himself able. We dined on fish we ourselves had caught, then took a ramble along the shores of Cash Creek, which will be recalled in the story of my icy journey up the Mississippi to Ste. Genevieve. We slept at the tavern before beginning our long walk north. One of two passengers who expressed a desire to accompany us said he hoped the lad could keep up—that for his part he had urgent business in Frankfort and must push ahead pretty fast.

It was past noon before we crossed Cash Creek. One of our fellow travellers, a delicate and gentlemanly person named Rose, acknowledged that he was not a good walker. He was glad my son was along, because he felt he might keep up with a mere youth. The other one, a burly, tall personage, at once pushed forward. We walked in Indian file along the narrow track cut through the sugarcane, on past a woodyard. We entered a burned forest full of logs and briars that drove us out toward the dry, pebbly river bed instead. Sometimes my son went ahead, sometimes he dropped behind, until we neared the best house that the village America afforded. There Mr. Rose became purser for the party, and paid the bill for our repast.

We walked on for another seven miles along the river's edge, having already covered twelve tough ones. At a house near the bank we met a woman picking cotton in a small field. She agreed to let us stay in her cabin for the night if we would make the best of the fare on which she and her husband lived. While she cooked supper, my son, Mr. Rose and I were refreshed by a swim, leaving our fellow traveller to stretch himself on a bench by the door.

It was sunset. Thousands of Robins were flying southward in the calm, clear air. The Ohio spread before us smooth as a mirror. The good man of the house, a tall, rawboned fellow with bronzed honest face called us to the frugal meal. We came in a trice. The four of us lay down in a large bed spread on the floor. The good couple went aloft, promising to call us at daybreak.

The woodsman roused us but recommended a place seven miles farther on for a much better breakfast than what he could provide. He would take no money but accepted my gift of a knife. My dear boy appeared very weak at the outset but began to gain momentum about the time our more redoubtable companion showed signs of lassitude. We reached the cabin of a lazy man blessed with an industrious wife and six hardy children all laboring for his support. Her manners and language suggested much higher birth than her present circumstances. A better breakfast I never ate: bread of new corn freshly ground on a tin grater by the beautiful hands of our blue-eyed hostess; chicken cooked by one of her lovely daughters; good coffee and fresh milk. As she watched with pleasure how heartily we ate she held a babe to her bosom. The children went to work. The lazy husband went to the door to smoke a corncob pipe. Into the ruddy hand of the chubby urchin we pressed a dollar and bade his mother farewell.

Again we trudged along the beach. After a while we took to the woods. My son became faint, dear boy! Never can I forget how he lay exhausted on a log, large tears rolling down his cheeks. I bathed his temples, spoke soothingly to him. A fine Turkey cock ran close by and so aroused his attention that he got up and ran a few yards towards the bird. He had new vigor after that.

That night, at Wilcox's wayside inn, we were reluctantly received, mostly ignored, but, at least, fed and lodged. At sunrise, beautifully reflected on the Ohio, we had a wonderful view of the river before setting out through dense woods to Belgrade two miles yonder, then Fort Massacre, before breakfast. Our tall friend grumbled that he was not used to "skulking through the bushes or tramping over stony sandbars in the beating sun." The other one kept up about as well as Victor. I, rather than the previously impatient stalwart, now led the way.

Toward sunset we were opposite the mouth of the Cumberland. A solitary woman, wretchedly poor, assured us that she could feed us and give shelter for the night, but that her skiff could ferry us on our way by moonrise if we wished. We lay down on the browned grass, hungry and fatigued, to await either a meal or the return of the ferry. I grated corn, made a fire, and was about to roast some chickens when a cry of "Boat coming!" roused us all. We crossed half the Ohio, to reach Cumberland Isle, walked across it, then after another ferry ride found ourselves in Kentucky. I was within a few miles of the spot where my horse had been fatally struck from under me by lightning some years before.

No need to protract this narrative. Five days out of Trinity we began to travel over ground glittering with hoar frost that melted as the sun rose. My pleasure in the beauty of Nature was considerably dampened by the spectacle of my weary son's limping along like a winged Turkey. Not that the other two were much better off. While Victor smiled and straightened himself in an effort to keep up, the poor stalwart, who had been leader at first, panted many yards behind us and began to talk of buying a horse. Tolerably good roads helped. That evening we reached a house, with the prospect of supper, and some beds. I went inside to inquire. When I came out I found Victor asleep on the grass. Mr. Rose was examining his sore toes. The former stalwart was finishing a jug of Monongahela whiskey.

Next day as we trudged along we saw a fine black Wolf, quite tame and gentle, whose owner had refused a hundred dollars for it. At an orchard we filled our pockets with October peaches. We found Trade Water River so low that acorns that drifted on its shallows were picked up by Wood Ducks darting about. No sign here of the bulls that once scraped the earth at a large Buffalo Lick, in the love season, or in battle!

Rose's feet became sorer every day. Mr. "Stalwart" was almost ready to give up. At the house of a magistrate in Union County we were given directions for the next lap of our journey. But these were so elaborate as to confuse us, until a man came along on horseback to explain the way. That night, at Highland Lick, we stumbled on a cabin, its door held open by an overturned chair. Inside on a dirty bed lay a man. I saw a table with a ledger on it. Near the fellow was a small cask, over his head a brass pistol, by his side a long Spanish dagger. He rose and asked what was wanted, then pointed toward the house we mentioned, five miles onward. The others had seized the chance to warm themselves by the fire of the salt kettles near by, leaving to me all conversation with this man, an overseer. Off we went across the creek into hilly, "clay-ey," slippery country. Mr. Rose was limping like a lame duck, and his friend was cursing, but Victor was keeping up like a veteran.

On our seventh morning out of Trinity the other two were so nearly done in that they urged us to go ahead without them, over the pleasant barrens and agreeable road just ahead in the beautiful weather. Two hours later Victor and I were in the Green River ferry boat, hanging our legs in the water. At Smith's Ferry the stream looked like a deep lake. The thick cane on the banks and the over-hanging willows formed a fine picture. Smith gave us a good supper, sparkling cider, and a comfortable bed. Here our walk of two hundred and fifty miles ended. Smith made arrangements for us to be driven, by Dearborn wagon, a hundred miles north to Louisville, Kentucky.[66]

The virtue of hospitality, although agreeable to the stranger, is not always duly appreciated. The travelling celebrity often receives a sort so much alloyed by the host's obvious self-interest that the favors he confers are marred by an interminable flow of requests for tales of perilous adventure. The stranger may be received by persons possessed of all that life affords in the way of comforts, but with pomposity. They may lead him through their spacious mansion to a solitary apartment, bid him good-night, and, because he is thought unfit to be presented to a party of "friends," leave him alone to amuse himself. Still another kind of host is the congenial spirit who receives him with open arms. He offers servants, horses, perhaps even his purse, to forward the journey, and parts from his guests with regret. In all these cases the traveller feels more or less obligated, and is accordingly grateful.

It is the woodsman, the man who can offer only humble shelter and homely refreshment, that leaves the deepest impression of any. His kind of hospitality I myself have frequently received in our American woods. After Victor and I had walked for days from Trinity village, we set out by wagon with one Mr. Flint of Smith's Ferry at the rising of the moon, two hours before dawn. Off we went at a round trot, dancing in the cart like peas in a sieve. The rut-filled road was just wide enough for passage; here and there we rumbled over trunks and stumps. Flint, the tavern landlord, boasted of his perfect knowledge of the country. Willingly we confided ourselves to his judgment as he hazarded a shortcut. Before we reached the road again a change from fine, frosty weather to torrential rain occurred. The thunder bellowed. The lightning blazed.

By evening all was black and dismal. Cold and wet, silent and melancholy, we jogged along with no better prospect than a night beneath the wagon and what shelter it might afford. To stop would have been worse than to proceed. In the faint hope that the horses would drag us out of our forlorn state if given free rein, we found our course suddenly altered by the team. Soon a glimmer of light appeared in the distance. We heard the barking of dogs about the same moment. Before a high fence our horses began to neigh—and I myself to haloo, and at such a rate that in a moment or two we saw a flaming pine torch cross the gloom in our direction. The Negro boy said his master had sent him to show the strangers to the house. Much relieved, we reached the gate of a little yard and could see a small cabin.

A tall, fine-looking young man stood in the open door to welcome us. "A bad night, strangers," he called out to us. "You must have lost your way . . . there is no public road within twenty miles." Flint granted that we had, indeed, but thanked God for this reception. "Reception!" laughed the woodsman—with the assurance it would be nothing much, but that it was our safety that counted. He turned out to be the nephew of my Henderson friends the Rankins of Meadow Brook farm. Willy Speed, a bridegroom, turned to his black boy Jupiter and asked him to fetch wood for the fire. He had his wife "call up" the other servants to look after our comfort. Eliza Speed brought us a dry shirt and socks while our wet clothes hung by the fire.

Knowing my countrymen I was not much struck by all this. But my stripling son drew near me, to remark how good it was to have found such good people. Flint helped to put the horses up. Two Negro lads took a look at us; soon the squawking outside promised that good cheer was at hand. A fresh blaze illumined the room. The young bride moved about as if all she did were a pleasure to her.

All gathered round. Willy Speed regretted that we had not arrived three weeks sooner—for his wedding day and a housewarming that would have provided better fare than bacon and eggs and broiled chicken. Thereupon, he galloped three miles to his father's place, through torrents of rain, to bring a keg of cider. At this moment I was struck by the kindness of our host. The generosity of these young hearts knew no limits, despite means barely sufficient for their own comfort in a beautifully clean, new, tulip-tree log cabin. On one side hung homespun gowns and petticoats, on the other male attire. A large spinning-wheel with its rolls of wool and cotton stood in a corner. A small cupboard full of new dishes, cups, plates and tin pans filled another. The small, quite new, walnut table was polished as bright as could be. A fine counterpane on the only bed visible proved the young wife an expert at spinning and weaving. A fine rifle ornamented the chimney-piece of a hearth so big as to make one wonder whether it had been built to leave room for any number of progeny resulting from this happy union.

Jupiter ground coffee. The bride baked bread on a flat board before the fire. Bacon and eggs began to murmur and sputter in the pan. A pair of chickens puffed and swelled on a grid over the embers in front of the fire. Just as clattering hoofs announced Willy's return, a cloth was laid and the table set.

"Just think, Eliza," he said, his eyes sparkling as he came in with a two-gallon keg, "father wanted to rob us of the travellers and was coming to ask them to his place—just as if we could not give them enough—come gentlemen, sit down and help yourselves." From among six new Windsor chairs and some made by Willy I chose one of the latter. Its seat of deer-hide afforded much comfort. While we set to, our hostess resumed her spinning, our host dried out beside the fire. He would be twenty-two on Christmas Day, he told us. Like his aunt Elizabeth Speed Rankin, his father had come as one of a family of nine children to this wilderness tract, from a wornout Virginia farm. All of the nine had married and settled nearby on this land divided among them. Willy had cleared a field or two and planted an orchard, with the help of two Negro boys, during the two years before his wedding. His father had helped him raise the cabin, and had given him cattle, hogs and four horses. His bride had brought another servant.*

Speed offered us a choice of sweet or sour milk. The latter—

* Audubon consistently avoids the term "slave" in his writings, though he himself, like his father before him, had been a slaveholder.—*Ed.*

buttermilk—is considered a treat by some farmers. I chose to stick to cider, for my part.

After supper and a chat by the fire we were ready for the conversation that followed. Willy asked Eliza what sort of bed she could fix us. She said smilingly that she would divide their bedding with us, put half on the floor to enable us to sleep very well—"the best we can spare." I immediately objected. I said I would rest in a blanket by the fire. Neither one would listen, but instead began arranging the bedding for us. Pretty soon Mr. Flint was lulling us travellers to sleep with a long story to show us how passing strange it was that he should have lost his way.

Soon Aurora's light turned off Nature's "sweet restorer, balmy sleep." I really believe that young Speed was glad to find the weather too bad for us to start out. But I had Flint see about his horses. The couple whispered together; then, over our protests, they made breakfast. By nine we were on our way as the weather began to brighten. Willy guided us on horseback to the next road, a few hours away, before we headed for the main one and regretfully parted with our woodsman host. Telling Flint with a smile that he hoped we might follow the longest trail for a "shortcut" again some time, he bade us adieu, to trot to his happy home.[67]

I entered Louisville with thirteen dollars in my pocket. My plan was to rent a room in Shippingport before I placed Victor as a clerk apprentice in the Berthoud countinghouse concern. I myself planned to take whatever artisan tasks I might find before proceeding to Philadelphia in the spring, in the interest of my *Birds of America*.* I was advised to make a painting of the Falls of the Ohio. This made me resolve to paint one hundred views of American scenery. It would not surprise me, I said, to find myself seated at the foot of Niagara, one day.[68]

For nearly twenty years my life had been a succession of vicissitudes. I had tried various branches of commerce but all proved unprofitable, doubtless because my whole mind was ever filled with my passion for rambling. I had had to struggle against the will of all who during that period called themselves my friends . . . except my wife and children. Breaking through all the bonds I gave myself up to my pursuits. Anyone unacquainted with my extraordinary desire to see

* The mission to Philadelphia failed.—*Ed.*

and judge for myself would doubtless have pronounced me callous
to every sense of duty. I undertook long, tedious journeys, ransacked
the woods, the lakes, the prairies, and the shores of the Atlantic.

I reached Philadelphia on April 5, 1824. But I soon found myself
compelled to seek elsewhere for patronage. I visited New York . . .
ascended the Hudson to our broad lakes . . . wildest solitudes . . .
and forests, where I began to fancy my work already "multiplying"
through the efforts of some engraver. Dreams!—I wondered whether
a free, unaided individual like myself might possibly accomplish the
grand scheme. . . .[69]

Artists—and I know not if I can be called one—too often imagine
they must excel. That foolish idea leads them to go on spoiling much
paper and canvas instead of employing themselves in a different
manner. But digressions aside—I directed my steps towards the Falls
of Niagara, to put them on paper and so amuse my family. I reached
its tavern with little more than some drawings of rare birds and
plants after a tedious journey. My plight was such as would have
deterred most individuals from intruding upon polite society. A long
time had passed since the last of my linen had been removed from
my body and used to clean my gun. Dressed like an Indian of the
poorer variety, I was even more disagreeable, to the civilized eye,
for not having trimmed my beard or hair. The painter Hogarth could
not have asked for a better model for Robinson Crusoe. My beard
covered my neck in front; my hair fell over my shoulders; my leather
dress needed mending. A large knife hung at my side. My rusty tin
box of drawings and colors I kept wrapped up in a wornout blanket
that served me as a bed when it was not buckled to my shoulders.
To all who saw me I must have seemed in the depths of poverty,
or perhaps despair. But, unconcerned for my appearance, I strode
into the sitting room to unstrap my little burden and ask how soon
breakfast would be ready.

In America, to which so many come in search of opportunity, no
one is ever refused admittance to an inn. The landlord looked at
me with a quizzical eye. He answered that breakfast would be served
when the guests came down. I told him of my avocations to convince
him that he could feel safe on the score of remuneration. This put me
on a footing of equality in the house. He talked a good deal of the
many artists who had visited the Falls that season, and offered me
accommodations well suited to the task of finishing the drawings I
proposed to make. Once he had left me I looked about the room

and saw several views of the Falls. These so disgusted me that I suddenly came to my senses. "What!" thought I. "Have I come here to mimic Nature in her grandest enterprise—to add *my* caricature of one of the wonders of the world to those which I see here? No—I give up the idea as a vain attempt. I will look on these mighty cataracts and imprint them on my mind—there alone can they be represented!"

Had I undertaken a view, I would in any case have expected to describe the form, height, and the tremendous roar of these Falls. I might have spoken of the people who imperil their lives by venturing between the rock and the sheet of water; calculated the density of the atmosphere; related wondrous tales of Indians shooting the depths in their canoes; and described the narrow, rapid, rockbound river that leads the Erie waters to Lake Ontario, while remarking, *en passant*, the Devil's Hole and much besides. But to those who had seen this most magnificent of the Creator's works, my description would prove useless, quite puny, as would the picture I might have attempted for my family. Not all the pictures ever made, or all the descriptions of Niagara ever written, could evoke more than a glimmer as faint as that of a glow-worm beside the overpowering glory of the meridian sun.

I breakfasted amid a crowd of strangers who gazed and laughed at me. I paid my bill. I rambled about the Falls for a while. Several young gentlemen were *sketching on cards* the mighty mass of foaming waters.

At Buffalo, to which I walked, I bought new apparel and sheared my beard.[70] This village, utterly destroyed by fire in the War of 1812, now had about two hundred houses, a bank and daily mail. I found it filled with Indians, come to receive their annuity. The chief Red Jacket was a noble-looking man; another, called Devil's Ramrod, had a savage look. I took deck passage by schooner to Erie, Pennsylvania. Louisiana, by way of Pittsburgh, the Ohio, and the Mississippi, was my destination.[71]

Not all the incidents in the life of a student of Nature are agreeable in kind. This truth an extract from one of my journals bears out. The theft of my money on the shores of Canada during my journey to Niagara was as adroitly managed as any ever brought off in notorious Cheapside, London. The thing could not be helped; to have pined over it would have been unmanly. I told my travelling companion, an itinerant artist, found on the way to Erie, to keep a good heart. I felt satisfied Providence had something in store for us. The entire sum of our wealth was just seven dollars and a half—reckoned while I was still fifteen hundred miles from home.

At the entrance to Presque Isle Harbor the schooner could not pass the bar on account of a violent gale that came towards us. We dropped anchor and remained on board throughout the night, seasick at times, as well as sad that we had taken so little care of our money. How long we might have remained at anchor I cannot tell, had not that Providence on whom I never cease to rely come to our aid.

Never shall I forget that late August morning when the United States Navy commandant at Presque Isle sent a rowboat with six men to our rescue. My drawings were put into the craft with utmost care before we ourselves took our places, to be rowed ashore and safely landed. I gave the sailors one of our dollars for them to drink to the "freedom of the waters."

At a humble inn my companion and I had bread and milk while considering how to proceed from Erie. Our luggage was rather too heavy, so we hired a cart to carry it to Meadville for five of our vanishing dollars, along with ourselves. Had it not rained nearly all day, the country we passed through might have been favorable to our pursuits. We spent the night, a Sunday, at our driver's house. The good folks had not yet returned from their distant meetinghouse, but his grandmother, a cheerful dame, bestirred herself, got up a fire to dry our clothes, and put enough bread and milk on the table for a small army.

Fatigued from the jolting of the cart, we asked for a place to rest. As the good woman showed us into a room filled with beds I remarked that I would paint her portrait for her children in the morning. My companion and I were asleep and would probably have remained so, till morning, if a light—carried by three damsels— had not awakened us later on. As quickly as they saw us they blew out their candle, supposing us asleep, and got into a bed opposite our own. We heard them say how delighted they would be to have their portraits taken, as well as their grandmother's. In the backwoods one room often suffices for all the members of a family. Soon we were all asleep without more disturbance.

At dawn we found we were alone again. The good country girls had dressed in silence and left us before we wakened.

No sooner had I made known my intention to portray the girls, after I had been well greeted by the family below, than my young subjects disappeared to deck themselves out in their Sunday clothes. My black chalk went to work—to their delight—while the fumes of breakfast that whetted my sensitive nose redoubled my ardor for the task . . . soon over, along with breakfast.

While our guide, Maxon Randall, hitched his cart I played a few airs on my flageolet. By 10 A.M. we were under way. My companion and I enjoyed our journey with all the happy-go-lucky spirit of our artistic characters. Heavy timber threw its mellow shade over the land. There were pines, evergreens above all, and also trees loaded with fruit. The hay was still standing. The peaches were quite small and green, and the oats were just being reaped on account of the lateness of the crops that year.

At last we reached French Creek, Pennsylvania. At Meadville we paid Randall his promised five dollars before he cracked his whip and faced about. We were now down to a hundred and fifty cents. There was no time to lose. We put our baggage and selves under the roof of the Traveller's Rest before walking out to survey the little village that was about to contribute to our support. It appeared rather dull. But, thanks to God, I have always found something of His grand and beautiful works to admire on all such rambles. Moreover, I had a portfolio of drawings under my arm and some credentials in my pocket. Up Main Street I walked, eyeing different *heads* from left to right as I went. My eyes rested on that of a shopkeeper whom I thought a likely subject. I begged permission to sit down, then fell silent, to await his curiosity about what was "in that portfolio." At these three words I opened it to his view. The Hollander complimented me on the birds and flowers. I showed him a sketch of one whom I called my best friend—my wife—and asked if he would like one of himself in the same style. He not only answered yes, but promised to exert himself in helping to find as many more customers as he could.

Supper was ready at the Traveller's Rest: *table d'hôte* as is generally the case in America. Because of my flowing hair I was taken for a missionary and asked to say grace, which I did with a fervent spirit.

At daylight I visited the groves and woods . . . returned, breakfasted. It was ten o'clock before the sitter was ready at the store, eager though I was to begin. I ascended a crazy flight of steps from the rear storeroom to a large garret that extended over the place. Four windows at right angles posed a problem. I took a blanket to close those openings that interfered with a *painter's light*. In one corner a cat nursed her young among a heap of rags destined for the paper mill. I saw at a glance two hogsheads of oats, a parcel of Dutch toys strewn on the floor, a large drum, a bassoon, fur caps on wall pegs, and the clerk's portable bed that swung like a hammock near the center.

First the merchant had his son pose, to test my skill. I finished his phiz, which was approved of. The merchant then took the chair; I had the good fortune to please, with him, also. Little by little the gentry of the village had been crowding in to watch. Some laughed, others wondered. My work went on in spite of all. Huidekoper, the store-keeper, invited me to spend the evening at home for some flute and violin music, after which I returned to my companion in good spirits. Judge of my pleasure on finding he also had made two sketches!

I felt gratified, by the end of another such day, that the talents hidden by my gray coat had made their way out. I was pleased to realize once more that first-rate talents without industry count for less than moderate abilities with the same. Our hearts were light, our pockets replenished. We walked to Pittsburgh—happy as our circumstances permitted—in just two days.[72]

I spent one month in Pittsburgh, and continued drawing. I scoured the country for birds. A merchant, Henry Baldwin, volunteered to subscribe for my constantly dreamt of book of birds. His was the three-hundredth such promise. The Reverend John H. Hopkins and his ministry brought me to think more than I usually did about religious matters. (I confess I never think of churches without feeling sick at heart at the sham and show of their professors. To repay evil with kindness is the religion I was taught to practice, and this will forever be my rule.)

Late in October I bought a skiff to go down the Ohio and Mississippi, in company with an artist, a French doctor named Lamotte, and an Irish crewman. At Wheeling the artist and doctor became disgusted with boating, wet, and rain; the Irishman was tired of his bargain. They left. To repair my very low finances I sold my skiff and took passage on a keelboat for Cincinnati. I got a loan cheerfully and reached my son in Shippingport. Too much notice was taken of my rough appearance. I decided to move on quickly to Bayou Sara, and open a school that would enable me to complete my ornithological studies [and reach England]. I rejoined my wife, still a teacher at Beech Woods plantation, in my tattered clothes—looking, with my uncut hair, like the Wandering Jew. I was put ashore about midnight.

On that dark, rainy, sultry night I groped my way to the village, about a mile away. That awful scourge, the yellow fever, prevailed. It had been carrying off victims more relentlessly than ever before. The desolation made itself felt at once. I walked into one large hotel, to find it deserted, its doors standing open. All had withdrawn to the pine woods. On rousing the postmaster I learned to my joy that my wife and son John were well. In the calm, heavy, suffocating atmosphere it seemed to me as if I were breathing death. The tavern had no bed to spare but sent me to a villager, the German, Nübling, who, though he could not take me in, gave me supper and offered me a horse like the good and kindly lover of natural sciences that he was.

To reach my beloved wife and child I took a straight course through woods I thought I knew thoroughly, hardly caring where I might have to cross the bayou. Two hours later I reached its shores. The horse refused to enter the water, snorted, and made off through the woods as if wanting to cross elsewhere. We returned to the shore and crossed over safely. Stars at last peeped through the overcast sky to help me make my way through the gloom. Mosquitoes were plentiful. I thought I recognized a spot where I had once watched a Wild Cat or Deer. But at dawn I found myself in woods unknown to me. I met a black man who told me I had gone two miles beyond Beech Woods. I spun about, and spurred my horse into a brisk gallop that soon brought me to the plantation. It was early, but I found my beloved wife up and busily giving a piano lesson to one of her pupils. I held and kissed her. All toils and trials were forgotten. I was once more happy.

After a few days' rest I began to think of the future and how to hasten the publication of my drawings. My wife was earning a large income that she generously offered to share in order to help forward my aim. Numerous pupils wanted lessons in music, French and drawing. From nearby Woodville came an invitation to teach dancing. A class of sixty was organized.

One day I went over to begin my duties. I dressed at the hotel, then with my fiddle under my arm entered the ballroom. My music was highly appreciated at the start. I placed the gentlemen in line, thinking to let the young ladies compose themselves a little. How I toiled before

I could get one graceful step or motion! I broke my bow and, nearly, my violin in my excitement and impatience! Next I had the ladies, alone, take the same order and try the same steps. Then I tried both together —pushed one here, another there—all the while singing to myself to assist their efforts. The many parents who were looking on seemed to be delighted. At the close of this first lesson I was asked to *dance to my own music*. This I did—until the whole room came down in thunderous applause, in the clapping of hands and shouting. Thus ended my first lesson and an amusing comedy. Lessons in fencing, for the young gentlemen, came next. I went to bed extremely fatigued. Nevertheless, the dancing speculation was to fetch two thousand dollars.[73]

Never shall I forget an encounter of one of those Bayou Sara days.

Late one sultry afternoon I emerged from a swampy place of baneful effluvia to head towards home. Besides my heavy gun I was laden with a pack of five or six Wood Ibises, but moved along at a lively speed. I thought that to wade through a miry bayou that I came to might be dangerous, although it was only a few yards wide. On account of the mud I could not ascertain its depth, especially under such a burden. So, one at a time, I threw my birds across it, then my gun, powder flask, and shot-bag. To defend myself I drew my hunting knife from its scabbard, to be ready for Alligators. Carefully and slowly I waded in, followed by my faithful dog "Plato" who enjoyed the cooling of his fatigued and heated body. The water deepened, as did the mire of the bed; but with a stroke or two more I gained the opposite shore.

Scarcely had I stood up on the bank when my dog ran to me in terror, his eyes bursting from their sockets, his mouth grinning the hatred expressed by his stifled growls. Thinking this due to the scent of a Wolf or Bear, I stooped to take up my gun.

"Stand still or die!" I heard a deep voice command me.

Such a *qui vive* was as unexpected as it was rare. Instantly I cocked my gun, ready to shoot, but saw no one. I meant to resist the peremptory command that blocked my way here. Presently a tall, sturdy Negro emerged from the bushy undergrowth where he had crouched out of sight. In a voice still louder he repeated his order. Had I pressed a trigger his life would have ended in a flash. But I saw that the gun he aimed at my breast was a wretched rusty piece from which fire could hardly be produced. Feeling little fear I did not judge that the occasion warranted so rash an act, but instead laid my gun by my side.

I tapped my dog lightly to silence him, then asked the man what he wanted.

The stranger's long habit of submission—and my own forbearance—had their effect. "Master, I am a runaway," he said. "I might perhaps shoot you down. But God forbids it. For I feel just now as if I saw Him ready to pass judgment against me for such a foul deed. I ask your mercy. For God's sake, do not kill me, master!"

"Why have you left your quarters where certainly you must have fared better than in these unwholesome swamps?" I asked him.

"Master, my story is a short but sorrowful one. My camp is close by," he said, "and as I know you cannot reach home tonight, depend upon *my honor* that if you will follow me there, you shall be safe till morning, when I'll carry your birds to the main road, if you will let me."

His large intelligent eyes and calm manner and tone of voice induced me to risk the venture. I felt myself at least his equal in any case; moreover, I had my dog to second me, if need be. I noticed his emphasis on the word *follow* when he asked me to follow him. But when he handed me a butcher knife and threw away the flint of his gun I was confounded. This was too much—I refused the knife and told him to keep his gun in order, for a Cougar or Bear if we should meet one.

Generosity exists everywhere. All, from the lowliest to the proudest of those that encircle the throne of a monarch, experience the results of the impulse, the overpowering sentiment on occasion. I offered to shake hands with the runaway. He thanked me humbly, and gave me a squeeze that impressed me both with the goodness of his heart and his great physical strength. From then on we walked through the woods together. When my dog heard my usual tone of voice return, he stopped his suspicious sniffing, left us, and roved as long as my whistle went unused.

I remarked that we were moving towards the setting sun, away from my homeward course. "Merely for our security," the man replied with utmost simplicity. At each bayou that we reached he threw his gun and knife across, then waited for me to go over first. Coming to an immense canebrake where I had often driven and killed Deer, we began to walk, and to move on "all fours," by turns. Through the tangled stalks the Negro led the way. Solicitously, he helped me over fallen logs. That he was a perfect "Indian" in his knowledge of the woods I saw, for he kept as direct a course as any Redskin I ever followed. Suddenly he gave a loud shriek—not unlike that of an Owl—that so startled me I once more levelled my gun. But he was only letting his wife and children know of his approach. A tremulous answer of the same nature echoed through the treetops. The beautiful ivory teeth of the runaway smiled through the dusk. In gentle tones full of delight he told me that his wife, though black, was as beautiful to him as the President's wife to her husband. She was his "queen," and his sons "so many princes," as I should see for myself.

There, in the heart of the canebrake, we came upon a small fire with slices of venison broiling on the embers. A lad of nine or ten was blowing the ashes from some fine sweet potatoes. A large pallet of Bear and Deer skins seemed to be the family resting place. The wife did not raise her eyes. The three little ones withdrew into a corner like so many uneasy Racoons. But the runaway, bold now, and happy, spoke cheering words to them. They began to look on me as one sent by Providence to relieve them of all their troubles. They hung my clothes up to dry. The Negro asked to clean and grease my gun. The wife tossed a piece of Deer's flesh to my dog that the children, already, were caressing.

Here I was, ten miles or more from home, four or five from the nearest plantation—in the camp of runaway slaves and quite at their mercy. Their strong desire to make me a confidante and friend destroyed any lingering suspicion. By now I was in a condition to relish much less savory fare than the tempting venison and potatoes this family shared with me—for as hearty a meal as I had ever enjoyed.

After supper, when the fire was put out and a small pineknot lighted and placed in a hollow calabash, the runaway unburdened himself of this story that I encouraged him to tell:

A certain planter not very far off was obliged, about eighteen months before, to put up his slaves at a public sale. Their value was well known. The auctioneer was to sell them in lots and singly, depending. The plantation overseer bought the runaway whose value brought an immoderate price, second only to that paid for his wife, bought by a planter from a hundred miles away. For her, eight hundred dollars were bidden. The children were shown, and brought high prices that were to scatter them on different places along the river. The heart of the father was torn by this calamity. For a while he pined under his new master. He feigned illness—if it could be said that he *feigned* it in his grief— refrained from food for days, and disappointed the overseer in the bargain he had driven to acquire him.

On a night of furious winds the poor Negro made his escape through the swamps into the heart of the canebrake. A few nights later he reached his wife and led her away. The children he succeeded in stealing, one after another, until at last all the objects of his love were under his care again. To provide for five was no easy task in those wilds which planters, up in arms, were ransacking. Necessity, the saying goes, brings the Wolf from the forest. The runaway had been stealing back to his first master's plantation whose house servants gave him provisions to take back to the camp at dawn. Once he had set a gun and returned to find a dead Bear in front of the muzzle. The same friends kept him in ammunition which, on damp and cloudy days, he ventured to use near camp. Courageous, active, he grew careless of the distance. It was on one such excursion that I met him. He assured me that the noise I had made in passing through the bayou had caused him to lose a chance to shoot at a fine Deer with his old musket. It missed fire "sadly too often."

Both the runaways rose, their eyes full of tears, after making known their secret. "Good master, for God's sake, do something for us and our children," they sobbed with one accord. Their little ones lay sound asleep in the fearlessness of innocence. Who could hear such a tale without emotion? I promised my most heartfelt assistance. I slept close to their urchins as if on a bed of the softest down while they sat up, that night, to guard my repose.

Day broke, so fair, so pure, so gladdening that I told them this must be a good omen, and that I had little doubt of obtaining their full pardon. I promised to accompany them to their first master, and said I desired the children to come with them. They gladly obeyed.

My Ibises hung round their camp. I notched several trees as a memento of my having been there. The owner, with whom I was well acquainted, received me with the usual, generous kindness of the Louisiana planter. Within an hour the family were again looked upon as his own. He later bought them back and treated them with his former kindness, so that such happiness as is to be found among slaves of the region was once more theirs. The devotion that had led to their adventures in the canebrake continued unbroken.

I have since been informed that it has become illegal to separate members of slave families without consent.[*74]

* Audubon cites no authority.—*Ed.*

VIII

Shape of Destiny

A MERICA having by now become my country, I prepared, and with deep sorrow, to leave it, after having tried in vain to publish in the United States. (In Philadelphia, Alexander Lawson the engraver of the ornithologist Alexander Wilson, and others around him, had expressed the opinion that my drawings of birds could never be engraved. Other difficulties that presented themselves in New York City immediately after my visit to Philadelphia made me determined, in spite of all, to carry my collections to Europe.) I knew not an individual in England; and although I was the bearer of letters from American friends and statesmen of great eminence, my situation appeared precarious in the extreme.[75]

On May 17, 1826, I left New Orleans on the *Delos,* commanded by Captain Joseph Hatch of Kennebunk, Maine, bound for Liverpool.

The steamer *Hercules* towed us several miles outside the Balize. About ten hours later she left us, but there was still not a breath of wind to bear us off. The waters were smoother than the prairies of the Opelousas in Louisiana. Notwithstanding our big sweep of canvas, we lay floating at the mercy of the currents like a dead Whale, under skies uncommonly fair and in excessive heat. The sailors whistled for wind, then raised their hands in all directions for the feel of some motion in the air, but to no purpose. This was a dead calm. We concluded that Aeolus had agreed with Neptune to detain us until our patience had been tested or our sport exhausted. For sport we certainly had, both on board and around the ship, during this sleepy fit of the god Aeolus on whom we depended for our progress toward merry England.

About the end of the week we had lost sight of the Balize, although our captain had had to mind the tug of the helm but rarely. Vast numbers of beautiful Dolphins glided along beside us, gleaming like burnished gold by day, and like burning meteors by night. The captain and his mates lured them expertly with baited hooks as well as with those five-pronged instruments called grains. I was delighted with the sport because it afforded opportunity to observe and note some of the habits of this beautiful fish and others.

The hooked Dolphin flounces vigorously, shoots off with great impetuosity to the very end of the line, then—suddenly checked—it often rises perpendicularly several feet out of the water, and shakes violently in the air to disentangle itself and escape. But if well secured it is not played very long before the experienced fisherman can haul it, exhausted, on deck. If pulled in at once it may shake itself forcefully enough while out of the water to drop back in. Dolphins move in shoals of four or five to twenty. Like Wolves on land they hunt their prey in packs—generally the Flying fish, now and then the Bonita, or the little Rudderfish under the stern if nothing better can be had. For a while the velocity of the Flying fishes lets them escape, sometimes by spreading their broad winglike fins to scatter and sail through the air like a covey of timid Partridges before the rapacious Falcon, straight ahead or to left and right, until they drop once more into their natural element. But all the while their keen and hungry pursuers follow in their wake like Greyhounds, leaping in mid-air again and again, as they gain rapidly on the quarry that they often seize as it falls back into the sea.

Dolphins manifest a very remarkable sympathy with each other. The moment one is hooked or grained the others make up to it. They remain around until the unfortunate fish is pulled on board, then move off together. Seldom do they bite at anything thrown out to them as they go—or at least this is true of the larger ones, which in any case keep apart from the young in the way several species of birds may be observed to do. Large shoals of smaller Dolphins remain under the bows of a ship and bite, one after another, at any sort of line, as if determined to find out what became of their lost companion—until all may be caught.

You must not suppose that the Dolphin is without its enemies. Who in this world, whether man or fish, has not enough of them? It may be about to swallow, not what it takes for a Flying fish, but a piece of lead with a few feathers fastened to it, when an insidious Barracuda happens along—to seize and cut it in two. I saw the sharp teeth of one of these carry off part of a hooked Dolphin that had already been hoisted to the surface of the water.

Dolphins caught in the Gulf of Mexico during the calm were suspected of being poisonous. To make sure about this, our African Negro cook never boiled or fried one without first placing a dollar inside it, to see if the silver would tarnish. If not, the fish was served to us as perfectly good. Inasmuch as not one of a hundred caught turned silver into copper, I suspect that our African sage was no magician.

One sultry morning late in June a surprise awaited me when I got out of my hammock that was slung on deck. The gleeful sporting of a swarm of Dolphins all around betokened wind. The sailors watched them, murmuring, "Aye, and a fair breeze too." I caught several within an hour, by which time few remained about the ship. But not a breath of air was stirring on that day or the next. The sailors were in despair. I would probably have desponded also, had not my spirits been raised by the tug of a very large Dolphin on my hook. I hauled it in—to find a magnificent creature. The biggest I had ever caught, its tail flapped the hard deck rapidly, so that the sound was like the roll of a drum. Its beautiful color changed from blue, then to green, silver, golden, and burnished copper—all the colors of the rainbow—until the quivering agony of death turned it dull. It settled into a deep calm that seemed, symbolically, to have stilled the winds and quieted the proud ocean waves.

Shark's flesh in long strips makes the best bait. I think the Dolphin prefers it to the simulated Flying fish, which it rarely seizes except when the ship is under way, and it is made to rise to the surface. But hunger and the absence of prey will induce the Dolphin to dash at any sort of bait—even a piece of white linen fastened to a hook. Its appetite is as keen as a Vulture's. Given the chance, it gorges itself until it becomes easy prey of its enemies, the Barracuda and the Bottle-nosed Porpoise. One that had been lazily swimming under the stern before we grained [speared] it had a stomach crammed with Flying fish, all lying side by side with tails downward—which is a way of saying, also, that the Dolphin always *swallows its prey tail foremost*. They looked, in fact, like so many salted Herrings packed in a box. We counted twenty-two Flying fishes, six or seven inches long.

The Dolphins in the Gulf of Mexico averaged about three feet. I saw none more than four feet and two inches long; one of these weighed only eighteen pounds, because of its narrow form. I noticed that the upper fin of a fish just caught reaches from the forehead to within a short distance of the tail, and is of a fine dark blue. The upper part of the body is azure, the lower a golden hue mottled irregularly with deep-blue spots. Along the Florida coast they may, like their kinsman the "Cavalier," be seined in shallow water. As food it is not equal to the Barracuda, which is as good a fish as any in the Gulf. When eaten for many days in succession its firm, white flesh, which flakes when cooked, becomes insipid to the taste. Yet at first it tasted delicious to me.[76]

The irregular currents had been carrying us hither and thither. At one point we thought we might drift to the Florida coast, at another to Cuba. A slight motion would revive our hopes, swell our sails a little, carry us through smooth waters like a skater gliding on ice, only to lapse again into a dead calm a few hours later.

One day several small birds alighted on the spars, then on the deck. One, a Rice Bunting, held my attention as a beautiful Peregrine Falcon descended in her wake. The plunderer hovered about for a while before alighting. Then, after stationing himself on the end of a yard-arm, he pounced on the little gleaner of the meadows, to clutch and carry her off in exultation. I was astonished to see the Falcon feed on this Finch while on the wing, and with precisely the ease and composure that the Mississippi Kite might show in devouring—while in the air—a Red-throated Lizard swept from out of some magnificent tree of the Louisiana woods.

On board there was a pet, nothing more nor less than the female companion of a cock. In other words, she was a common hen that some liked because now and then she dropped a fresh egg, so rare an article at sea, even aboard the *Delos*. Others liked her for the pleasing simplicity of her character; still others because when they pushed her overboard it amused them to watch the poor thing flail the water with her feet in an effort to reach her floating home. This she never failed to accomplish with the kindly aid of our humane Captain. Several weeks out to sea, she accidentally flew overboard as we were scudding along at a furious rate. I thought I saw a tear in the eye of Joseph Hatch as he watched her float, panting, in our wake.

That was after we were no longer becalmed, and after we were heartily displeased at old Aeolus for overlooking us. One windless afternoon we caught two Sharks. In the female we found ten young ones, all alive and quite able to swim, as we soon found out by casting one into the sea. It made off as if quite able to shift for itself. The head half of one that was cut in two swam off out of sight. We used the rest as bait for Dolphins.

Rudderfish were plentiful astern. To amuse me, the Captain dressed some hooks beneath sails that began to bulge a little and bear our ship through the water, then he handed me one of the thread-lines baited with bits of bacon. From a cabin window we dropped out lines among myriads of delicate little fishes. They rose in such rapid succession that in about two hours we had caught a delicious mess of three hundred and seventy. (If ever I am becalmed again in the Gulf of Mexico I shall not forget the Rudderfish!) The little things are three inches long; thin, but deep from ventral to dorsal fin. So voracious were they, as they kept en masse to the lee of the rudder that they actually leaped at the bait the way "sunnies" do in our rivers. But the instant the ship was becalmed again they scattered and would bite no more. Not one did I ever see, when crossing the north Atlantic in after years, among many kinds that came close to the stern of various ships, though some were called Rudderfish as well.

A Porpoise, caught by moonlight, weighed about four hundred pounds and was about two yards long. It was grained [speared] rather than harpooned, and held fast while it flounced and beat about the bows, until the Captain took over the grain-line, so as to let the grainer slide down the bobstays with a rope, and then with some effort run it around the tail of the fish. The crew hoisted it on deck. It gave a deep groan, flapped with great force, and soon expired. Eight hours later we opened it, to find its intestines still warm. In its paunch were several partially digested Cuttlefish. In its upper, slightly protruding jaw were single rows of conical teeth about half an inch long and dovetailing, one by one, when the jaws were closed. Its eyes were extremely small. Some of the men on board considered its flesh delicate. If it be good, then in my opinion that of a large Alligator is equally so. And on neither do I myself intend to feast for some time. The Captain told me he had seen Porpoises leap perpendicularly out of the water to a height of several feet. He said small boats have been sunk by Porpoises that chanced to fall into them while sporting.

All the while we were becalmed flocks of Pigeons were crossing the Gulf between Cuba and the Floridas. Many a "Rose-breasted Gull" [?] played around by day. Noddies alighted on the rigging by night. Now and then the Frigate bird [Man-o'-war] ranged high overhead in the azure, cloudless sky. So calm and sultry was the weather that we had a large awning spread on deck, where we took our meals and slept. We got so wearied of the calm that I began to think the very sailors would leap overboard and swim to land. Our Captain kept trying the direction of the currents. An extraordinarily handy gentle-

man, he had a genius for turning powder horns and other articles
into admirable scrimshaw* at his leisure.

On the thirty-seventh day out of New Orleans a smart breeze that
began to overtake us caused much bustling on board the *Delos*. In
a few hours we reached the open Atlantic. Aeolus had finally awakened.
On the nineteenth day after we left the Florida capes we landed at
Liverpool.[77]

To Britain I owe nearly all my success. She furnished the house
of artists and engravers, R. Havell & Son, through which my labors
have been presented to the world. She has also granted me the highest
patronage and honors. To Britain, therefore, I shall ever be grateful.[78]

I was received by the most notable people in and around Liverpool.
In Edinburgh the engraver William Home Lizars offered to bring
out my *Birds of America* in the size of life, beginning in November,
1826.[79]

About the middle of April I reached Newcastle-upon-Tyne, on my
way to London. The Lark was in full song. The Blackbird rioted
in the exuberance of joy. The farmer was cheerfully pursuing his
labors. Although a stranger in a foreign land, I was delighted with
all around me. I had made kind, courteous friendships, and entertained
hopes that these would continue. I was not disappointed. I had looked
forward to meeting the celebrated engraver on wood, Thomas Bewick,
whose works mark the start of an era in the history of art.

Bewick must have heard of my arrival at Newcastle before I had
time to call. For he sent his son to me with the following note:
"T. Bewick's compliments to Mr. Audubon, and he will be glad of
the honor of his company this day to tea at 6 o'clock." His few
words at once revealed his kindly nature.

I had seen little of the town and until I set out with Bewick's
son had never crossed the Tyne. First the fine church of St. Nicholas
caught my eye. Beyond an arched stone bridge lay the wharves and
ships, some American vessels among them. The shores were pleasant,
the ground undulating. I noticed windmills and glassworks among
the buildings. On the Tyne were odd boats manned by long oars
and heavily laden with local produce.

At once I was shown to the old engraver in his workshop. Tall,
stout, full of life although seventy-four, he came forward to welcome me

* Engraved or carved whale's tooth or jawbone.—*Ed.*

with a hearty handshake like the perfect Englishman he was. For a moment he removed his cotton nightcap that the coals of Newcastle had soiled a little, and bared his large head. His smiling eyes were set farther apart than any I had ever seen. He had been at work on a small vignette on a block of boxwood, about two by three inches. It represented a dog frightened by spectres, in the night, among rocks, and the roots and branches of trees, and other things that resembled men. Like all his works this curious piece was exquisite. I felt strongly tempted to ask for a whittled fragment.

Upstairs all the best artists of Newcastle had assembled. But first I was introduced to the amiable and affable Bewick ladies. A miniaturist who had finished a well-drawn portrait of the engraver was among those present. The old gentleman and I remained beside each other, he to talk of my drawings, I of his woodcuts. Now and then he would take off his cap and draw up his gray-worsted stockings to his knee breeches. But when our conversation became animated the cap stuck to the back of his head as if by magic. The neglected hose resumed their downward trend. His fine eyes sparkled. The free, vivacious way that he voiced his sentiments pleased me enormously. Having heard that my drawings had been exhibited in Liverpool he expressed anxiety to see some. This wish I proposed to gratify next morning.

I asked Bewick where I could obtain a copy of his *Quadrupeds* for my sons in Kentucky, a work they wished to own. Immediately he answered—"Here!"—and presented me with a beautiful set.

The tea-drinking came to an end. Young Bewick brought out his new Durham bagpipes and, to amuse me, played some Scottish, English and Irish airs, all sweet and pleasing to my taste. I could scarcely understand how his large fingers managed to cover each separate hole. The sound put me in mind of a hautboy. It had none of the shrill, warlike booming of the pipes of the military Scotch Highlanders heard in Edinburgh.

That night when I parted from Bewick I knew I parted from a friend.

I received another note from him while I was showing some callers my drawings in town. It was an invitation which I understood to mean dinner. Judge of my surprise on discovering at 5 o'clock that, despite my arrival with an appetite becoming the occasion, tea was served. However, the mistake was speedily cleared up to the satisfaction of all concerned. An abundant supply of eatables was placed on the table. A local clergyman joined us. At first the conversation wandered in desultory fashion. But after the repast Bewick took his place by the fire and the two of us discussed our more immediate concerns. I was invited to return for breakfast at 8 A.M., by which time I found the whole family so kind and attentive that I felt quite at home.

Bewick laughed that he would show me how easy it was to cut wood. I soon saw, however, that cutting in his style and method was no joke, easy though he wished it to seem. He himself had made all his delicate and beautiful tools. I may say, with truth, that his shop was the only artist's "shop" I ever found perfectly clean and tidy. He subscribed for my work in behalf of the local Literary and Philosophical Society; but in this his own enthusiasm misled him, for the learned body did not see fit to ratify the act.

Soon again he invited me back to Gatehead. "I could not bear the idea of your going off without telling you, in writing, what I think of your *Birds of America,*" he said. "Here it is in black and white, and make what use of it you may, if any." I put the unsealed letter in my pocket, and prize it as much as a manuscript, the *Synopsis of the Birds of America,* that Wilson gave me when he was in Kentucky. We chatted a while about natural history. Now and then he would start up, exclaiming, "Oh to be young again—I would go to America too. Hey! what a country it will be, Mr. Audubon."

"Hey! What a country it is already, Mr. Bewick!" I retorted.

He drank my health and the peace of the world in hot brandy toddy. I returned the compliment by wishing the health of all our enemies. His daughters enjoyed the scene. They had not seen their father in better spirits in years, they said.

On my next and last visit, when we parted, Bewick repeated three times, "God preserve you, God bless you!" He must have seen how moved I was, even though I could not reply.

A few weeks before his death about a year and a half later, the engraver and his daughters paid me a call in London. I was far from thinking that this interview would be our last and that the death of Bewick, who looked so well, would soon be announced in the papers.

My opinion of this remarkable man is that he was a son of Nature, purely and simply, and that to it he owed nearly all that characterized him as man and artist. Warm in his affections, of deep feeling, highly imaginative, keenly observing, he needed little else to make him what he became: the first English engraver on wood. Where is anything livelier to be found than the vignettes of Bewick, now of the glutton that precedes the Great Black-backed Gull, now the youngsters flying their kite, or the disappointed sportsman who by shooting a Magpie has lost his chance at a woodcock, or the horse trying to reach water, the bull roaring near the fence-style; the poor beggar attacked by the rich man's mastiff? Every leaf of his admirable books excites admiration. Perhaps no one has equalled him in his peculiar path. Thomas Bewick may be rivalled or even excelled in after years, but he must forever be considered, in the art of engraving on wood, what Linnaeus is to natural history. While not the founder he was yet the benefactor, enlightened exponent, and illustrious advocate.[80]

I shall try to give some idea of the Liverpool jail that I have visited. Its fine situation near the mouth of the Mersey River commands an extensive view of the Irish Channel and the mountains of Wales. A large building, it is set in eight walled acres and includes a Court of Quarterly Sessions.

Imagine cells for each female prisoner, but only one cell for perhaps two or three males . . . large apartments for cooking, washing and the like; council rooms, storerooms. . . . I confess that I think the treadmill infamous. Conceive of a wild Squirrel within a round wheel, moving without progress. The labor is severe, the true motive of correction destroyed, because there are no mental resources attached to this laborious engine of mere shame. Why, the stranger wonders, should each prisoner not be taught trades that would enable them, when thrown again upon the vile world, to support themselves more honestly and save them from those temptations which necessity, inevitably, will force upon them? Knowing nothing but the uphill walk, they have a choice between being dragged again and again to the treadmill and sheer despair. Trades would be four times more profitable to the institution than the present grinding of flour that is done; and they would be worthier of the place and its good intentions. I condemn the treadmills not only as machines of labor without either general or personal benefits but as extremely prejudicial to health. Think of those poor miserable beings, obliged either to weigh heavily on one paddle or to raise their own weight to the next. The same effort is cost in walking up a steep hill constantly, for four to six hours, or averaging five, while the man might instead be making a good pair of shoes, cutting nails, or working at some other useful trade.

The wheel of the treadmill is only six feet in diameter, so that the accelerated motion demands steps in quick succession. From experience I know that a quick short step is more fatiguing than a long one and ultimately lowers resistance. The sallow, withered, emaciated, thin visages and bodies of the men at work proved this to my eyes, as well as did my calculation. The wheel forces thirty steps to every revolution, all of them uphill and therefore longer and more laborious than steps on level ground. The wheel goes round once per minute, so that if a man takes steps of two-and-a-half feet each he may take 45,000 in a single day. He receives his neighbor's breath in exchange for his own in this place where free circulation of air is wanting. The body and mind suffer in an exchange of the most debased conversation. I was sorry to find that female deportment is more difficult to manage there than that of men; for the want of tobacco the *ladies* smoke their *petticoats*. I entered a room thick with smoke—most disagreeably so. Each female proceeded to hide the cause of it in her bosom, no fit receptacle for a filthy pipe.

I felt glad to leave this abode of misery with my companion, a Quaker lady of great benevolence and solid understanding. Her committee goes there daily to superintend purchases and sales for the institution. I would write more but I am not the poet and author William Roscoe.[81]

In January, 1829, I made up my mind to go to America, and with much labor and some trouble I made ready. My excellent friend John George Children of the British Museum kindly offered to see to the engraving of my work. I took passage on the packet *Columbia* on account of her name, and paid thirty pounds for passage out of smoky Portsmouth, England, on April 1. I sought new species for the continuation and eventual completion of *The Birds of America*.*[82]

* Robert Havell & Son of London took over the engraving of the Folio of *The Birds of America* (1827–38), after the engraving of the first ten plates by W. H. Lizars of Edinburgh.—*Ed.*

PART THREE

I

*"America, My Country!"**

I<small>N</small> Camden, New Jersey, where I went to watch the passage of certain Warblers on their way north, I took lodgings in a street ornamented with tall Lombardy poplars. In one of these I had the pleasure of finding the nest of the interesting little Warbling Vireo, just beneath my window. Never before had I been able to observe it to such advantage. I had cut down nests from high trees with rifle balls, but had not come upon one so low or open to my gaze as this. The nest is fixed between trunk and branch at a very acute angle. For eight days, mostly in the morning and evening, the birds kept busy, after first examining the tree and warbling congratulations on their good fortune in finding so snug a place. Then they attached blades of grass to the knots of the branch and the bark of the trunk in a circle; on this they worked down, and outwards, until their delicate tenement was formed. Before the end of the second day they had pushed bits of hornets' nests and cornhusk within the grassy rows and fixed them with a silky substance. On the third day the birds could be neither seen nor heard. Thinking a cat might have caught them from the edge of the roof, I despaired of seeing them again.

However, next morning their notes caught my attention before I rose to watch them weaving still more, extremely slender grasses around the frame. They would disappear for an hour at a time before returning with the grass from, presumably, a considerable distance. I went into the street to follow their direction as they flew from tree to tree towards the river. There they paused and seemed to be carefully watching me, until they could safely resume their journey. I retired a little way. Their course then led me out of the village to a large meadow with an old haystack. There each selected a blade of grass. They returned

* Motto on Audubon's seal.

by the same route, but moved so slowly, from tree to tree, that my patience was severely tried. For two days they travelled for the same kind of grass. On the seventh day I saw the female at work with wool and horsehair. The eighth was spent, almost entirely, in smoothing the inside of the nest. They would sit in it, turn round, press the lining —a hundred times or so in an hour, I should suppose. The male had ceased to warble. Both exhibited great concern, going back and forth so often that I actually became quite tired of this lesson in the art of nest building. I should perhaps not have looked at them more that day had not the cat of the house made her appearance just over my head on the roof, within a few feet of the nest. At times she came so near the frightened, innocent creatures that I gave chase to Grimalkin and saved the Vireos—at least for that season.

Within five days five eggs were laid. . . . On the twelfth day of incubation the young came out. . . . I thought I saw them grow every time I turned from my drawing board to peep at them. . . . On the sixteenth day they took to wing. Never had the noted François Huber* watched the operations of his bees more intently than I these Vireos, and I bade them adieu at last with great regret.[83]

After I had spent the spring observing the migratory warblers and other birds which arrive in vast numbers in the Camden region, I prepared to visit the seashores of the state of New Jersey, to acquaint myself with its feathered inhabitants. The country seemed to smile, in the pleasant June weather, at the prospect of bright days and gentle gales ahead.

Professional fishermen gunners passed daily, between Philadelphia and the various small seaports, in Jersey wagons laden with fish, fowl and also the produce needed for the families of these hardy boatmen. I bargained with one to take me and my baggage to Great Egg Harbor.

One afternoon about sunset the vehicle halted at my lodgings. My trunk and guns were thrust into the wagon. The driver whistled to his steeds which made off at a round pace over the loose, deep sand of the roads. After a while we overtook a whole caravan of such wagons moving in the same direction. It being Saturday night the merry wagoners drew up to gather round and relate their adventures

* François Huber, born and died in Geneva, 1750–1831: *Nouvelles Observations sur les Abeilles* (Geneva, 1792).—*Ed.*

of the week . . . the number of "Sheepsheads" he had taken to market . . . the number of Curlews lingering on the sands . . . the harvest of Marsh Hen's eggs. An elderly man assured me the Fish Hawk would be plentiful near Great Egg Harbor. With a laugh he asked if I had ever seen the "Weak Fish" along the coast without the bird in question. Not knowing this animal I confessed my ignorance, whereupon the whole party burst into a loud laugh in which I joined, there being nothing better for it.

About midnight the caravan reached a halfway house for rest. There the wagons took various roads, except for one that remained to keep us company. The bright sand indicated our course very distinctly through the gloom and the dark. The galloping of horses suddenly struck my ear. I looked back, to realize that in another instant we would be in danger. My driver leaped down, to draw his team aside barely in time to let the runaways pass without harm to us. On they went at full speed. Pretty soon their owner came panting up to us. He said his animals had bolted with fright at some noise in the woods. He hoped they soon would stop. Just then we heard a crash. Then all was silent. From the neighing of the horses we knew they had broken loose. When we reached the spot we found the wagon upset. A few yards away were the horses, quietly browsing by the roadside.

Dawn in New Jersey in June is worth a better description than I can furnish. Therefore I shall only say that the moment the sun-beams blazed over the horizon, the loud and mellow notes of the Meadow Lark saluted our ears. On both sides of the road were open woods. I saw several Fish Hawks' nests on the tallest trees. Above, the white-breasted bird slowly winged its way toward the ocean whose salt air filled me with delight. In half an hour we were in the center of Great Egg Harbor.

I had the good fortune to be received into the house of a veteran fisherman and gunner, only a few hundred yards from shore. Thanks to his wife, an excellent woman, and little daughter, as playful as a kitten though wild as a Sea Gull, I was soon quite at home.

Oysters are reckoned out of season at this period, but if eaten when fresh from their beds they are as good as ever. My first meal consisted of some as large and white as any I have eaten. The sight of them, before me on a clean table, and the honest industrious family in my company, never failed to please me more than the most sumptuous fare could have done elsewhere. Gaiety shone in every face during our simple, harmless conversation. The good man rubbed his hands with joy as I explained the object of my visit: shooting and fishing, and long excursions into the surrounding swamps and marshes.

My tall, strong-boned, muscular host of the dark complexion and eyes as keen as a Sea Eagle's [Bald Eagle] proved himself a tough walker undaunted by obstacles. He could pull an oar in competition with any man. As to shooting, rarely did I see him miss. Whether he or an Indian Isle hunter of my acquaintance would have proved best I have often since wondered.

We were off at daybreak, I with my double-barrelled gun, he with a long fowling-piece, a pair of oars and a pair of oyster-tongs. The wife and daughter who had brought the seine to our boat watched us sail away, along the inlet, on a good and gentle breeze. Except for the Florida Keys, Great Egg Harbor probably affords the naturalist as varied a field as any part of our Atlantic seaboard. Birds, fishes and testaceous [hard-shelled] animals abound. The forests shelter beautiful plants. Even on the driest sandbar insects of the most brilliant tints may be seen. The "Lawyer Bird" [Pelican?] happened to be the object of our search, that morning, for several miles of winding inlet waters that brought us into a vast marsh, its nesting place.

When we returned to the channel where we had left our seine to fill, we found the tide out and a number of fine fishes inside. We cooked and ate a few of them on the spot. One seemed to me so curious that I saved it to send to the Baron Cuvier of Paris. We returned to the marshes to continue our researches until the tide came in. On our return to the fisherman's house we dragged the seine successfully several times on the shore in front of his door.

I passed several weeks here . . . one day in search of Herons breeding in the swamps . . . another among the joyously crying Marsh Hens . . . or among the White-breasted Sea Gulls. We hauled the fish called the Sheepshead from an eddy along the shore, or watched the gay Terns dance in the air before they plunged after tiny fry in the waters. Many a drawing I made, many a pleasant day I spent at Great Egg Harbor. Much pleasure would it give me to visit, once more, the good and happy family in whose house I resided.[84]

I left Philadelphia at four in the morning, by coach, with only the bare necessities for the jaunt I now intended to make. These consisted of a wooden box holding a small supply of linen, drawing-paper, my journal, colors, pencils, twenty-five pounds of shot, and some flints; enough cash, my gun "Tear-jacket," and a heart as true to Nature as ever.

Our stagecoaches, none of the best, do not move with the speed of those of some countries. It was 8 P.M. on a dark night when I reached Mauch Chunk, eighty-eight miles from Philadelphia. To reach this place celebrated for its rich coal mines, I had passed through country both highly cultivated and wild (the latter much more agreeable to me). I was shown to the traveller's room, and, unlike most who travel here for the very simple pleasure of being dragged on the railway, received a special rate from the fine-looking young landlord who approved of my plans and had me comfortably fixed inside of four minutes.

The cocks of the village had no more than announced the dawn than I marched out with gun and notebook. I covered much ground, crossed many steep hills, to be much disappointed by the extraordinary scarcity of birds. So I bargained for a ride by cart to the middle of Great Pine Swamp. A heavy storm was rising but that did not stop us. We wound round many mountains before we crossed the highest in tremendous, drenching weather that failed to budge my resolution that compelled the boy to keep driving. Fifteen miles beyond Mauch Chunk we left the turnpike for a bad, narrow road that seemed to have been cut merely to enable the people of the Great Pine Swamp to receive supplies. In the dusk, after making some wrong turns, we were directed to the Jediah Irish place—my destination. We rattled down a steep incline with almost perpendicular rocks on one side, and a chattering stream that seemed to grumble at us strangers on the other. Laurel and pine formed a mass of darkness around us.

The door was already opened for us, because the sight of strangers is nothing unusual in our woods, no matter how remote. I went in while my driver put up his horses in the stable. My expressed wish to remain in the house for some weeks met with the approval of the lady of the house. Her husband was absent from home and not expected for some days. My questions about birds, the country, prompted Mrs. Irish—more *au fait* to household affairs than ornithology—to send for her nephew at once. His appearance and speech were that of an educated person, decidedly solicitous and kind.

The sun shone on the foliage by morning. The always sweet and mellow notes of the Wood Thrush greeted my ears, as did those of other songsters. I had not gone far into the woods before I found a lovely Sylvia which until then I had always sought in vain. I needed no more to convince me that much of value was in store. My young companion offered to accompany me through the woods, but I was anxious to put the beauty of the little bird in my hand on paper. I had him break a twig of blooming laurel for the picture.

A few days passed. I became acquainted with my hostess and her sweet children, and made occasional rambles, but spent most of my time drawing. One morning I saw a tall, powerful man alight from his horse. He removed its bridle, for it to betake itself to the brook to drink while he approached the house. (In America business comes first, and rightly so; I heard him below, then saw him cross to his mills and stores nearby.)

Jediah Irish, a man of qualities impossible to describe, not only made me welcome. He promised to help increase my knowledge. I can never forget our long walks and long talks, or the many beautiful birds we admired and pursued; or the juicy venison, excellent Bear's flesh, and delightful Trout that we enjoyed. While I smoothed and softened the drawings before me he read aloud from his favorite writer, the poet Robert Burns. This was enough to recall my boyhood impressions of the Golden Age—it became reality here.

The Lehigh River courses through these mountains. Its frequent waterfalls form deep pools that lend themselves to mills of any kind. My host had for some years been millwright for the Lehigh Coal Company. He had been manager for the cutting of timber on the mountains. Young, robust, industrious, he and his men had cleared the road over which I came. He erected the mills, and put up his house and buildings. The pass here is so narrow that it looks as if a mountain had split to form it. Both sides ascend abruptly. The settlement is hard to reach, even by the road in its present, more travelled state. So great, he said, was the difficulty in reaching this spot that for months barreled provisions were lowered by rope to the camp below. But axes soon began felling the trees. Greedy mills were soon telling their sad tale of the destruction of the noble forests that in a century will perhaps have disappeared entirely. Many mills rose; many dams defied the impetuous Lehigh. A third or more of the trees have been turned into lumber and floated as far as Philadelphia. They have to be hauled to the edge of the mountains bordering the river, where they are launched into the stream and guided to the mills over shallows and around obstacles. To see them tumbling from on high, glancing off a rock here and there with the elasticity of a football, to fall at last with an awful crash into the river, is too awesome for description. I have seen masses of five

23   JOHN SWIFT,
ASLEEP. Aboard the
Delos. A page from
Audubon's 1826 journal.
—Henry Bradley Martin
            Collection

22   AT WORK ON
THE FORECASTLE,
LARBOARD SIDE.
Aboard the *Delos.*
A page from Audubon's
1826 journal.
—Henry Bradley Martin
            Collection

24   AUDUBON AT
GREEN BANK,
ALMOST, HAPPY!!
—Sep.r 1826. Self-
portrait, Black chalk.
            —Courtesy of
B. L. Rathbone, Esq.

21 OAKLEY PLANTATION.   —Louisiana State Parks Commission

20   MOCKINGBIRD. The snake is from a study made at Oakley in 1821, the birds
and jessamine from the Beech Woods drawing of 1825. (Original study for Plate
217, *The Birds of America*.)   —New-York Historical Society

18 JOHN WESLEY
JARVIS inspired
Audubon's episode,
"The Original Painter."
Oil by Henry Inman.
  —National Collection
          of Fine Arts

19 A CREOLE
GENTLEMAN. Not
Lafayette, as sometimes
hinted. Black-chalk
wash and crayon signed:
"Audubon 1821."
  —John Scott Lansill

25　AMERICAN HARE. Water color by Audubon.　—The American Museum of Natural History

26 CORMORANT. Male adult. Spring Dress. View of Florida Keys. (Plate 252, *The Birds of America*.)

—U. S. Library of Congress

27 GREENSHANK. View of St. Augustine and Spanish Fort, East Florida. (Plate 269, *The Birds of America*.)

—U. S. Library of Congress

28   DEER. Water color by John Woodhouse Audubon.
                    —The American Museum of Natural History

29 AUDUBON WITH GUN AND DOG. *Ca.* 1842. Oil by John Woodhouse
Audubon.   —Robert Gwynne Stout Collection

30   AUDUBON. *Ca.* 1842. Oil by John Woodhouse Audubon.
—The American Museum of Natural History

31   ARCTIC TERN. Drawn June 25, 1833, Labrador. (Plate 250, *The Birds of America*.) —The American Museum of Natural History

32   FORT UNION. Ackermann aquatint (1841) from the oil by Karl Bodmer
(1833) in the collection of Prince Maximilian of Neuwied.

—Joslyn Art Museum, Northern Gas Company, Omaha

33 BUFFALO HUNT. Day & Haghe lithograph of the oil by George Catlin.

—U. S. Library of Congress

34 BLACK RAT. This watercolor and oil was "drawn from Nature. Minnie's Land. Sep.r 1st, 1842. J.J.A." (Plate 23, *Quadrupeds of America*.)

—The American Museum of Natural History

35 SWIFT FOX. Watercolor by Audubon. This Swift or Kit Fox was brought live from Fort Union, North Dakota, and painted at "Minnie's Land. Jan. 18th, 1844." (Plate 51, *Quadrupeds of America*.)

36   PENNANT'S MARTEN. Water color by Audubon. —Wadsworth Atheneum, Hartford

thousand heaped together. My friend Irish says the number is much greater at some seasons. The river becomes completely choked with logs.

Irish described what he calls a "frolic." When the water is running high he leads his men to the upper leap. Each has his wooden hand-spike and short-handled axe. They take to the water like so many Newfoundland Spaniels, be it summer or winter. They separate the logs, to send them floating downstream and whirling round and striking against rocks. The logs have to be forced along shallows with the hand-spikes. At the edge of the dam they are pushed over, until all dams have their logs. Not until then do the drenched leader and his sixty men enjoy the evening of frolicking at a dance that awaits them after a good supper. In the morning a horn calls all the sawyers, millers, rafters, and raftsmen to work. The logs are split, that they may be milled into board. The boards are launched into the stream, to be formed into temporary rafts for the run to market. A lock at the breast of the lower dam releases a pool, held there during seasons of shallow waters in the Lehigh, and the approaching raft shoots through with lightning speed. The water suffices to float them to Mauch Chunk's canals.

Game was extremely abundant in that range before it began to be settled. Elk browsed high in the mountains. Bear and the common Deer are still hunted there, as well as the fairly abundant Wild Turkey and Grouse. As to Trout, the angler should go there; I have been made weary by pulling the sparkling fish, in its zest for the struggling grasshopper on my line, from those rivulets.

Something comical happened one afternoon, when some of Irish's raftsmen were returning from Mauch Chunk. This was when the huckleberries were plentiful and ripe. The sound of snuffing suddenly alerted them to the presence of Bears close by. No fewer than eight of the bruins made their appearance. The men faced about with their axes, ready and willing for the scratch. But claw and tooth drove them off in a twinkling as the assailed turned into assailants. Down the mountain the men rushed. When they returned with their rifles no Bears were to be found. Nightfall forced them to give up and go home, with a laugh that concluded the affair.

I spent ten weeks in the Great Pine Forest. (*Swamp* it cannot fairly be called, although it sometimes is.) The time came for me to follow the migratory flocks southward. I bade adieu to the excellent wife and children of Irish who shouldered his heavy rifle to trudge along with me over the mountains. We reached Mauch Chunk in time for dinner. May I have the pleasure of seeing that good, that generous man again![85]

One of my forty-eight new drawings made beneath the roof of Jediah Irish was of the diminutive Winter Wren. Its sweet song came to my ear at a time when I was on my guard against venomous reptiles in a tangled wood. It so cheered me that I lost all apprehension. I pressed forward through rank briars and stiff laurels in hopes of finding the bird not far from its nest. As if bent on puzzling me, the Wren rambled among the thickest bushes now singing near by, now from a different direction, with uncommon cunning. Finally, much fatigued, I saw him alight close to the roots of a tree where his warbling exceeded anything before this, it seemed to me.

Suddenly another Wren appeared, then both vanished. Without taking my eyes from the spot for an instant, I walked up to it and found a protuberance covered with moss and lichens. It was like most excrescences that are seen on forest trees, but with the difference that its opening was perfectly rounded, clean, and smooth. I put a finger in and felt the pecking of a bill. A querulous cry sounded. I had, in a word, found the nest of our Winter Wren for the first time in my life. Gently I forced the tenant out, before scooping up the eggs—six in all. The little bird called to her mate, and their united clamor induced me to leave their treasures with them. I was just about to go off when it struck me I ought to take a description of the nest, since I might not have the opportunity again. I hope all will believe that when I resolved to sacrifice the nest, it was as much on your account as on my own.[86]

The civil engineer, White, visited me at the Inn where I paused, and he looked at my new drawings. News of my sons, then in Kentucky, made me more anxious than ever to move in that direction. A sharp frosty breeze was my sole companion on the way to Philadelphia. Left to my thoughts I marvelled that such a place as the Great Pine Forest should be so little known to Philadelphians, scarcely any of whom had been able to direct me towards it. How regrettable, thought I, that the young gentlemen there, so much at a loss to know what to do with their leisure, should not visit these wild retreats so valuable to the student of nature. If they were to occupy themselves with the contemplation of those riches, or in seeking specimens for the Peale Museum—once so valuable and so finely arranged—instead of spending weeks in the smoothing of a useless bow or walking out in full dress in order to display the make of their legs, how different they would feel! But alas!—no. They are, none of them, aware of the richness of that place, nor are they likely to know the hospitality to be found there.

Night came on as I was thinking of such things. I was turned out of the coach in the streets of the fair city just as the clock struck ten. I cannot say my bones were much rested. But not a moment was to be lost. I had a porter take up my luggage and follow me to the nearest wharf for the ferrying of the Delaware to Camden. The lights of Philadelphia's parallel streets, all tranquil and serene, were shining as I crossed to the river. The *Baltimore* steamer, later than usual, broke the evening silence, then ferried me over. A bribe that I offered to a bystander after I landed sufficed to bring me and my luggage to my former boardinghouse. The entire household was in bed, but my voice afforded ready entrance.[87]

I have so frequently spoken of the Mississippi that an account of the progress of navigation on that extraordinary stream may not be out of order.

I shall commence with the year 1808 when most of the "Western" country, and the river's banks, particularly from above Natchez, were in their natural state. To ascend it was an adventure of no little difficulty and risk, because of its powerful current . . . stronger wherever islands occur. Another hazard, its thousands of sand banks, change and shift like the alluvial shores themselves. At every deep bend those shores give way as if crushed by the weight of forests, and they sink into the muddy waters by the acre. Innumerable logs called "sawyers" and "planters" raise their heads above the water as if to bid defiance to all that passes. Few white settlers had marched to its shores, and these few were of a class little able to assist the navigator. Here and there lone Indian encampments on shore raised doubt. Encroachment of the white men upon their lands had made many foes among the natives. Small canoes, piroguas, keelboats, some flatboats and a few barges were to be seen. The canoes and piroguas were often laden with furs from the headwaters country. The craft were of little worth after their run to the New Orleans market and seldom returned. Flatboats were demolished for firewood. Besides furs the keelboats and barges conveyed lead, flour, pork and other items. They returned with sugar, coffee and dry goods for Ste. Genevieve, St. Louis, and Upper

Mississippi markets, sometimes branching off and ascending the Ohio to the foot of the Falls near Louisville.

As a rule ten hands, mostly Canadian French, manned the keelboats under one patron or master. Seldom did they carry less than twenty or thirty tons. The barges, manned by forty or fifty men, carried fifty or sixty tons. Both bore a mast, square-sail, and coils of cordage called *cordelles*. They carried their own provisions. At points that project from shore and cause a strong, eddying current—as powerful as the one in midstream—the bargemen row close to the bank, up to the current then row for the opposite shore. Rarely can they proceed along the same side. There may be a drift of a quarter of a mile downstream before the strong current is overcome. Exhausted, the men tie up to the shore or a tree, to receive a small measure of whiskey before they cook and eat their dinner. An hour's repose, and they recommence their labors, advancing slowly. At large sandbars they pole their craft along if the bottom of the river is hard. Two bowsmen remain at the prow to help the helmsman manage the boat and keep it headed against the current. The other crewmen keep to the land side of the vessel, poling it with all their might. As each in turn arrives at the stern he then crosses to the other side, runs along it, and comes forward to the landward side of the bow—to start his poling over again. Meanwhile the barge ascends at a rate of not more than one mile an hour. Once the bar is behind and the shores become straight, and the current uniformly strong, poles are laid aside. The men on the river side take to their oars; those toward land seize branches overhead and slowly propel the boat. When a fallen tree trunk projecting from the bank impedes their progress, they strike it with iron points of the poles and gaffhooks. At sunset they tie up in the best harbor available. They cook supper, then betake themselves to their blankets or bearskins. Sometimes they light a fire to avoid the persecution of swarms of mosquitoes. They have done well if fifteen miles have been covered by the end of such a day.

If the wind is favorable they may set their sail, to avail themselves of every advantage. But a headwind along treeless shores occasions a halt. The cane grasses on the bank are too thick and stout, perhaps, for use of the *cordelles,* but not for the men to cut through them in search of abundant game. Three days may pass before the wind changes, thus allowing the boat to proceed. It may run on a log, swing on the current, yet hang fast with the lee side almost under water. Out come the poles again, with all hands busy. Toward sunset, perhaps, the bustling and pushing succeed in freeing the boat, for the weary crew to take it to shore for the night.

I could tell you of crews that abandoned both boat and cargo, and of countless accidents and perils. Suffice it to say that a boat that left New Orleans on the first of March often did not reach the Falls of the Ohio until the month of July . . . or even October . . . and, after all this trouble . . . with a cargo of a few bags of coffee and at most one hundred hogsheads of sugar.

Such were things in 1808, when not more than twenty-five or thirty barges, their burden not exceeding a hundred tons or so, plied the rivers. The barge that came up in three months was thought to have done wonders. Few made it in that time.

If I am not mistaken the first steamboat to descend from the Ohio to New Orleans was named the *Orleans,* under Captain Ogden in the spring of 1810. Next came a vessel from Pittsburgh, until, before many years, the steamers became a common sight. By 1826, by which time our population had doubled, the navigation of the Mississippi had so improved, both as to facility and speed, that I know of no better way to give you an idea of it then to present an extract of a letter from my son, who copied it from the records of my brother-in-law, Berthoud:

"1823, from Jan. 1 to Dec. 31, 42 boats : 7,860 tons. 98 trips. 19,453 tons.
1824   "   to Nov. 25, 36   " : 6,393   " . 118   " . 20,291 tons.
1825   "   to Aug. 15, 42   " : 7,484   " . 140   " . 24,102 tons.
1826   "   to Dec. 31, 51   " : 9,388   " . 182   " . 28,914 tons.

"The amount for 1827 will be much greater than the above. The number of flatboats and keels is beyond calculation. The number of steamboats above the Falls I cannot say much about, except that one or two arrive at and leave Louisville every day. Their passage from Cincinnati is commonly 14 or 16 hours. The *Tecumseh,* 210 tons, arrived here in 9 days, 7 hours, from New Orleans . . . 1,650 miles . . . one of the quickest trips made. There are now 140 or 145 boats on the waters west of the Allegheny Mountains. Last spring we had a very high freshet (1826) which came 4½ feet deep into the countinghouse. The rise was 57 feet 3 inches perpendicular."

When steamboats first began running regularly, a cabin cost one hundred dollars from Shippingport, Kentucky, to New Orleans, and one hundred and fifty for the return. In 1829 I paid twenty-five to go from Shippingport to Natchez. In 1830 it cost me sixty dollars for two staterooms on the New Orleans to Philadelphia run; a trifling accident lengthened this trip by fourteen days. The real distance is probably less than the estimated 1,650, above. Abler hands have described these steamers. I shall desist.[88]

What a wonderful spectacle to the eye of the traveller is a *booming flood* of our gigantic streams. A sudden rise of temperature, the swift melting of snows, the southeasterly winds that blow rain until the deluge fills rivulets, ravines, creeks and small streams, are the cause. These flow into the great streams which rise to a surprising height, to overflow their banks wherever the land is low. The Ohio is at once splendid and appalling enough, but, when its waters mingle with those of the Mississippi below, an American flood may be seen in all its astonishing magnificence.

The water at the foot of the Falls of the Ohio will rise sixty feet above its lowest level as it receives the full force of numberless tributaries. Beginning at Pittsburgh, nearly seven hundred miles above, the flood sweeps violently along, taking fences and dwellings. Dreadful are the effects of such an inundation. I have known a cow to swim through a window seven feet above ground, and sixty-two feet above the low-water mark. Yet the family did not leave the house surrounded by water, but instead moved into its upper storey after opening the doors and removing the lower window sashes.

Spread over neighboring swamps the Mississippi looks like an ocean overgrown with stupendous trees. The Indian has fled to the inland hills. Cattle and game swim to dry strips of land, or grapple with the waters until they perish from fatigue. Settlers near the shore put their livestock and provisions on rafts which they tie fast to big trees. Then they watch the current carry off their houses and woodyards in pieces. Only the Squatters have little to lose, and they make off in canoes to collect the Deer and Bear for their saleable skins. They resort to low ridges surrounded by water, to destroy thousands of Deer, leaving the flesh behind.

No large vessel, unless under steam, can make its way against the current of rolling, swollen waters. But small boats and their produce crowd onto it. Yellow foam, and pumice from the Rockies, cover the eddying surface. Trees give way and fall. Forests are undermined. Here and there a Vulture or Eagle perches on a bloated animal carcass in the water, as indifferent to the flood as it would ordinarily be to the sawyers in the river while it tears its prey. Floating trees and logs break the steamer's paddles. Dry wood to fuel it is hard to obtain.

You will see a whole community out working to repair the levees, or artificial barriers, where these exist. In spite of all, a dreaded *crevasse* opens, for the water to rush in upon the fields of plantations and lay waste the crops blooming in all the luxuriance of spring. This opens a new channel which, for all I know, may run to the Gulf.

I have floated on the Mississippi and Ohio in a canoe when they were in flood and travelled across immense portions of the country when it was under water. On the Mississippi bottom lands little or no current is met with except on a bayou. All is silent, melancholy, except for the mournful whinny of the hemmed in Deer, the dismal scream of an Eagle, or of a Raven as the foul bird, disturbed by one's approach, rises from a carcass. Bears, Cougars, Lynxes and other quadrupeds that can ascend trees may be seen crouched among the top branches. Hungry in the midst of abundance, they see their prey floating around them but dare not venture to swim out to them. Fatigued by the effort of reaching dry land, some will stand near the hunter's fire as if to die by a bullet rather than perish amid the waste waters. Thus they fall by the hundreds.

Opposite Natchez, which stands on a high bluff, the inundation of a thirty-mile tract by the Mississippi and Red Rivers is immense. The mail-bag may have to be carried by canoe through the immersed forest a long distance, for forwarding to Natchitoches.

The gradual subsiding of the flood effects mighty changes. Everywhere the earth is covered by deep deposits of muddy loam. This splits into deep, narrow chasms when dry, which in warmer weather give off noxious exhalations that fill the lower air like a dense fog. The river banks are broken in greater or less degree. New large streams are found to exist where, before, none had been seen. These force their way in direct lines from the upper parts of the river bends. Some of these "shortcuts" have proved large enough to change the navigation of the Mississippi. One, the Grand Cut-off, only a few miles long, diverted the river from its natural course and shortened it by fifty miles. The upper part of the river islands is a mass of trees that have lodged there. Large sand banks have been removed and deposited elsewhere, so that the navigator must note their new situation and bearings in his log-book. Trees bend over the stream like the arms of giants. Everywhere the lamentations of farmer and planter may be heard. Work to repair the damage goes forward.

At one *crevasse* an old ship or two that has been dismantled for the purpose is used to close the gap. Squatters shoulder rifles as they make

their way through the morass in search of lost stock that they hope
to drive home if any have survived. New fences and new houses begin
to rise; this time an elevated platform supported by pillars made from
tree trunks will be a precaution. The land is ploughed anew if it seems
that a crop of corn and potatoes may yet be raised. But the rich prospects
of the planter are blasted. Travel is uncertain . . . a bank of sand may
give way beneath the wayfarer's horse which, the next moment, sinks
in quicksand—to the chest in front, and over the crupper behind, leaving the rider in a situation not to be envied.

Unlike the mountain torrents and the small rivers of other parts of
the world, the Mississippi rises slowly during floods. The increase is at
the rate of an inch a day over a span of several weeks. At its height
it fluctuates little for some days. It subsides as slowly as it rose. Four
to six weeks is the usual duration, although it may last two months.

Everyone knows how floods and cataclysms affect the theories of the
geologist. If European streamlets afford illustrations of formation of
strata, how much more must the Mississippi teach, with its shifting
sand banks, its crumbling shores, enormous masses of drift timber . . .
the source of future coal beds . . . its extensive, varied alluvial deposits,
and its mighty mass of waters, rolling sullenly along like the flood of
eternity![89]

By autumn I was in Lower Louisiana where the Opossum abounds.
The Zoological Society of London had asked me to forward some live
ones of this species. By offering a little more than the common price
I soon had twenty-five brought to me. I put the excessively voracious,
cowardly animals into a large box with a quantity of food and then
onto a steamer bound for New Orleans. Two days later I arrived there
to send them off to Europe. But, to my surprise, I found that the old
males had eaten off the heads of the younger ones until only sixteen
were left. I put each one in a separate box, and was to see a good
number of them in the Zoological Garden on my arrival in London.

The Opossum is more or less abundant in the Southern, Western
and Middle States of the Union. Other writers on its habits have said
nothing of its talent for dissimulation. Like other animals that feed
principally on flesh, it is also frugivorous and herbivorous. When hard
pressed it seizes various insects and reptiles. It is so fond of grapes that
one species now bears its name. It greedily eats persimmons; and in
severe weather I have observed it eating lichens. Fowls of every kind,

and quadrupeds less powerful than itself, are its habitual prey. By no means does it confine its predatory ranging to night despite its fondness for seclusion by day.

Like a fat foal it moves two legs of one side forward at an ambling gait if it supposes itself unobserved. (The Newfoundland dog shows a similar propensity.) Its constitution, hardy as that of most Northern mammals, enables it to stand the coldest weather, despite a covering of hair and fur comparatively scanty even in winter. A thick layer of fat compensates for its coat. The Opossum does not hibernate. It carries its curious prehensile tail high as it ambles rather slowly along, its rounded ears forward, its pointed nose on the scent at almost every step. Methinks I see one slowly and cautiously trudging over the melting snows beside an unfrequented pond. It noses along as it goes after the fare that its ravenous appetite prefers. Now it comes upon the fresh track of a Grouse or Hare, raises its snout, and snuffs the keen air. It decides on its course, then speeds onward at a man's ordinary gait—stops—seems at a loss which direction to go, because of a leap its prey had taken, or a backward cut, before it, the Opossum, caught the track. It rears up on its hind feet, looks around, snuffs the air again, moves on towards the foot of a noble stand. There it halts, walks round the base of the huge trunk among whose snow-covered roots it finds an opening. At once it enters. Several minutes later it reappears with a lifeless Squirrel in its mouth. Slowly it climbs. The first fork it reaches will not do; perhaps because it is too exposed to the view of some wily foe. It reaches a cluster of branches intertwined with grapevine, composes itself, twists its tail round a twig, and devours the unlucky Squirrel which all the while it holds in its fore paws.

Pleasant days of spring arrive. Vigorously the trees shoot forth their buds. The Opossum is almost bare. Apparently almost exhausted, too, by hunger it visits the margins of creeks and is pleased to see the young Frogs—a tolerable repast. By and by when the pokeberry and nettle shoot up, it gorges itself on the tender, juicy stems. Morning calls of the Wild Turkey cock delight the ear of the cunning creature who well knows he will soon hear the female whose nest of succulent eggs he will discover. Through the woods, aloft from tree to tree, or on the ground, moves the Opossum. A rooster crows. Then, instinctively, the Opossum responds, advancing on the hen house, where at last it conceals itself.

Honest farmer, why did you kill so many Crows last winter?—! Aye, and Ravens too? Well, you have had your own way of it. But now hie to the village for ammunition, clean your rusty gun, set your traps, and teach your lazy curs to watch the Opossum.

There he comes! The sun is scarcely down, but the appetite of the prowler is keen, as the screams of one of the best chickens testify. The cunning beast makes off with it. Nothing can be done. You, farmer, can only stand there while Fox and Owl exult that you killed their enemy, your own friend, the poor Crow. Another hen under whom, last week, you placed a dozen eggs or so is now deprived of them. Heedless of her angry outcries and the ruffling of her feathers, the Opossum has removed the eggs one by one. Look at the poor bird as she moves across your yard. If not mad she is at least stupid, for she scratches here and there, calling all the while.

All this comes of your shooting Crows. Had you been more merciful or more prudent, the Opossum might have kept within the woods, to content itself with a Squirrel, young Hare, Turkey eggs, or the grapes that hang in such profusion on forest boughs. But I talk to you in vain.

There can be no better example of maternal tenderness than that of the Opossum. Just peep into that curious sack that conceals her young. Each is attached to a teat. She nourishes them and protects them from their enemies. Like the Shark she moves with them. In the thick foliage, high aloft in tulip-trees, she hides them until, after two months, they begin to shift for themselves according to particular lessons given to each one.

But suppose the farmer has surprised an Opossum in the act of killing one of his best fowls. In his anger he kicks the poor beast which, conscious of its inability to resist, rolls off like a ball. The more the farmer rages, the more reluctant the animal becomes to show resentment. At last it lies there—not dead, but exhausted, its jaws open, its tongue extended, its eyes dimmed. And there it would lie until the bottle-fly came to deposit its eggs, if its tormentor did not at last walk off, saying to himself that surely the beast must be dead. But no, it is only " 'possum-ing." No sooner has its enemy withdrawn than it gets gradually upon its legs and once more makes for the woods.

Once I was descending the Mississippi in a sluggish flatboat. During a hunt I chanced to meet two full-grown Opossums that I brought alive to the "ark." Immediately the crew began to tease them. Following their natural instinct they lay as if dead. As an experiment, both were thrown overboard. Only their desperate situation made them, after a moment or two, begin to swim towards our uncouth rudder that was formed from a long tree and extended from the middle of the boat thirty feet beyond the stern. Both got upon it. We took them up and afterwards let them go free in their native woods.

The flesh resembles that of a young pig and would perhaps be as highly prized were it not for the prejudice of some "very particular persons," some of whom, despite, have pronounced it excellent eating. Its body is suspended for a whole week in the frosty air after cleaning, but never eaten in summer. Place it on a heap of hot wood embers. Sprinkle it, when cooked, with gunpowder. Then tell me whether it is not equal to our famed Canvas-back Duck? You may see it in our markets among the best of game.[90]

After a passage of twenty-five days my wife and I arrived safely in Liverpool, on the *Pacific*, in the spring of 1830. In England everything had gone well, and although my list of subscribers to *The Birds of America* had not increased, it had not much diminished. I intended to revisit America as soon as possible.

On September 3, 1831, we again landed in New York, that I might winter in the Floridas and enrich my collection of skins and drawings.[91]

One beautiful November morning I left Charleston with my host the Reverend John Bachman for a visit to Cole's Island, twenty miles distant. When our shooting was over we left our various birds in a summer cottage, then we separated. Some of the crew went off to fish, others to gather oysters. We gunners made ready for the arrival of the Long-billed Curlews at sunset. They began to appear in twos, threes, or fives —by no means shy—and were the same that we had seen near the salt marshes on our way. The number of Curlews increased with the lowering of the dusk. Flocks, in quicker succession, came not in lines but in a long, regular mass not more than thirty feet above, with individuals no more than feet apart. Not a note or cry did they sound. They would flap regularly for ten or more yards, then sail for a few seconds, their long bills and legs stretched to their full extent, directly toward the "Bird Banks." There they alighted without performing the evolutions that they exhibit at their feeding grounds. We followed them to these small sandy islands, but the moment they saw us land, the flock of several thousand rose, performed a few evolutions in silence, and alighted again with one accord on the far edges of the sand bank close to tremendous breakers. It was now dark, but flocks were still arriving as we left the place.

We had procured fish, fowl and oysters, in addition to delicacies—beefsteaks and beverages—taken with us from Charleston. We had no cook, however, but your humble servant. Onto a blazing fire that lighted the cottage we tossed our fish and oysters. The steaks we stuck on sticks before the blaze. Our salt was gunpowder, as many a time, for me, in the past. To our keen appetites the steaks were quite as savory as any ever cooked and seasoned at home. Our fingers and mouths may have borne the marks of the "villainous saltpetre," or rather of the charcoal with which it was mixed; for plates and forks we had none, a lack which only increased our mirth. Our supper over, we spread our blankets on the floor, stretched out with feet towards the fire and arms folded under our heads for pillows. I need not tell you how soundly we slept.[92]

The different ways of hunting Deer are so well known and so cleverly practiced in the United States that despite the almost incredible abundance of these animals in our forests they may soon, because of the havoc being wrought among them, become as scarce in America as the Great Bustard is in Britain.

The first mode, called "still hunting," is by far the most destructive. The second, "firelight hunting," is the next so. The third, a mere amusement named "driving," destroys many Deer if by no means so perniciously.

Frontiersmen follow "still hunting" as a kind of trade. Much activity, expert marksmanship, along with knowledge of the forest and habits of the Deer, are required. Not only must the hunter know the ways of the animal at different seasons of the year but at every hour of day in order to find it. Let us suppose we are about to follow the true or "still hunter" through tangled woods, across morasses and ravines —like spies bringing up the rear to watch his agility, patience and careful motions. He wears a leather hunting shirt, leather trousers, a belt round his waist, and moccasins. His heavy rifle rests on his shoulder. A pouch of shot hangs by his side along with a powder horn that came from a Buffalo that was once the terror of the herd. His scabbarded butcher knife is caught by the same strap through which his tomahawk is thrust. Few could keep up with his rapid step for more than a short distance. He has looked to the flint of his gun, its priming, and the leather cover of the lock. He keeps an eye on the sky, to judge the likeliest direction for game.

Already the dewy emerald leaves begin to turn. The red glare of the morning sun gleams from clear heavens. A light frost shines on fence rails on the cornfields. The hunter scans the dead foliage before him for signs of the hoof of a buck. He bends down, sees something that impels him to alter his course, swiftly, towards a hill. He moves more cautiously from tree to tree, peeps ahead, as if within shooting distance of game. Again he advances, but how very slowly! On reaching the slope he takes his gun, throws aside the cover of the lock, and wipes the edge of the flint with his tongue. Like a statue he stands and calculates the distance between him and a buck before firing. One shot suffices. The hunter prepares for the skinning by hanging the Deer on a branch. The carcass is left to the Wolves. The hunter flings the venison in the skin and straps it to his back as he goes on with his gun, ready to drop more game.

If the weather had been warmer the hunter would have looked for Deer along the shadowy side of the hills, rather than in the sunlight. If the season had been spring instead of autumn he would have led the party through some thick canebrake to the margin of a lake. Deer would have been seen standing up to their heads in water. If the time had been winter and the earth snowy he would have searched the low, damp woods where mosses and lichens abound and which the Deer feed on. There might have been signs that the animals had been scraping the velvet from their horns against the low stems of bushes, or that they had been digging the earth with their fore hoofs, or feeding where persimmon and crab apple abound. In early spring our hunter would imitate the bleating of the doe and in that way overtake both her and her fawn. Or, like some Indians, he would put the head of a Deer on a stick and creep among the tall prairie grass with it until he decoyed Deer within range of his rifle.

Hunting by "firelight" or "forest light," observed for a first time, never fails to cause a very strange feeling . . . of its awful grandeur on the one hand, of its fear for the hunter on the other. He jumps his horse over huge fallen tree trunks. He rides through thick undergrowth and straggling grapevine. Stubborn saplings come smack in his face. He runs the risk of breaking his neck by pitching headlong onto the ground at the same moment that his horse sinks in a moss-covered hole. But to begin from the beginning: The hunter waits for nightfall. He gathers pine knots and takes along a frying pan so old that for all I know it may have been used by his great-grandmother. He and his servants ride to the woods. They strike fire with flint and steel to light the resinous pine knots which they place in the pan. This blaze lights the riders' way a little through the darkness, until the leader sees that the eyes of a Deer or Wolf are reflecting the light that he holds high. To the unaccustomed witness these eyes look like those of some lost hobgoblin. The spectre remains quite still. The hunter who is nearest the bearer of the light draws close enough to discern the form before he shoots. Thus he hunts through the night, taking the skin only and what he may want of the flesh. Besides five to ten Deer as well as a Wolf or two, he may shoot a stray horse or cow by accident.

For the third kind of hunt, picture a good-sized Virginia-bred horse —listen for the bugle and horn, the clamor and yelping of a pack of hounds! The party gathers in the shade of a wood to "drive" the lightfooted Deer, oblivious to the distance they may have to travel. They gallop pell-mell through the woods to some likely spot. The servants, now called "drivers," keep ahead, urging the hounds before them. The dogs rout a Deer. The chase is on. The horn blows louder and more clearly. The riders dismount to take their stand beside a tree as the Deer is driven towards them. It stumbles, but the dogs drive it on —so near that it will be within range in a moment. How beautifully it bounds over the ground! What a splendid head of horns! How fleet it is! But its flight is in vain. Someone fires. The animal plunges, then doubles its speed. A second, better aim brings him to earth. Dogs, servants, sportsmen rush to the spot. Congratulations are in order. After that the chase is resumed somewhere else.

Deer are fond of following and retracing familiar paths, even after having been shot at more than once, as hunters who seek their tracks well know. A Deer "stand" may be a road, a field, or a small stream where the animal has been seen more than once. There the hunter watches; or several hunters may form a line, to await the passing or crossing. The servants will then start the Deer with hounds, and, by good management, make it run the course to its death. But a cautious Deer may take another route. Hunters and horses will gallop to intercept it. Horns and the baying of hounds guide them for the kill. The sport proves successful on almost every occasion.[93]

The Black Bear, however clumsy in appearance, is active, vigilant and persevering, possesses great strength and courage, and endures hardships and fatigue, imposed by the hunter, with little injury. Like the Deer it changes haunts each season—and for the same reasons: the desire to find food in more inaccessible, more secure places, away from its most dangerous enemy, man.

In spring it searches the low, rich, alluvial river borderlands, or along the shores of pondlike lakes. There it finds succulent roots and tender juicy plant stems. In the heat of summer it enters the gloomy swamps, wallows in the mud like a hog, and contents itself with Crayfish, roots and nettles; or, if hard pressed by hunger, it seizes a young pig, a sow, or even a calf. As soon as berries begin to ripen on the mountains the Bear goes up into the mountains with her cubs. In regions without hills it visits cornfields, to ravage them for a while, afterwards turning to nuts, acorns, grapes and other forest fruits called "mast." It robs every "bee-tree" of the woods like the expert it is. A good climber, it sometimes houses itself in the hollow trunks of large trees, there to suck its paws for weeks together.

The Black Bear will carefully examine the bottom of a tree trunk, all the while snuffing the air and looking around to make sure no enemy is near. It then embraces the trunk with its forelegs. With teeth and claws it tears at the bark for several minutes, until its jaws are foaming, after which it continues its rambles. I have heard woodsmen discuss this singular action. They imagine the Bear behaves in this way to leave a sign of its size and power behind it. It can be measured by its scratches on the bark. The hunter can anticipate its size. My own opinion is that the Bear scratches the tree merely to sharpen its teeth and claws, to enable it to handle a rival Bear during the mating season when this action occurs. The Wild Boar of Europe drives its tusks and scrapes the earth with its hoofs. The Deer rubs its antlers for the same purpose.

One night in the house of a friend I was awakened by a Negro servant bearing a light. He handed me a note to his master from a neighbor who asked us to join him at once for a hunt. He wanted us to help kill some Bears that were in the act of destroying his corn crop. I dressed in a hurry, you may be sure. I found my host in the parlor, ready and waiting except for the casting of some bullets by a Negro. The overseer's horn began calling the other Negroes from their cabins. Horses were saddled. The cur-dogs of the plantation were rounded up. All was bustle. Within half an hour four stout Negroes armed with axes and knives, and mounted on strong nags of their own (for you must know that many of our slaves raise horses, cattle, pigs and poultry of their own) were following us at a fast gallop through the woods.

The night was none too favorable. A drizzling rain made the air thick and rather sultry. At the neighbor's house, five miles distant, three of us accompanied half a dozen servants and a good pack of dogs of all kinds towards the field where the Bears were at work. The animals had been visiting the corn for some days. At least five had been seen by a Negro sent to find out where they entered. According to the plan of attack, the bars at a gap in the fence were noiselessly lowered for the men and dogs to enter, then to separate in two parties to surround the Bears. A horn was to sound the charge towards the center of the field. All were to shout as loudly as possible to frighten the animals off into dead trees that dotted the cornfield.

The horns sounded. The horses galloped forward. The men shouted. The dogs barked and howled. The shrieks of the Negroes were enough to frighten a legion of Bears, let alone those that fled. We heard the Bears scrambling into the treetops.

The drizzle had ceased. The sky was clear. The glare of crackling fires lighted by the Negroes enabled us to shoot, immediately, two cubs among the Bears that were crouching, terrified, in boughs near the trunks. We had the Negroes cut down the tree in which the mother Bear perched. First the dogs had a battle with her, after one of her hind legs had been fired at to keep her from escaping. The work of felling the tree was extremely tedious, meanwhile. At last it began to vibrate at every stroke. Shortly it came crashing to the ground in such a terrifying way that Bruin must have felt the shock as severely as we would feel the collision of the globe with a comet.

The dogs now charged on the Bear from all sides while we riders surrounded the poor animal. With all her might she defended her life. One second she was killing a dog with a single stroke, the next she was dealing one a blow in the forelegs that sent it yelping piteously off and *hors de combat*. A cur dared to seize her by the snout and hang on while a dozen more scrambled over the back of the now infuriated and vengeful animal. We had about decided to finish off the fray when, to our astonishment, she gave us a look and suddenly shook off all the dogs. Before we could fire she charged a Negro on a spotted horse. With teeth and claws she clung to the breast of the snorting, plunging steed. The capital horseman kept his seat, although only saddled on a tightly girthed sheepskin. He called out not to fire. But when we saw horse and rider come to the ground, our anxiety for the safety of the youth reached fever pitch, notwithstanding his coolness and courage. But we were relieved to see the masterly way that Scipio dealt with his foe in the next instant. A blow of his axe and a deep growl announced her death. The valorous Negro sprang to his feet unhurt.

About two hundred yards away, by the light of dawn, we discovered two more Bears lodged in a tree. We circled them but found them quite unwilling to come down. We piled brushwood and branches around the foot of the tree. The fire that we lighted ascended and caught hold of the dry bark, until a pillar of flame sent the Bears scampering into the topmost branches. There they began to totter, then to fall through the cracking and snapping boughs, bringing down a mass of twigs as they struck ground. The dogs soon worried these cubs to death.

The party returned to the house in triumph. The severely wounded horse was turned loose in the field in order to repair his strength by eating the corn. A cart brought the game. But, before we left the field, the horses, dogs and Bears, together with the fires, had destroyed more corn inside of a few hours than had the poor Bear and her cubs during all their visits.[94]

II

The Floridas

IT was neccessary, and somewhat difficult too, to bring my stay in
Charleston to a close. . . . But my mind was among the birds farther south—the Floridas, Red River, the Arkansas, that almost unknown
country California, and the Pacific Ocean. It was necessary to tear myself away from the kindest of friends.

With my assistant artist and my bird-skinner I embarked on the
packet schooner *Agnes* for the Floridas. Off Georgia the wind put us
back into St. Simon's Island Bay. This was one setback that proved
fortunate for me. I made for shore, presented my card to a man on the
beach and was immediately invited to dinner. His gardens and our
agreeable conversation made me wonder whether I had landed on one
of those fairy islands said to have existed in the Golden Age. Thomas
Butler King urged me to spend a month at his hospitable mansion.
He subscribed to my *Birds*. But the wind shifted. The voyage to St.
Augustine resumed.[95]

In St. Augustine I followed my usual avocations, but with little success on account of winter.[96] However, at the plantation of my friend
John Bulow of Bulowville, I heard so many wonderful accounts of a
certain spring near the St. Johns River sources that I resolved to visit it
and judge for myself.

On January 6, 1832, I set out with a Scottish engineer who was
employed by the planters to erect their sugar refineries. We rode strong
horses of the Indian breed. If the weather was pleasant, our route
surely was not. No sooner had we left the old Spanish "King's Road"
than we entered a thicket of scrubby oaks that led into a denser mass
of low palmettoes. For three miles our nags picked their way among
the roots before we entered the great Pine Barrens. Sand—nothing
but sand, and the palmettoes which at times so covered our narrow
Indian trail that it took all our sagacity and all the instinct of our

horses to keep it, was what we saw as we approached what seemed the farthermost end of the world.

My companion had travelled over this perfectly flat, wild, scraggly country before, at seasons when the barrens were covered with water fully knee-deep. Even now we passed through muddy pools to the depth of our saddle girths. Here and there were large tracts of tall grasses, not unlike our Western prairies to the view. Lowlands, wherever they occurred, were covered with cypress draped with Spanish beard moss and dense bushes of the magnolia family, growing in black mud.

Three times we crossed Haw Creek at its branches, a quarter to half a mile wide, and with extreme difficulty. While we were in the middle of the stream, my companion told me that his horse once placed its forefeet on the back of a large Alligator there. None too pleased to be disturbed in his repose, the reptile had reared up and his monstrous jaws had snapped off a part of the lips of the frightened pony. After a few terrified plunges the horse managed to carry its rider to safety —to be honored forever after by the appellation of "Alligator."

At high noon, twenty miles upon our way, we dismounted, for our horses to graze on the herbage along the little pool.

All at once, after we went on at two and a half disagreeable miles per hour, a wonderful change took place. We came upon higher, undulating country of red oak, live oak, magnolia, and pine. Thousands of Salamander "mole hills" and Gopher burrows appeared; now and then the horses stumbled in these at the risk of breaking their legs and our own necks. Sometimes they sank to the depth of a foot.

Beautiful, pure lakes lay before us, becoming larger and more numerous the farther we advanced. Some were several miles long and twenty feet deep. Because their shores were destitute of vegetation we saw no birds, but only Tortoises basking in the sun (until our approach sent them plunging into the water). Not a trace of a man . . . scarcely a bird . . . not a single quadruped, even a Rat, had we seen in the unimaginably poor, desolate country beyond the Halifax River. But before we had travelled much deeper into this undulating, lake country we saw the Negro huts of a planter whom we had come to visit. No pilgrim to Timbuctoo had ever approached his destination with more excited curiosity. Our horses, catching on to our anticipation, trotted at a smart rate toward the plantation entrance. Just at sunset we leaped from our saddles, in time for supper and an evening of agreeable conversation with Colonel Rees.

In the morning I walked over the place. The ground—a reclaimed swamp—was black, rich, fertile—much of it on the lake border under cultivation. Seven miles up the lake lay St. Johns River, navigable for vessels of not more than fifty or sixty tons.

After breakfast our host showed us to the celebrated spring. It more than made up for the tediousness of the journey from Bulowville. From the center of a circular basin about sixty feet in diameter water gushes with great force, though to a height of only a few inches above the ground level. The whirlpool deposits vast quantities of shells, bits of wood, gravel and the like that have coalesced into solids of odd appearance. The dark yet transparent water is so impregnated with sulphur that it emits a highly nauseous odor. Its surface lies fifteen or twenty feet below the level of the neighboring lakes; its lowest depth, reached in autumn, is about seventeen feet. Probably the spring is formed of water collected from the lakes by infiltration or a subterranean outlet; at any rate the lakes' shells are the same. Actually, the lakes are reservoirs that hold the residue of the rainy seasons. They supply the St. Johns River.

The spring pours its waters into Colonel Rees's lake through a broad, deep channel called Spring Garden Creek—fully sixty feet deep in places, but shallow towards the entrance of the lake, which is a mud flat under fifteen inches of water. The mud, four or five feet deep, has a fine bed of white sand beneath. Sulphurated hydrogen gas sends air bubbles out of the dark, greenish mud that reeks of sulphur.

The mouth of the curious spring is believed to be two and a half feet square, its velocity during rainy seasons three feet of water per second, or about 499,500 gallons per hour. We saw the remains of another such spring that had dried up from some natural cause.

One day Colonel Rees took me by boat towards the St. Johns River. As we crossed his lake I noticed the deep cypress swamp on its northeastern shores, and the marshes and islands of pine, live oak and orange trees across from these. We followed Spring Garden Creek for about two miles. Except for its very narrow channel it was covered with nymphae, and its waters and margins were filled with Alligators and birds —the White Ibis, Gallinule, Anhinga, Coot, Cormorant and—overhead —the sailing Fish Hawk whose nests could be seen in the broken trees. We passed a mud bar then entered Dexter's Lake. The bar was stuck full of Unios. Each time the Negroes thrust their hands into the mud they took up several of these inedible shellfish. This lake, though transparent, was of a dark chestnut hue when we saw it—five feet deep throughout and about eighty by three miles long and wide. We crossed it to a creek that led to Woodruff's Lake which empties its still darker waters into the St. Johns River. I shot a pair of curious Ibises here. One of the small islands of the lake was covered with fresh, luxuriant, highly fragrant wild-orange trees—like a rich *bouquet* formed by nature for the weary traveller, cast down by the dismal swamps, pools and rank grass around him. Under the beautiful evergreens, and in the midst of golden fruit that covered the ground we spread our cloth. Humming-birds fluttered over our heads. Colonel Rees informed me that this was only one of numerous *terrae incognitae,* and nameless lakes. He said that henceforward the charming retreat would bear the name of "Audubon's Isle."

Lest I forget—the spring here described had its current directed to turning a mill that would grind all the Rees sugarcane, thanks to my friend the engineer.[97]

While I was at Mr. Bulow's I visited a long, tortuous bayou almost daily, to watch the Anhinga or Snakebird. But I found it impossible to get near their roosting place, a large dead tree, either by cautiously advancing in the boat or by creeping among the briars, cane, and tangled palmettoes on the banks. So I paddled directly to the place with my Newfoundland dog. The birds flew off, up the stream. I knew they might remain away for hours. I therefore ordered the Negroes to start any up that way that they could see. I hid myself and my little bark in among the plants, then with my gun ready I kept my eye on the tree until I could see the beautiful bird alight. Unaware, it came, looked about to see if all was right, but then fell into the water at a shot that reverberated until all the birds around took flight. My dog, obedient as the most submissive of servants, never stirred until I ordered him to bring me the bird, after which he lay gently down again in his place. . . . With what anxiety have I waded towards these "Grecian Ladies," to watch their movements while I left behind me myriads of hungry sand flies, gnats, mosquitoes and ticks that had annoyed my overheated body for hours! . . . On several such occasions the Anhinga watched my approach or that of my dog. It stood erect with head drawn back and bill open, its throat swollen with anger until the chance came to thrust its head forward and inflict a severe wound. Once one struck at my dog's nose and hung on until it was dragged thirty paces to my feet. When seized by the neck they scratch severely with sharp claws, and beat their wings about you with much more vigor than you would suppose they possessed. . . .[98]

I shall ever feel grateful to John Bulow, one of the most generous of men, for his unremitting efforts to make me comfortable and to promote my researches. Thanks to him I put off with a fair wind, and a pure sky, about eleven miles down a torpid creek lined with thousands of acres of marshes, grape and high palm trees, toward the Halifax River, an inland arm of the sea nearly a mile wide at points. Besides "three white men"—I, Bulow and a friend—six hands manned our boat, bound eighty miles inland from St. Augustine.

Next morning I and four of the Negroes went in search of birds and adventure. I wanted twenty-five Brown Pelicans, for a new drawing of an adult male and for their skins. So abundant were the fish in the narrow, shallow bay along which we proceeded that—believe it or not—large or small, they obstructed our way. We reached a point, when lo! we came in sight of several hundred Pelicans perched on mangrove branches, seated in comfortable harmony, and as near each other as the strength of the boughs would allow. I ordered the hands to backwater, that I might wade to shore under cover of the rushes. I then examined the countenances and behavior of the "reverend sirs" that lay fast asleep until I fired my piece and dropped two of the finest I ever saw.

We returned to Live Oak Landing. With the prospect of a severely cold night, with the tide against us, and with the wind in our teeth, we headed back. But our bark was as light as our hearts. All pulled well and we went merrily on until dark. The wind freshened and the cold increased as our supplies diminished and the waters dropped, leaving us little besides our enterprising dispositions. Fast in the mud, about three hundred yards from a marshy shore, where we had not the least hope of being able to start a fire, we were in straits. There was nothing but palm trees, and these not the *grand Diable* himself could ignite. We made up our minds to roll up in our cloaks, the best way we could, at the bottom of our light, beautiful bark.

Good God, what a night! To sleep was impossible. The cold and the breeze increased. Every moment seemed an hour. But morning came —clear as a morn ever was—and with it a northeaster as cold as ever blew in this latitude. Our crew were stiffened, exhausted with cold, and lightly clothed. Our only hope of reaching shore was to leap waist-deep into the mire and push the boat to a point some five or six hundred yards away, whose scrubby trees seemed to have grown there expressly to save our lives, this time.

"Push, boys, push, push for your lives!" cried the good Bulow and poor Audubon.

Aye, and well we might push, through mire now up to our breasts. Our limbs grew stiffer with every step. We moved along as if dragged down by heavy chains. We were two and a half hours reaching the point but did get there, thank God. It was well we did, for, at the edge of the marsh, two of our Negroes fell down as senseless as a torpid Alligator or Snake, and would certainly have died but for the presence of *the white men*. We carried them into the grove to which, I believe, we all owed our lives. In a crack I struck a fire—and in five minutes I had the indescribable pleasure of seeing a bright, blazing pile of logs to warm our shivering party. We wrapped the Negroes in their blankets, and boiled water for tea that we made them swallow to revive them. May God preserve you from ever being in such a plight as ours, with scarcely a man able to stand and the cold wind keen as ever. Two hours later I saw cheerful faces again. However, we were confined in a large salt marsh, without provisions, and still fifteen miles from Bulowville.

Not a moment was to be lost. I prophesied a much colder night. Once more we manned the boat, toward the creek, in hopes of enough water there to float her. It did so happen, thank God! As we once more saw our bark afloat, our spirits rose. Indeed they rose to such a pitch that we, in fun, set fire to the whole marsh. *Crack, crack, crack,* went the reeds in a rapid blaze! The Marsh Rabbits scampered off by the thousands as we pulled our oars.

Nevertheless, the northeaster had well-nigh emptied the creek a bit further on. We had to leave the boat behind and tramp through sand that sent our feet back six inches at every step, for many a long mile, redeemed only by our picking up a shell here and there (shells nowhere else to be found). But finally we reached the Bulow landing, and were glad to see the immense plantation, and the large house that promised a good dinner. We were none the worse for our adventure, except for my stiff left leg, the result of nearly six weeks of daily wading through swamps and salt marshes, or scrambling through the vilest thickets of scrubby live oak and palmetto, evidently created for no other purpose than to punish us for our sins.[99]

I carried letters from the Secretaries of the Navy and Treasury to Revenue Service commanders, directing them to afford me any assistance in their power. To the schooner *Spark,* bound up the St. Johns River, I presented my credentials at St. Augustine, where Lieutenant Piercy took me and my assistants on board.

The strict attention to duty, even on this small vessel of war, surprised me. Things went on as regularly as a chronometer. Orders were carried out before they had time to vibrate fully on the ear. The crew were as neat as the white planks of the deck; the sails were perfect. Built for swift sailing, the *Spark* went gamboling from wave to wave. But alas!—how fleeting are our enjoyments. When we were nearing the river the wind changed and the skies began to cloud over. Before many minutes the little bark lay "like a duck." It blew a hurricane. Back we turned to St. Augustine.

Our next attempt was successful. A few hours after we crossed the bar we saw the great lantern at the entrance of the St. Johns glimmering like a star. It was near dawn. Only when the tide is up can the treacherous sand bars at its mouth be safely crossed. A gun was fired to signal a Government pilot, then another to bring him reluctantly from his couch by canoe. My own eyes were not on the barely sufficient depth of the channel but on high where thousands of White Pelicans, frightened from their roosting grounds by our signals, were performing their broad, beautiful gyrations. How matchless was the marshalling of their files, after a while, as they flew past us!

We moved apace on the tide. Myriads of Cormorants covered the face of the waters. Innumerable Fish Crows were already arriving from their distant roosts. At one place where we landed to search for birds whose charming melodies had caught our ear, we added some young Eagles to our collection. The river did not seem to me to equal the Ohio in beauty. But its often low, swampy shores were the delight of vast flocks of Herons that moved along in their gracefulness, and grim Alligators that swam about in sluggish sullenness. Up a bayou we caught many young Alligators for the purpose of our experiments. On February 12, after we had taken soundings, bearings and angles in every nook and crook of the sinuous stream, we anchored a hundred miles up the river. The fog was so thick that neither shore could be seen. So wonderfully plentiful were the "blind mosquitoes" everywhere, even in the cabin, that more than once they just about put out the candles while I was writing in my journal, until I closed it in despair, and crushed more than a hundred of the little wretches.

[Midges?] Bad as they are, they at least do not bite. To render our situation doubly uncomfortable, the breezes from a beef-jerking establishment to windward came to us laden with far from sweet odors. It was 90° F. on shore, but 75° on board.

By morning the country still lay under thick fog. I could plainly hear the notes of birds on shore, but could see nothing beyond the bowsprit. Guided by the scent of the beef-jerker's works we went ashore through the close, sultry air. The jessamine blossoms lay steeped in dew, the humming bee was collecting her winter's stores from the snowy orange branches, and little warblers frisked along the twigs of smilax. At last the dense mists began to dissolve as the bright luminary and her rays shone forth. Some friendly "live-oakers" whose camp was near guided us around the woods.

After a while we returned to the *Spark,* to glide silently along beneath her sails. We spied a Seminole Indian approaching in his canoe. This poor, dejected son of the woods, endowed with talents of the highest order—talents that the usurpers of his native soil rarely acknowledge—had just finished a night and morning in the swampy thickets. He was coming to offer us some brilliant wild birds. Alas, fallen descendant of an ancient line of freeborn hunters, that I might restore to you your birthright, your natural independence, and those generous feelings that once your brave heart knew! But the irrevocable deed is done. I can only admire your perfect symmetry. Dexterously the Seminole threw his Trout and Turkeys on the deck. Without smile or bow, or acknowledgment of any kind, he received his recompense, after which he started off with the speed of an arrow from a bow such as his own.

The heads of fishes that the many Alligators had snapped off floated around us on the dark waters. Now and then a shot sent into one of the big ones caused a tremendous lash of its tail. One morning I saw a monstrous fellow on shore. Anxious to make a drawing of his head I approached him cautiously with one or two of our sailors. One shot, and we watched him slowly raise his head, curve upwards, open his huge jaws, swing his tail to and fro, then rise on his legs. He blew in a frightful manner, then fell to earth. Contrary to my instructions, one sailor leaped ashore to catch hold of the animal's tail. This aroused him from his trance. With one last effort he crawled slowly towards the water and plunged heavily into it. Had the monster once thought to flourish his tremendous weapon, he might have ended his assailant's life. Fortunately, he went peacefully to his grave where, on account of the depth of the water, we had to leave him.

That morning we saw another Alligator, attracted by the gentle ripples of the *Spark,* swimming directly for the bows. A shot sent him tumbling and rolling at a fearful rate. All the while he blew most furiously.

Early one morning my two assistants and I bade the *Spark* adieu. I hired a boat to take us and our baggage ashore. My intention was to return to St. Augustine by a shortcut, forty miles down river. We reached the point about 4 P.M., thinking to hire a wagon, but were doomed to disappointment. I decided to leave our things on the bank for bird-skinner Henry Ward to look after until I sent for him by wagon from St. Augustine. Lehman, and my Newfoundland dog and I, set off at a good rate to try to put eighteen miles behind us before sunset.

A pine barren that we entered was as level as a floor. Our path, narrow and well beaten, had been used by the Seminoles for ages. The weather was calm and beautiful. By rivulets we now and then quenched our thirst. Magnolia and flowering plants relieved the dull sameness of the woods. When the path forked, mystifyingly I would follow one branch, Lehman another. If we did not soon meet again, one would cross the intervening forest to the other.

The sun went down behind a cloud. A southeast breeze sprang up among the tall pines. Along the eastern horizon a black vapor slowly rose, then covered the heavens. The hot, oppressive air told us that a tempest was approaching. Plato now became our guide. His white markings were all we could make out in the darkness. As if aware of his usefulness, he kept only a short distance ahead on the trail. If we had thought ourselves more than a few miles from St. Augustine we would have made camp here for the night. But our belief that the distance could not be great kept us trudging along.

Large drops began to fall from the murky mass overhead. Thick impenetrable darkness surrounded us. To my dismay my dog refused to proceed. Upon groping with my hands along the ground I discovered that several trails branched out at the spot where he threw himself down. But when I chose one for him he went on. Vivid flashes of lightning streamed across the heavens. The wind rose to a gale. The rain poured down upon us like a torrent. Soon the water almost covered our feet. But on we went, slowly heading against the tempest.

Here and there a tall pine, on fire, presented a magnificent spectacle.

The trees around it were illumined. The halo of dim light was abruptly bordered by the deep black of night.

At one point we passed through a tangled thicket of low trees. At another we crossed a stream flushed by heavy rain, before we reached the open barrens.

How long we groped our way, half-lost, is more than I can tell. The tempest passed over. Suddenly the clear sky became spangled with stars. Soon after, we smelled the salt marshes and walked directly towards them like pointers advancing on a covey of Quail. At last, to our joy, we descried the beacon light of St. Augustine. My dog began to run briskly around as he came to ground where he had once hunted. He took a direct course toward the great causeway across the marshes back of town. Lehman and I refreshed ourselves at the first orange tree that we met, to parch our thirst. In half an hour we were in our hotel, drenched with rain, steaming with perspiration, covered to the knees with mud, and cutting quite a figure in the eyes of the good people whom we found snugly enjoying themselves in the sitting-room.

In the morning a wagon and mules went with two trusty soldiers from the garrison for friend Henry and the luggage.[100]

As for the Live-oakers, one sees small parties of these men in the East Florida forests called the Pine Barrens, thinly wooded districts covered with pine of an indifferent quality and an undergrowth of rank grass, low bushes, and sword palmettoes growing in flat sandy soil. They are parched in summer and autumn, except for some stagnant waterholes. The dark hummocks of live oak and other trees that the traveller suddenly comes upon in these Barrens are places of unexpectedly luxuriant flowers, cooler air, and bird song. There are festoons of vines, jessamine, and begonia, and one finds clear springs that glide through the fragrant undergrowth. It is in these beautiful woods that the visitor can watch the Live-oakers at their labors.

Picture two men on opposite sides of a noble and venerable live oak. At first the small chips of their keen axes seem to make no impression on the trunk's mossy, wide-spreading roots. One of the men, a handkerchief around his head, climbs barefoot forty feet up another partly fallen tree, one with its boughs tangled among the branches of trees beside it. There he boldly swings his blade with sinewy arms until the tree, be it as tough as it is large, is severed except for one thin strip of wood. Taking a firm stance on the side of the trunk that still holds fast, he shakes it with all his might. The huge bulk above him sways, then strikes the ground with a force that echoes through the hummock. Every Wild Turkey within hearing utters a gobble of recognition. The wood cutter throws his axe to the ground and with the aid of the nearest grapevine slides down the broken trunk to earth in an instant.

Several men cut the prostrate trunk at its extremities in order to sound the bark and to discover whether white-rot is present. If so, the huge log will be left to crumble away. If there is no sign that the sap has already risen, and if its pores are sound, measurements are taken. The men first determine the forms and size of the timber to be hewn. They do so with the aid of models, in much the manner that the sections of a ship's skeleton are laid out. Because white-rot or some other disease has affected the quality of these trees that are attacked by Live-oakers in every known hummock, the woods are strewn with trunks found to be worthless. Every year these valuable oaks become scarcer. The destruction of young trees by the fall of the great trunks is of course immense. No trees of the kind are planted. Before long a good-sized live oak will bring an enormous price even while yet standing in the wood.

While I was far up the St. Johns in February, 1832, I went along one of its banks with a live-oak forest warden who received a good Government salary for his trouble. He pointed out some large hummocks of dark-leaved trees that he called live oaks. I thought differently. Our controversy became a little warm, so I proposed we row to the place, examine the leaves and decide the question. The trees turned out to be thousands of big "swamp oaks" without a single live oak among them. The moral is that live-oak hummocks are *not quite* so plentiful as represented. I continued my search for birds.

One dark evening I was sitting on the banks, wondering what arrangements I should make for the night. The rain began to fall in torrents. A Live-oaker invited me to his cabin. There I had supper with a number of Live-oakers. I did my best to help reduce the contents of the tin pans and dishes that my host's wife set before us. We talked of the Floridas and this peninsula until time to take to our bearskins for the night.

At daybreak I accompanied the wood cutters to a hummock of live oak that was destined for the building of a man-of-war. We shot a fine Wild Turkey on our way through a long pine barren. Other cutters were waiting at the shanty to give us breakfast. It was ready and waiting but for the Turkey that their Negro cook began to roast—to go with beef, fish, potatoes, vegetables, biscuits and tin cups of coffee. It was a repast to vie even with a Kentucky morning meal. The conversation of the hungry, happy men had a humorous lilt.

My host, the leader of the party, made little use of his axe other than to strip bark here and there to determine soundness of certain trees, as if he were none too well versed in his profession despite a general intelligence.

He gave me an account of the work. Live-oakers build shanties of small logs, preferably at hummocks near navigable streams, though timber is hauled five or six miles if need be. Beef, pork, potatoes, biscuits, flour, rice and fish, with excellent whiskey, are the daily fare of these mostly hale men, seasonal workers from the Middle and Eastern districts of the Union. The best time for cutting live oak is from early December to early March, or while the sap is completely down. When the sap is flowing, the tree is at "bloom" stage and easier "shaken." Only experts can detect the small round dots, meaning white-rot, on the outer bark. A hard stick may be driven into them for several inches. The disease follows the heart of the tree, up and down. But the spots are so deceptive that thousands of trees are cut and afterwards abandoned because of white-rot. Reports of the quantity of good oak here are much exaggerated. The once good constitutions of the Live-oakers, particularly those who bring their families to settle permanently rather than for the winter, are often impaired by the climate—that was the case with him who gave me this account and who helped my pursuits along.[101]

A certain Live-oaker was on his way from home to a hummock on one of those days when heavy fog, of a kind not infrequent in winter, gave no sign of lifting even when the sun was at its meridian. In woods where every tree looks like the next and where grass, if unburnt, grows as tall as most men (not to mention overgrown trails which often meet, and confuse), even the best woodsmen may find themselves bewildered for a while. (Well do I remember the time when *I* was lost after imprudently venturing to pursue a wounded quadruped that led me some distance from the track.)

The alarmed young workman imagined that he had sped past his destination, and accordingly turned his back on the sun in favor of a different route. The sun headed his course. Hours later it went down.

Still the air was enveloped. The huge gray trees spread giant boughs over head. Rank grass grew on all sides. Not a living being had the Live-oaker met on the path. The scene, silent and still, was like a dull, dreary dream of oblivion, in which he wandered like a forgotten ghost in the land of spirits but not one of whom he met, for a word of encouragement.

The dilemma of the man lost in the woods cannot be imagined by those who have not been in a like predicament. At first every object appears recognizable, while the mind is bent on searching for familiar signs. The farther he goes the more errors he commits. The Live-oaker in question watched the fiery ball of sun go down like a warning of a sultry tomorrow. Insects began to fill the air. The piping of Frogs sounded. Squirrels took to their holes, the Crow to its roost, the harshly croaking Heron to the miry heart of some distant swamp. An Owl hooted. Heavy, chilling dews were wafted by breezes that swept through the trees. There was no moon to light the dreary scene. The Lost One, weary and vexed, lay down on the damp ground. Prayer is always consoling to man in every difficulty or danger. The woodsman fervently prayed.

Imagine the length of that cold, dull, dark night. At dawn the poor man started to his feet with a sorrowful heart—again in fog—and began walking, scarcely knowing where. All day he sought the path home but in vain. At the return of night, terror stole upon him. Worn out, hungry, almost frantic, he beat his breast and tore his hair, and began to feed on weeds and grass around him. The night was one of agony and terror. He knew that if the Almighty did not come to his assistance he must perish. He believed he must have walked more than fifty miles, without coming upon a brook to quench his thirst or bathe his bloodshot eyes. He knew that he would have to find one or die. Deer and Bears were within a few yards or even feet of him but he had only his axe for a weapon. He began to run through the pine barrens, calling on God's pity.

What should he meet but a Tortoise. He gazed on it with amazement and delight, aware that if he were to follow it undisturbed, it would lead him to water. Instead he cut it in two with one stroke, to eat its flesh and drink its blood.

"Oh Sir," the Lost One told me. "How I thanked God whose kindness put the Tortoise in my way! I felt renewed. I sat down at the foot of a pine and gazed up at the heavens to give thanks, for I felt sure that before long I must recover my way and reach home."

There at the foot of the same tree he slept soundly. At dawn he resumed his weary march, following the direction of shadows cast in the sunlight. The dreariness of the woods was the same. He was on the point of despair, when he observed a Racoon squatting in the grass. What had happened to the Turtle now befell the Racoon. On the man journeyed, possessed of his faculties, but like someone groping in a dungeon without a door.

Days passed into weeks. The Lost One subsisted on cabbage-trees, even on Frogs and Snakes until, after forty days, he was so emaciated that he could scarcely crawl to the banks of the river when, at last, he reached it. His clothes were in tatters. His axe was rusted. His hair was matted, his bearded face grimy. It was little more than a parchment-covered skeleton that laid itself down to die. In his feverish fancy he thought he heard oars far away. This was indeed a dream. The last glimmer of hope, the light of life, were about to be put out. But again the oars woke him from his lethargy. The hum of a fly could not have escaped his eager ears. The measured beat of oars—joy to the forlorn soul!—began to mingle with human voices. As the little boat rounded the tangled undergrowth of the headland close by, its lusty rowers saw the poor man on his knees. He raised his feeble voice, suddenly, to a scream of joy. As the rescuers came near his heart nearly failed him. His sight was dim. His brain reeled; he gasped for breath that he, the Lost One, should at last have been found!

The amiable wife and loving children were present in the cabin of the once lost Live-oaker when he told me of this painful experience four years later. Never shall I forget the tears of the family as they listened to a more than thrice-told tale in the plain garb of truth. It only remains for me to say that the hummock to which the woodsman was bound was little more than eight miles from home. The point where he was found was thirty-eight miles away. He must have rambled some four hundred miles in circles as people usually do at such times. Nothing but his strong constitution and the merciful aid of his Maker could have sustained him for so long.[102]

I left the little port of St. Augustine on March 5 in the packet schooner *Agnes* which was bound for Charleston under an old experienced seaman. On the second afternoon out, heavy clouds darkened the heavens. In an ominous lull, before angry Nature inflicted her punishment on guilty man, I kept my eye now on the Captain's face, now on the distant cloud. Both were foreboding. Satisfied as to our safety in such a vessel, and with such a crew, I decided to remain on deck and witness the storm that was about to begin. In a twinkling all sails were so closely reefed in that the *Agnes* no longer resembled her former self. A minute later, down swept the blast that sent the spray leaping over the vessel. Onward and onward sped the *Agnes* unscathed, over the white-capped waves. I cannot say at what rate we were carried by the gale. Two hours later we anchored in the mouth of the Savannah River under a blue sky.

I went ashore to present my credentials to an Engineer Corps officer who was building a fort. He agreed to convey me and my assistants by barge to Savannah next day. I bought some shad to have it cooked on the *Agnes* where I spent the night.

Thousands of Canvas-back Ducks were swimming on the broad river as we ascended in the barge on a beautiful morning. Grackles, Red-wings, and Buntings rose in great numbers from the rice fields. The great Heron spread its broad blue wings and went screaming over. Presently the city of Savannah came into view. On arriving at the hotel I immediately took a seat in the mail coach bound for Charleston. But, before departing, I went to a certain merchant, William Gaston, to present a letter of introduction from Liverpool friends, the Rathbones, who had encouraged me to consign trunks to him on various occasions, and whom I wished to thank. While we walked together arm in arm, he talked of the many demands of charity on his money, the high price of *The Birds of America,* and his inability to subscribe. He expressed doubt that I could find even a single purchaser in Savannah.

My spirits were sadly depressed by this news, for my voyage to the Floridas had been expensive and unprofitable on account of my having been there at the wrong season. We walked on to Gaston's counting-house. There I came across a previous acquaintance, Major Le Conte of the U. S. Army. The conversation turned to the difficulties that authors have to face, even in their own country. I noticed that the merchant Gaston was extremely attentive—to the point of becoming ill-at-ease. He rose from his seat, spoke to his clerk, and sat down again. I was about to follow the Major as he departed but the merchant began to address me. He said he could not conceive why the arts and sciences should not be encouraged by Americans of wealth. At this point the clerk handed him some papers. Gaston turned them over to me, saying, "I subscribe to your work; here is the price of the first volume." He added that if I would accompany him he would obtain other signatures for me. "Every one of us," he said, "is beholden to you for the knowledge you bring us, and for things that might never have reached us without your zeal and enterprise. I shall make it my duty to serve you and will be your agent for Savannah."

Thus has poor Audubon watched art transported from a cold to a warm climate, from one mood to another, alternately, first desponding, then, inspired by a generous merchant, buoyant with hope! I was made to think much about the work going on in London without me, under the care of my British Museum friend, John George Children.

I showed the merchant my new drawings, spreading them, as I usually do, on the floor. This sent him off in search of subscribers. He paid me three more visits. Each time he brought along a friend. Two of these gentlemen subscribed. Gaston himself paid me for their first volumes. He thought others, absent from town, might have done the same. When I bade him adieu at the ferry boat—instead of the mail coach—I found it utterly impossible to express the gratitude I felt.

Almost as soon as I myself reached Charleston his remittance arrived, plus one more subscription. Before the week ended, two checks came, with two more names for my list. It was the merchant's realization of the difficulties that must be overcome by some, for success (despite often malevolent opposition from competitors) that so nobly impelled him to exert himself in the cause of science. As if this were not enough, he took it upon himself, a year or two later, to see that the death of three subscribers did not bring me a loss on the volumes.[103]

"I have much pleasure in furnishing Mr. Audubon with credentials to the officers of the Navy," wrote Secretary of the Navy, Levi Woodbury, to the Secretary of the Treasury, in my behalf. Soon after my arrival in Charleston the revenue cutter *Marion* took me aboard with my assistants Lehman and Ward.[104]

Long before I reached the lovely islets off the southeastern shores of the Floridas, I had heard accounts of the Wreckers. The tales deeply prejudiced me against these men and the cruel, cowardly way they were said to lure vessels toward perilous reefs for the sake of plunder. I had little desire to meet with such men under any circumstances, much less to become the prey of their "aid" which, for me, had come to mean piratical depredation, barbarous usage, and even murder.

One fine afternoon I was standing on the polished deck of the

Marion. A close-hauled sail, bearing in an opposite course, hove in sight. As she rocked in the breeze, the gentle rake of her masts put me in mind of waving reeds on the banks of the Mississippi. By and by she shifted her course towards our own. The *Marion* swept through the waters like a sea bird with wings spread and gently inclining to either side, while the unknown vessel leaped from wave to wave like the Dolphin in pursuit of prey. Soon we were gliding side by side. Our Captains exchanged salutes.

"What a beautiful vessel!" we all thought. "How trim, how clean-rigged, how well-manned! She swims like a duck."

With a broad sheer, she makes for the reefs a few miles under our lee. There in that narrow passage well known to her she rolls, rumbles, dances like a giddy thing. Her copper sheathing gleams. For a moment the waves conceal her, but as she hauls on the wind she resumes her former course. Gradually, the Florida Wrecker vessel recedes from view.

At the Tortugas I was to visit several vessels of this kind with our Captain, Robert Day. I admired the form of the largest of the schooners as we approached . . . its broad beam, light draught, correct water line, neatly painted sides, smooth and well-greased masts, and beautiful riggings. The typically frank greeting of these American tars whose quick, ready application to their tasks was the same on this as on any other vessel, was followed by silence and order on deck. The Commander and Second Officer led us into a spacious, well-lighted cabin furnished with every convenience for fifteen or more passengers. I had to take care, when the former brought out his collection of marine shells, not to admire any one of them too much, for if I pointed to any that I had not seen before, he offered it with much kindness. His many eggs of rare birds he handed over to me with the assurance that a new set could easily be gathered to replace it, there being "much idle time on the reefs at this season." These "down East" men, stout and active, and smart in their cleanly attire, thought my visit in quest of birds "a curious fancy." But they expressed pleasure, notwithstanding, on seeing some of my drawings, and they now offered to help provide me with specimens.

Dinner was served, all extremely social and merry. Expeditions far and near were proposed. We parted friends and agreed to meet next morning.

For our destination, a small Key called Booby Island about ten miles from the lighthouse, the Captain, some crewmen, and I set out in small Hampton boats such as the men of whalers and man-o'-wars also row with long, steady strokes. Sometimes the Captain sang. For a frolic we raced our own beautiful *Marion,* off and on. We had capital sport on the Booby Isle. These men knew more about Boobies and Noddy Terns than do nine-tenths of the best naturalists in the world. When business is slack the Wreckers are also wont to land on some such large Key to hunt Deer. Within a few hours they bring back a supply of delicious venison.

On another day the *Marion* took me on an expedition in quest of sea shells. We were all in the water to the waist at times, or much deeper. These men would dive like Ducks and come up with a beautiful shell. It was a sport they seemed to enjoy above all others.

Word that the *Marion* was about to sail drew me a last invitation. We went after some superb coral, shells, live Turtles of the Hawksbill species, and a quantity of eggs. Not a picayune would the Captain and crew receive in return. They only asked me to mail some letters for their wives "down East." So anxious were they to do all they could for me that they proposed that I keep just ahead of the *Marion* and meet her on the way, to be handed rare birds from haunts that they knew along that coast. Circumstances prevented. With sincere regret and a good share of friendship I bade these excellent fellows adieu.

"How different is the knowledge of things acquired by personal observation from that of hearsay!" thought I.

Never before had I seen the Florida Wreckers, nor has it been my fortune to fall in with any since. But my good friend Dr. Benjamin Strobel gave me a graphic account of a few days that he spent with them, which I now pass along.

Once, in September, five wrecking vessels, bound for Key West to renew their licenses, anchored in the harbor at Indian Key. Strobel had expected to see a parcel of dirty pirate ships, and a set of black-whiskered villains with murder in their looks, rather than these fine large sloops and schooners . . . regular clippers in first-rate order, under generally jovial, goodhumored sons of Neptune, so polite and hospitable as to afford persons passing up and down the Reef every assistance. The crews were hearty, well turned out, honest-looking men.

A day later the five Wrecker vessels got under way on a beautiful, soft, pea-green sea, smooth as a sheet of glass, and as transparent. Its surface was troubled only by the departing ships and the plunging of Pelicans after fish. Instead of following on his own much slower schooner, *Jane,* the Doctor accepted an invitation to sail with the fleet. Every sail was set to catch the breeze. White foam curled round the prows. The ships, like islands of flitting shadows, glided silently along on a motionless sea of light. Visible several fathoms below were fish diving and sporting among the sea grass, sponges, sea-feathers, and coral that covered the bottom.

To the right were the Keys which were like specks on the surface, until the ships drew near. Close at hand, the Keys rose as if by enchantment in the richest livery of springlike hues, which the brilliant sun in the clear sky rendered soft and delicate in color. The trade winds played about the fairy scene. The vessels of the fleet began a race toward the Bay of Honda. There being no prospect of reaching Key West that night, they entered the beautiful basin and dropped anchor about 4 P.M. Boats were lowered for the hunting parties that went in search of shells and birds. An Indian, picked up somewhere along the coast by a Wrecker, went after venison with only one ball in his rifle. A few hours later he returned with two Deer killed at a single shot. He had waited until both moved, side by side, within range.

Most of the game for an abundant supper was sent to the largest of the ships. As soon as the moon rose, row boats passed back and forth among the vessels, lying close by one another, in an exchange of festivities that suggested nothing of the professional rivalry among these men. About 9 P.M. many gathered for the supper. A German sailor played his fiddle on the quarter-deck for dancing until the meal was ready—a feast of venison, wild Ducks, Pigeons, Curlews, and fish. Afterward there was much toasting and singing. The German fiddler sang this chanty that the others said he himself had composed in characteristic style:

THE WRECKER'S SONG

Come ye, goot people, von and all,
　　Come listen to my song:
A few remarks I have to make,
　　Which vont be very long.
'Tis of our vessel stout and goot
As ever yet was built of woot
Along the reef where the breakers roar,
De Wreckers on de Florida shore!

Key Tavernier's our rendezvou;
　　At anchor there we lie,
And see the vessels in the Gulf,
　　Carelessly passing by.
When night comes on we dance and sing,

Whilst the current some vessel is floating in;
When daylight comes, a ship's on shore,
Among de rocks where de breakers roar.

When daylight dawns, we're under weigh,
    And every sail is set,
And if the wind it should prove light,
    Why then, our sails we wet.
To gain her first each eager strives,
To save de cargo and de people's lives,
Amongst de rocks where de breakers roar,
De Wreckers on de Florida shore.

When we get 'longside, we find she's bilged:
    We know vel vat to do,
Save de cargo dat we can,
    De sails and rigging too;
Den down to Key West we soon vill go,
When quickly our salvage we shall know;
When every ting it is fairly sold,
Our money down to us it is told.

Den one week's cruize we'll have on shore,
    Before we do sail again,
And drink success to de sailor lads
    Dat are ploughing of de main.
And when you are passing by dis way,
On the Florida Reef should you chance to stray,
Why, we will come to you on de shore,
Amongst de rocks where de breakers roar.

Between each verse the German played a symphony, remarking "Gentlemen I makes dat myself." Twenty or thirty voices trolled each chorus that rang out upon the stillness of the night.[105]

At Indian Key I observed an immense quantity of beautiful tree Snails of a pyramidal or shortly conical form, some pure white, others curiously marked with spiral lines of bright red, yellow and black. They were crawling vigorously on every branch of every bush where there was not a nest of the White Ibis. Wherever that bird nested not a live Snail was to be seen; hundreds lay dead beneath . . . because of the ordure of the Ibis?[106] There I also saw a pair of Nighthawks killed by lightning while they were on the wind during a tremendous thunderstorm. They fell on the sea. I picked them up to examine them carefully, but failed to discover the least appearance of injury to their feathers or internal parts.[107]

On Indian Key, also, I observed that largest of its species, the Great White Heron. When I was prevented from accompanying Egan the pilot of Indian Isle the day after my arrival, because of my anxiety to finish a drawing, he came in with two young birds and a nest cut from a mangrove. Imagine my delight to see at a glance that these were different from any I had ever seen! The beautiful white plumage was cream-tinged. The birds were remarkably fat and strong for their age—three weeks or thereabouts. We placed the nest and birds in the yard. Unless we extended a hand when we drew near, they seemed quite unconcerned by our approach. My Newfoundland dog came at my whistle. At the sight of him the Herons rose slightly, ruffled their feathers, spread their wings, opened their bills, and clicked their mandibles angrily without, however, leaving the nest. I ordered Plato nearer, but said not to hurt them. Despite the fact that one bill struck him and clung to his nose, he took it all in good part and merely brought the bird towards me. I seized it by the wings to make it to relax its hold on the dog. It walked off as proudly as any of its tribe. I was delighted to find it possessed of so much courage. I left these birds with the pilot's wife when I sailed south. On my return I found them well and much grown, but with bills broken by the force of striking at fish thrown to them on rocks in their enclosure. It is a curious fact that the points of their bills, broken by about an inch, grew back again and were as regular in shape as if nothing had happened. In the evening, or early in the morning, they would frequently set, like pointers, at moths in the Charleston garden to which eventually I took them. With a well-directed stroke of the bill they would seize the fluttering insect hovering over the flowers, and instantly swallow it. At last they began to pursue the younger children of the place. That ended their career. One Ibis was beautifully mounted by my taxidermist assistant, Henry Ward, for the Charleston Museum.[108]

Once the *Marion* was over the coral reef that stretches along the shore of Indian Key like a great wall reared by an army of giants, we anchored and I was in a row boat that soon put me on the beach. With what feelings of delight did we gaze about us—at the gorgeous flowers, the luxuriant trees, the singular and beautiful plants. The birds, more brilliantly colored than any I had ever seen before, were all new to me. I longed to become more intimately acquainted with those that gamboled happily among the bushes or glided over the light green waters.

Students of nature spend little time over introductions to persons likely to take an interest in their pursuits. In a trice I was in the boat and in the company of the Deputy Collector of the island with his pilot and his fishermen, bound for a large Key. There we began to bring down the objects of my desire. Some of the party headed into the tangled groves that cover the beautiful coral beach, and others kept close to the curious inhabitants of the deep. One of them even rushed into the waters to seize a Crab that prepared, with outstretched claws, to meet its adversary. A loud voice called out to warn of Sharks, as abundant as pebbles along these shores. The hungry prowlers could not have asked for a more savory dinner than this might have afforded.

Egan the pilot, besides being a first-rate shot, was intimately acquainted with the country. A former "conch shell diver," in quest of curious shells, no matter how many fathoms down to the craggy bottom seemed to him more pastime than toil. No Cormorant, Pelican, Flamingo, Ibis, or Heron built a nest unbeknownst to him. He knew Doves of these Keys better than many fops know the contents of their pockets. Every channel, every cranny, was familiar to him.

For years Egan was a professional hunter of Sea Cows or Manatees for the Havana market. He called his wonderful gun "Long Tom," and its large shot, "groceries." He never paddled his light canoe without a trusty javelin at his side for fishing. I doubt if his equal at attacking, or netting, or overturning Turtles ever lived on the Florida coast. From the moment of my arrival until I left Key West he was at my service and seldom out of my hearing. While the others gathered plants, shells and small birds, he tapped me on the shoulder, that first day, and said with a smile, "Come along, I'll show you something better worth your while."

With only the Captain and a pair of tars—for more, he said, would not do—we sailed in the yawl at a great rate until near a certain point. There the pilot alone did the "sculling" while the rest of us prepared for "rare sport." We stepped ashore and moved slowly and silently towards a thick wood of mangroves. There, before us, we beheld a multitude of Pelicans.

Half a mile away, at the end of the Key, we saw four hundred Cormorants' nests overhead. "Pull away, never mind those on the wing, for those black rascals don't mind a little firing," Egan had cried as we approached. "Now, boys, lay her close under the nests." There we were, under the sitting birds. The number that plunged into the water was such that I thought we had killed the whole colony by some unaccountable means, when we fired. But as one bird after another peeped up from the water, only a few were unable to take to wing. Most of our shots had lodged in the tough dry twigs of the nests. We had lost the more favorable opportunity of hitting them by not waiting until they rose.

"Never mind," said Egan. "If you wish, you may load that Lady of the Green Mantle, your ship the *Marion,* in less than a week." He promised we would bring down a score within ten minutes. And so we did.

A beautiful bird called Peale's Egret came up within range as we sailed round the island.

Three hours before sunset we returned to Indian Key. The others had brought their collections to the home of Egan for me. Mrs. Egan had a room ready for me to draw in. Lehman began a sketch of the lovely isle, and Ward to skin the birds.

Time is ever precious to the student of nature. I wired several birds in natural attitudes. I did not join the merriment at a dance of males and females at the house that evening. The thought of patrons of my work in America and Europe kept me "grinding"—not on an organ but on paper, that I might finish not only my outlines of the birds but also notes about all I had seen that day. Next to the room where I worked was the one that the merrymakers filled. Two miserable fiddlers sawed, not on catgut, but on screeching silken strings. The bouncing of the brave lads and fair lasses shook the premises to its foundations. One dancer slipped to the floor and drew a burst of laughter that echoed over the island. Diluted claret cooled the ladies. A more potent beverage warmed their partners. That night the Captain of the *Marion* returned to his cabin. My assistants and I slept in light, swinging hammocks under the eaves of the piazza.

This was at the end of April. The nights were short, the days long. Anxious to turn every moment to account, we were back in the Deputy's boat at three next morning. Soon we were on our way along those tortuous channels that keep crossing immense, muddy soaplike flats from the outer Keys to the mainland. Here and there, on our voyage of discovery, we came upon vast beds of floating seaweeds which are the refuse of the food of the Turtle. The Deputy, Thurston, mentioned that he had once been lost for several days and nights among these narrow channels while pursuing smugglers well acquainted with their windings. He had been unable to reach either Keys or mainland, though in full sight of them, until a heavy gale raised the water. He then sailed directly home over the flats because he was almost exhausted by hunger and his exertions. (Egan laughed that, had he himself been the pilot, "the rascals would not have escaped.")

We observed multitudes of Brown Pelicans and shot a good number. Several times Egan brought down a bird from a height of fully a hundred yards. Some, unaware of our range, sailed calmly along . . . for "Long Tom" to furnish us with as many as we required. Towards night we returned with our booty.

Next morning . . . delightful . . . clear . . . silent save for the long line of breakers that washed over the far reefs, we headed for Keys seldom visited by men. My soul was struck by the idea of the Almighty and his Power, at the sight of the sunrise, a burst of glory from the bosom of the waters. The moon, thin and pale, concealed herself in the dim West, as if ashamed of her feeble light. The waters, at once tremulous and smooth, fairly glistened. The deep blue of the clear heavens was pure as the world that lies beyond. The Heron flew heavily towards land like a glutton, retiring at daybreak, its paunch well-lined. The nocturnal Owl and Night Heron hurried to safety in the depths of some swamp. The ever-cheerful Gulls and Terns gamboled, exulting, over the waters abounding in food. I also exulted, and seemed to expand with hope. That Nature also had charms for the crew showed in their merry faces. How much of beauty and joy do they miss who never view the rising sun . . . they whose waking hours are seldom nocturnal!

Our men rowed twenty miles to bring us to Sandy Island. From its level shores we could plainly see the southernmost cape of the Floridas. The flocks of birds that covered the shelly beaches, and those that hovered overhead, so astonished us that at first we could scarcely believe our eyes. Our first volley brought down food enough for two days—sixty-five Great Godwits lay at our feet.

Rose-colored Curlews stalked gracefully beneath the mangroves. Purple Herons rose at almost every step we took. Each cactus held the nest of a White Ibis. The sky was darkened by whistling wings. Gallinules and other water birds floated about.

Under a shelter that we formed of sticks and grass the sailor cook set to work to supply our fatigued frames at day's end. Under mosquito nets we were lulled to rest by the cackle of the beautiful Purple Gallinules!

When we lay down in the sand to sleep, the waters almost bathed our feet. In the morning they were at an immense distance. Our boat lay on her side, looking not unlike a Whale reposing on a mud bank. Birds were flocking over the exposed sea bottom now turned into pasture. Apart from the many Ibises were the equally numerous Godwits. Thousands of Herons paced along, ever and anon thrusting their javelin bills into pools of water to draw out some unlucky fish. I could not estimate the number of Fish Crows. From the havoc they caused among the Crabs these animals must have been scarce by ebb tide. Brown Pelicans chased the Jaeger which in turn had just robbed a Gull of its prize. The Gallinules, timorous at the sight of us, spread wings and ran to the thickets.

It would have been too dangerous to venture out over the mud. Egan assured me that nothing could be lost by waiting. Off we went to a part of the island where "our breakfast, although uncooked, was waiting." Sailors followed us with baskets, others with tin plates. In a thicket of about an acre we found Ibis nests on every bush. The birds gave way to us and before long we had a heap of the large, beautiful eggs— delicious fare that we soon prepared in one way or other on the fire that we had kindled.

After breakfast we saw the tide beginning to come in. A foot or two of water is quite sufficient to drive even the tallest Heron or Flamingo off these enormous mud flats. The tide seems to flow of a sudden over the whole expanse. As soon as the water began forcing the birds back towards shore, the shooting from behind bushes began, until we had a heap not unlike a small haycock. Who would not help himself to a few of these birds? Surely not one as fond of these things as I am. Even the sailors tried their hands at the work of skinning.

Instead, Egan went after something else, marching quietly off with his "Long Tom" and fishing tackle. In about an hour we saw him returning, looking quite exhausted.

"There's a Dew fish and some Barracuda yonder, but I couldn't haul them here," he said. The sailors went back for the hundred-pound Dew fish which afforded excellent eating. As for the more dangerous Barracuda, "some of these gentry" had followed Egan on more than one occasion when he was waist-deep in water, until he had to spear "the gentlemen" before they cut off his legs or some other nice bit with which he was unwilling to part.

We filled our cask at an old well long since dug by Seminoles or Pirates in the sands of Cape Sable. Then at about full tide we left Sandy Isle. We had twenty miles to go, "as the birds fly," but actually about twenty-seven because of the winding course of the channels. At different Keys along the way we looked for nests and eggs of rare birds.

A black cloud obscured the rapidly descending sun. A breeze swelled our sails. Telling us to sit on the weather gunwale, the pilot warned that we were "going to catch it." One sail was hauled in, another reefed. A low murmuring sounded. The black cloud became a rolling, tumultuous mass that shot forth vivid flashes of lightning. Egan steered for the nearest land, and as he covered himself with his oil jacket he cried, "Blow, sweet breeze, we'll reach land before the blast overtakes us." Sailors passed their quids of tobacco from one cheek to the other. We all pulled on our jackets.

Furious indeed was the cloud that like a spread eagle approached as if in haste to destroy us. Close to shore the pilot commanded that all "sit quite still," or risk being carried overboard. The terrific grandeur of a tropical hurricane cannot be imagined. Not content with laying the land waste, it sweeps the shallows quite dry of water to quench its thirst. Nothing in its path escapes its fury for an instant. Like the scythe of the destroying angel it cuts everything by the roots with the careless ease of that reaper. Within its "eye" it collects a heap such as the harvester casts aside. On it goes with a wildness and fury until its force is spent, leaving in its wake Nature weeping, disconsolate, bereft of her beauty. A full century may be required for even her powerful energies to repair the loss. The planter has lost not only his mansion, crops and flocks, but he has to clear his lands of trunks and branches strewn everywhere. The boat that is overtaken by the storm is cast on the lee shore, to present a melancholy spectacle which nevertheless delights the Wreckers.

Our light yawl shivered like a leaf the instant the blast struck her sides. The next instant we thought she had gone over, but then we found ourselves on shore, and the waters were drifting like snow around us. The tough mangroves were hidden amid their roots, and the roaring waves were driving in among them. The tempest howled. It was not rain that fell, but masses of water—in a horizontal direction—which gave the exposed part of my body a smart blow.

But enough!—in half an hour it was over. Pure blue heavens returned. Night descended. Some spent the night in the boat. The pilot, my assistant Lehman, and I took to the heart of the mangroves. We kindled as good a fire as we could, spread a tarpaulin and, our insect bars over us, soon forgot, in sleep, the horrors around us.

Another day of cruising, and we anchored in a safe harbor for visits to other Keys. This brought us a hundred miles or so south of Indian Key.

One May morning we set out for a Key difficult to reach. At one point we had to haul and push our row boats over nine miles of mud flats before we came to one of those deep channels that usually ring the mangrove islands. Here, exhausted by our labor, we floated on the deep water to rest from the excessive heat, and under mangroves fanned by gentle breezes from the Gulf. Here, as elsewhere in the lower Floridas, we confined ourselves to fish and soaked biscuit. Water and molasses was our constant and only beverage. More substantial fare in these latitudes of alternating heat and moisture would have been a hazard. None of us ever complained of so much as a headache on this regimen.

Far away, on one of the flats, I saw the Heron *Ardea occidentalis* moving majestically along in a great flocks. The rising tide drove them toward us and the tallest trees. We shot as many as I wished. I took some of the young alive.

We found Mule Key, beyond, dismal in the extreme, and in no way profitable. Bales of cotton floated in all the coves. Spars of every description lay on the beach. Far off on the reefs lay the remains of a lost ship, her hull dismantled. The schooners of Wreckers were a sight from which I turned with heavy heart. Indeed I was in dread of meeting floating bodies of the crew cast upon the shore. I came much closer to a large Shark, while I was swimming in the channel of the isle than I ever wish to be again.[109]

The Tortugas, five or six extremely uninhabitable banks of shelly sand that are the resort of Wreckers and Turtlers, lie about eighty miles from Key West. Between these islands, the last that seem to defend the Florida peninsula, lie deep intricate channels well known not only to those adventurers but to revenue cutters on duty along that dangerous coast. About eight miles from the inhospitable isles, in the direction of the Gulf, stretches the great coral reef on which many an ignorant or careless navigator has suffered shipwreck.

The Tortugas are covered with Coral, Sea Fans and other marine animals. Curious and beautiful fishes fill the limpid shoals. Turtles resort to the banks to deposit their eggs in the burning sand. These, and the clouds of sea fowl that nest there, are followed by persons called Eggers. The ill-gotten cargo is sold in distant markets for the share of gold that all men seem bent on acquiring.

One day a few hours before sunset the *Marion* approached the islands on a fresh breeze. We dropped anchor before twilight. Those who have never seen the sun go down in these latitudes might well make a voyage for the purpose. I doubt that its departure is as gorgeous in any other corner of the world. The great red disk triples its ordinary dimensions as it sinks towards the horizon. From half way beneath the line of waters it still illuminates the heavens with a flood of golden light. Its refulgent glory blazes through purpling clouds and through masses of vapor which seems to turn into mountains of molten gold. Slowly, after the sun has disappeared, night begins to draw a curtain of gray from the east over the world as the dusk gathers.

The Nighthawk flaps on noiseless wings. The Terns settle on their nests. The Brown Pelicans wend their way to distant mangroves. The Brown Gannet, in search of a resting place, perches on the yard-arm. The heavily laden Turtles, anxious to deposit their eggs in the sands, slowly advance towards land with their heads above the rippling water. Dimly I see their broad bulk as they toil along, or I hear their suspicious, uneasy breathing. The moon begins to light the scene of the Turtle's slow and laborious landing. Over the sand she drags her heavy body by means of flippers far better adapted to propelling her through water. Up the slope, in spite of all, she works her way. Industriously she casts up the sand on either side of her before depositing layer after layer of eggs that she arranges in the most careful way. With her hind "paddles" she brings the sand over the last of them, then swiftly retires towards the shore, to launch again into the deep.

There are [five]* different species of sea Turtles: the Green Turtle, the Hawksbill, the Loggerhead, the Trunk [Leatherback], and [the Ridley]. All deposit their eggs in much the same way. I have several times watched them in the act. Nearing the shores on fine, calm, moonlight nights, the Turtle hisses loudly to warn any unseen enemies of her approach. At any noise or sign of danger she instantly sinks back and swims off. But if she sees nothing likely to upset her plans, and if everything is quiet, she crawls to a place suited to her purpose. She stretches her neck as far as she can as she gazes all around. Then she begins to scoop out the sand beneath her body, and works so skilfully that she seldom falls in. The sand piles up behind her to a depth of about two feet within nine minutes. It takes her perhaps twenty minutes to deposit nearly two hundred eggs, and she will not

---

* Namely, the *Chelonia;* the *Eretomochelys;* the *Caretta;* the *Lepidochelys;* and the *Dermochelys* (Source: Archie Carr, *So Excellent a Fishe,* New York, Natural History Press, 1967). Audubon omitted the Ridley, or "bastard turtle."—*Ed.*

leave off even if approached, or even if someone should come and sit upon her back. She seems to find it necessary to go ahead with her labors regardless of anything. She smooths the surface so that no passerby could possibly be aware of the nest where the heat of the sand will hatch out her eggs. Once this is accomplished she hurries off; not even a Hercules could very readily manage to overturn her and keep her captive. To do so he would have to fall on his knees, place his shoulders beneath her forearm, gradually raise her up by main force, and then with a jerk throw her over. Sometimes it takes several men to accomplish this. Some Turtlers dare to swim up to a Turtle and turn her over while she is sleeping on the surface of the water. Few Turtles can bite beyond the reach of their forelegs, nor can they regain their natural position when overturned. Nevertheless, it is necessary to tie their flippers with rope to prevent their escape, once they are taken up into a boat kept near at hand.

Turtles frequent many other of the Florida Keys, as well as various parts of the mainland. The Green Turtle, considered the best by the epicures, winters in deep waters and enters the bays, inlets, and rivers early in April. Twice in May, once in June, it deposits eggs. The first deposit is the largest, and the last is the least; and the total averages two hundred and forty eggs. The shell of the Hawksbill Turtle is a valuable article of commerce; its flesh is next in quality. It resorts to the outer Keys only, to deposit about three hundred eggs, all told, in July and again in August. It is seen, searching the beaches for a safe place to deposit them, much earlier in the season. Between April and late June the Loggerhead lays an average of one hundred and seventy eggs in three sets, in the Tortugas. The Trunk [Leatherback] Turtle, sometimes of enormous size, has a pouch like a Pelican. Its shell and flesh are so soft that one may press a finger into it, almost as if into a lump of butter. It is seldom eaten, except by Indians who carry off the eggs first, before catching the Turtles. The average seasonal deposit, in two sets, may be three hundred and fifty eggs.

The Loggerhead and Trunk Turtles are the least cautious in choosing a spot for their eggs. The Green and the Hawksbill species search for the wildest, most secluded spots but deposit eggs in the sand in the same way as the other two kinds of sea Turtles just mentioned. The Green Turtle chooses either mainland shores between Cape Sable and Cape Florida, or enters the Indian, the Halifax or other large rivers and inlets from which it retreats to the open sea as speedily as possible. Great numbers of the Green species are killed by Indians and Turtlers, as well as by Cougars, Lynxes, Bears, Wolves, and the like. The Hawks-bill is more wary than the Green, and always the most difficult to sur-prise. It keeps to the sea islands. All species employ nearly the same method of laying eggs, as I have seen for myself.

Persons in search of eggs go along the shores probing the sand, near tracks of the animals, with a light stiff cane or gun rod. Beasts of prey also discover the spots where hundreds of Turtles form holes within the space of a mile—a new one for each deposit, the second generally nearby, as if the animal were quite unconscious of what had befallen the first. It will readily be understood that the numerous eggs seen in a Turtle, on cutting it up, could not all be laid during the same season. The whole number deposited by one in a season may reach four hun-dred; yet if the Turtle is caught on or near her nest, the remaining eggs —all small and shell-less, and threaded like so many large beads— exceed three thousand. I found that number for one Turtle weighing nearly four hundred pounds. Soon after the young ones, scarcely larger than a dollar, scratch their way through their sandy covering, they take to the water.

The Green Turtle feeds on marine plants, especially grass-wrack that it cuts near the roots for the most tender, succulent parts. As I said earlier, masses of these plants float on their feeding grounds, the flats, or along the shores. The Hawksbill Turtle feeds on sea weed, crabs, shellfish, and fishes. The Loggerhead eats large conch shells mainly, crushing them to pieces with powerful beak as easily as a man might crack a walnut. We brought one aboard the *Marion*. It made a deep indentation in the flook of one of the anchors, much to my surprise. The Trunk [Leatherback] Turtle eats mollusks, fish, crustaceans, sea urchins, and marine plants. The speed of the Green and the Hawksbill in the water, and the ease of their motions, bring the flight of a bird to mind. It is therefore no easy matter to strike one with a spear, as accomplished Turtlers do.

While at Key West, and on other of the coastal islands of the Floridas, I needed to buy some Turtles to feed to my friends the Herons that I was taking alive in coops to John Bachman of Charleston. So I went to a "crawl" to price some. The smaller ones not above ten pounds were dearer than the larger ones. The Turtler assured me that although the "monsters" were better meat than the small ones, there was no disposing of the meat because he could not get it to a distant market. Its flesh would keep little more than a day. So I bought eight or ten small ones for my Heron friends. While I gazed on a

Loggerhead of more than seven hundred pounds that cost little more than a Turtle of only thirty pounds, I thought what a "Lord Mayor's dinner" it would have supplied . . . or what a curious carriage its shell would have made for Venus to sail the Caribbean, drawn by tender Doves if no Shark or hurricane upset it.

Turtles are caught in various ways on the coast, estuaries, and rivers of the Floridas. Great nets set across the entrance of streams have large meshes that the Turtles can enter part way, only to become the more entangled as they struggle to be free. The nets serve either at flow or ebb of the waters. The harpoon is also used.

In my opinion the method employed by Egan my pilot at Indian Isle was best. An extraordinary Turtler, he had an iron instrument called a "peg," with bradlike points at each end, resembling the beak of an Ivory-billed Woodpecker in shape. Between the two shoulders of this instrument a fine tough line, fifty or more fathoms long, was fastened by passing one end through a hole in the center of the peg. The line was carefully coiled and placed in a convenient part of the canoe. One end of the peg entered an iron sheath loosely attached to a long wooden spear, until the Turtle was pierced through the shell by the other end. Egan would paddle away as quietly as possible when he spied a basking Turtle. From a distance of ten or twelve yards he would throw the spear to hit the animal about where an entomologist would pin an insect to a piece of cork. As soon as the Turtle was struck, the wooden handle separated from the peg because of being loosely attached. The longer the peg remained in the shell the more firmly fastened it seemed to become on account of the pressure placed upon it by the shell of the distraught animal. After being allowed to run like a Whale until fatigued, the Turtle was hauled in with care. Egan said that one man could catch as many as eight hundred Green Turtles a year in this manner.

Each Turtler has his "crawl," a square wooden building or pen made of logs standing upright in the mud, and far enough apart to let the tide pass through freely. The Turtles are kept and fed there until sold. If they have not yet laid their eggs, they drop them there, and the eggs are lost. At Key West the price of Green Turtles was four to six cents a pound.

Mating is conducted in a most extraordinary manner which I must pass over here. One habit, however, I cannot omit, although I have it only at second-hand. When I was in the Floridas several Turtlers assured me that any Turtle taken from the shore of its choice and carried on the deck of a vessel several hundred miles would, if set free, certainly be found again where it had been before, perhaps in the following breeding season. Should this be true, and it certainly may, how much will the belief of students in Nature's laws be enhanced on finding that the Turtle, like the migratory bird, returns to the same locality, and perhaps with the delight of the experienced traveller who comes back to the familiar environment from distant countries?[110]

In the calm of a fine moonlight night, under clear heavens reflected across the broad glare of the trembling waters, I had a conversation with the officer on watch, a one-time Turtler and a great hunter to boot. Although a man of humble birth, his energy and talent, along with his education, had raised him to a higher station. Our talk ranged over a variety of subjects—principally, you may be sure, of birds and Nature. He told me of a disagreeable adventure he once had while hunting in a certain cove on the shores of the Gulf.

He was paddling towards a sandy, grass-covered shore one quiet summer evening with the thought of pitching his mosquito net for a night in the wilds. The Bull Frogs were bellowing by the thousands. He thought they would lull him to sleep, and that the flocks of Blackbirds would keep him company in this secluded retreat. As he was paddling upstream to a safe place for his canoe in case of a sudden storm, he came upon a beautiful yawl, the sight of which, in this unfrequented region, made his heart stand still. His paddle dropped from his hands for an instant. But with mixed fear and curiosity he drew nearer. He began to notice bloodstains on its sides. He glanced anxiously over the gunwale and to his horror saw two gory bodies that he at once took for victims of pirates or Indians. Naturally, his anxiety mounted and he could feel his heart missing a few beats, there, near sunset, where all was consternation and despair. How long his hesitation lasted he did not know, but only that he was roused from reverie by groans of a man in mortal agony. He felt almost refreshed by the cold sweat that began to bathe his body, as he reflected that he was at least well armed and might hope for the protection of the Almighty. He might even, out of humanity, render assistance or perhaps save a life unless surprised and overpowered. Buoyed by the thought, he urged the canoe ashore and taking it by the bow sprang it high among the grasses. He cocked and primed his gun, to be ready to shoot the first head that might arise as he moved towards the groaning sound. Sud-

denly he saw a hand wave from among the weeds in the most sup-
plicating way. Just as he levelled his gun in that direction, the head
and breast of a man covered with blood rose before him. A faint,
hoarse voice pleaded for mercy and help! A fall to the ground was
followed by a deathlike silence. He kept his eyes on everything about;
his ears strained for the slightest sound. The situation seemed one of
life and death. Still the Frogs croaked on; the last Blackbirds alighted.
He moved on towards the victim, his pity mixed with horror. The poor
being prostrate at his feet was so weak from loss of blood that there
was nothing to fear.

He ran to the water to fill his cap and bathe the weather-beaten,
seamy face of the once powerful man of the broad chest and frightful,
even disgusting features. The groans continued in an appalling fashion,
along with the choking struggle for breath. As my friend the officer
rubbed the throbbing temples with the contents of a phial that he kept
about him for snakebite, he noticed the large pistol thrust in the man's
bosom, the naked cutlass near by on the ground, the red silk handkerchief that bound his jutting brows, the loose-fitting trousers stuffed in
fisherman's boots. Here, in short, were the marks of a pirate.

The exertions were not in vain. But darkness, deep darkness, had
enveloped the two. My friend's offer to make a fire for the pirate whose
pulse was growing stronger drew protests. But he nevertheless went to
the yawl and with his hatchet soon splintered the rudder, benches, and
oars for a blazing fire. Half in English, half in Spanish, the pirate asked
him to put out the flames. Only a draught of spirits quieted the man,
who still bled freely from gashes in his side and shoulders. At the mention
of the want of food he sullenly turned his head.

The talk drifted to religion, but the dying man hardly believed in
the existence of a God. He said he knew nothing of His ways—that
he was an outlaw—for years a pirate, and perhaps in his rescuer's
regard a wretch. "The teachings of my parents were of no avail, for I
always believed I was born to be a most cruel man," he said. "Here
I lie, among the weeds, because I would not listen to those early
admonitions." He admitted that he had murdered his mother with his
own hands, and so deserved the death in store for him. He felt grateful
for the presence of another human being to witness his last agony.

All urging that he rally proved vain. He felt resigned to death. "I
am glad that the villains who gave me these wounds did not win over
me." Then he asked for water and to be left to die alone, without
begging pardon from any man.

In hopes of learning more about the pirate's dead comrades, the rescuer fetched another capful of water which the other gulped down while being urged to bare his whole story for the good of his soul. The pirate said there was not time—that the beating of his heart told him so—that long before daylight he would lie motionless, most of his blood gone from his body to make the grass grow. His wounds were mortal, and he vowed to die without saying more.

My friend pointed towards the majestic rising of the moon, and asked the pirate to recognize in it the presence of a higher power. This had the effect of persuading the dying man that his interrogator wished to finish him off if he refused to speak. But he concluded that because he did not care a jot about death except for the pain, he might as well tell what was "proper" to this stranger who had undeniably befriended him.

To quicken his mind the pirate was given a swallow of spirits. His eyes seemed to dart fire as a heavy, deep sigh swelled his chest and struggled through his throat. Raised a little, he began to speak a jargon of Spanish, French and English. He asked to know how many bodies lay on the deck and what kind of garb they had on. The answer convinced him that they were the "scoundrels" who followed him in an "infernal Yankee barge." Their craft was too broad for the channel, so they left it to wade after the pirate, all his comrades having already been shot in the chase. The pirate had thrown most of the bodies overboard to lighten the yawl. While he was still at it, two of his pursuers seized his gunwale and struck his head—but not until after he had mortally wounded both.

"The other villains carried off my schooner and one of our row boats," the dying man continued. "Perhaps by now they have hung the rest of my companions. I have commanded my beautiful vessel for years, captured many ships, sent many rascals to the devil. I always hated the Yankees, and only regret I didn't kill more of them. I myself come from Matanzas. I have often been in league with others. My money—and how much of it I have I do not know—is buried where it will never be found. Useless to try and tell you where."

His throat filled up, his voice failed, the cold hand of death lay upon his brow as he muttered a feeble farewell. The rattling in his throat marked the end. With an insupportable heaviness the body fell back on the arms that held it. One last, frightful groan issued from the bleeding mouth of that foul spirit.

My friend assured me that his feelings, during the remainder of that night, could not possibly be described. He dug a grave at dawn with the paddle of his canoe, then rolled the body in and covered it up. Buzzards were already at work on the deck of the boat. He tried to drag the bodies to shore for burial. This proved impossible. He covered them over with mud and weeds, before launching his canoe and paddling out of the cove. Although elated to be escaping, he felt his relief overshadowed by a dreadful sense of gloom and abhorrence.[111]

III

Northward

IN August my wife and sons accompanied me on a journey to Maine and the British province of New Brunswick.

Before sailing up the St. John River we spent a morning with Sir Archibald Campbell and his delightful family at Government house. The *Favorite*, a mere scow, was commanded by a person of rather uncouth aspect and rude manners. It had one cabin for my family (all fortunately well, and luxuriating in happiness, as a result of the kindness shown us in Frederickton) and, in addition, nearly a score and a half of assorted individuals. Two sorry nags drew the tow line. On the line nearest us rode a less than half-clad Negro youth with a long switch in one hand and a pair of bridles in the other, urging the team along at something more than two miles an hour.

We had provided ourselves with a large basket of picnic foods. Although it was by this time late in September, the mowers were still cutting grass along the delightful shores and on the undulating hills that were now and then under cultivation, now and then interrupted by steep rocky banks. Gardens showed patches of green peas. Apples were still green. The vegetation reminded us that we were in a northern latitude.

In the afternoon the changing of our jaded horses afforded us a chance to go ashore. An election was going on. No dinner could be obtained at the big place on the hill where we saw groups standing around. So, on the greensward, we refreshed ourselves with the contents of our basket.

Our second set of horses was worse than the first, something I have seen happen over and over in every country. To tell how often the tow line gave way would amuse the listener perhaps as much as it annoyed us while we plodded on. Once our "Commander" was pulled into the stream. He managed to climb back into his gallant bark and consoled himself with a volley of blasphemies unfit for repetition. Where we slept that night I would be ashamed to relate.

Before daylight the *Favorite* was not far upon her way before every able man aboard went ashore to take a hand with the tow. Farther on, a curious cataract of the "Pokioke" River forced "Sambo" to guide his steeds up the high bank. Suddenly he and the whole party came tumbling down like so many hogsheads of tobacco rolled from a store-house to the banks of the Ohio. The Captain hoped "the black rascal" had broken his neck, but "Sambo," alert as an Indian chief, leaped on the naked back of one of the horses as they got on their feet and, showing his teeth, laughed at his master's curses. Before long our boat caught, very snugly, on top of a rock in the middle of the stream, opposite the mouth of the Eel River.

Chapfallen but none the worse for all this, we landed at Woodstock village. After dinner the family hired a cart and driver and started towards Houlton, Maine, glad enough to return to our country after all our mishaps. In bidding farewell to the beautiful St. John River, I ought to mention that it is seldom navigable for more than eight months of the year. The breaking up of the ice in spring (ice known to jam to a height of nearly fifty feet) is awful, they say. The floods that follow cover even the plateau of Frederickton to a depth of four feet. Fortunately, such an occurrence is rare on our own great rivers of the West and South.

Major Clarke, U.S. border garrison Commander, received us most kindly. His officers and men joined us next day on a long though fruitless ornithological excursion that yielded not one bird of any use. Nor did any of those few days at Houlton, before we moved on again in another hired cart, or at Bangor our destination. The straight road that the soldiers had begun to cut through the forest, one destined to become among the finest in the Union, was still unfinished at points. The rain fell in torrents that reduced the loose earth to a complete bed of mud. Once our team went so deep in mire that it took two oxen to save us from spending the night in that spot. Luckily for us, a lighthearted wagoner with an excellent team of horses was induced, by a little "siller" across his palm, to hitch them to our cart for the rest of the ride to Cross Roads Tavern. Deer, Trout, Bear, Grouse—and the Great Gray Owl!—abounded in the neighborhood through which we were about to pass.

We resumed our journey next morning. Nature was displaying all her loveliness . . . the mellow tints of Autumn, her glowing fruits, and her rich fields of corn. Reaping had barely begun. The fruit of orchards and the mast of the forest hung in clusters above us. At the sight of the broad, clear Penobscot River, we were overjoyed! Canoes filled with Indians were gliding swiftly in every direction. They stirred the timorous water fowl flocking in from the North. Behind lay the beautiful—even majestic—mountain peaks. The Canada Jay leaped gaily from branch to twig. The Kingfisher, unwilling to be so suddenly surprised, rattled loudly as it flew off. The Fish Hawk [Osprey] and Eagle spread their broad wings over the waters not far from where we picnicked, before procuring our share of rare birds.

The Penobscot kept us company as we trotted on for several hours over a firm and level road. We came to a deep creek; the bridge was undergoing repair. Much surprised to see us, the workmen nevertheless helped us over by leading our horses onto a temporary raft to take them across, then the cart, and then ourselves. These good fellows were so averse to accepting what we deemed a suitable reward, or indeed anything at all, that we had to force one upon them.

We began to note changes in the country next day. At Old Town, a village of sawmills and manufactories, the people are noted for that industry and perseverance which assure the miller that the saws and floating timber in his dams will yield a fair return in time. Pine tracts to the north draw many an Old Town miller on long journeys of speculation. One, a Mr. Gillies, had just returned from an exploratory tour begun early in August by a party of sixteen under his leadership. Besides their axes and knapsacks they had two hundred and fifty pounds of pilot bread, a hundred and fifty of salted pork, four of tea, two large loaves of sugar, and some salt. They went twelve miles north to Bangor in light canoes, up the Penobscot as far as the Wassataquoik, then northwest along the river branch to the Seboois Lakes, with short portages between. From these lakes they carried their canoes west to the great lake "Baamchenunsgamook" . . . and north to "Wallaghasque-gantook" Lake . . . along upper "Umsaskiss" Pond, until they reached the "Albagash" River that leads to the St. John. Gillies assured me that not even the Indians had visited some of these regions. Their travels down the St. John brought them to Grand Falls and a portage of half a mile toward "Meduxmekeag" Creek a little above Woodstock. From there the party walked to Houlton. They had travelled twelve hundred miles, almost in a circle, by the time they returned to Old Town on the Penobscot. They had climbed to the high points, and up the tallest trees there, to inspect distant pine woods with their telescopes, noting its proximity to water, and, like the excellent judges and observers that they are, never afterwards forgetting the likely spots. They saw few birds and quadrupeds, apart from some Porcupines. Cranberries were plentiful on the lake and river borders; wild white onions in the uplands; and a variety of black plum. Some of the party went on up the Eel to Mattawamkeag River, due southwest of the St. John, before portages brought them back to the Penobscot.

I planned to accompany Gillies on a journey of this kind. But then I concluded that a visit to the more distant country of Labrador, later on, would be more useful and interesting to me.

Our road from Old Town to Bangor teemed with Penobscot Indians returning from market. At that beautiful town we found an excellent hotel for the night, before travelling in the mail stagecoach to Boston.[112]

[To speak further of our Maine journey . . .] Those men called Lumberers who cut trees and convey logs to mills or shipping points labor continually. Before the first winter snowfall they enter the woods in heavy sledges drawn by oxen. Sometimes they have to cut their way past huge, decaying tree trunks felled by age or fire, with branches so filled with undergrowth as to pose an impassable barrier. Again they may have to form causeways over miry ponds—the time to watch the exertions of their fine oxen. No rods are used, nor are oaths ever heard to fall from the lips of these industrious, temperate men (any more than from those of most Easterners, education and habit having tempered their passions and conditioned them to harmony). Indeed the sobriety of Maine towns I admit I have often considered as carried to excess; for not a drop of brandy, rum or whiskey could I obtain. Now and then I saw some good old wines, but these were always drunk in moderation.

But to return to the oxen—the Lumberers speak to them as if they were rational beings. A few words sufficed to bring their whole strength into play, quite as if in gratitude for so much gentlemanly and humane treatment. (Once near Boston I saw fifty or more ploughs, drawn by fifty pair of oxen that performed their work with such accuracy and regularity, under nothing more than the verbal mandates of the plough-men, that I was perfectly astonished.)

As soon as the Lumberers reach the spot which they had in mind they clear space for a camp and begin to build a low cattle shed. Then they raise the cabin and rough, corner bedsteads. The chimney consists of a frame of mud-plastered sticks. Skins of Deer and Bear serve as bedding along with blankets. Homespun clothing, guns, and various necessities hang from pegs along the walls. Some men prefer to take the provender of their oxen from the roof of the shed and sleep on sweet-scented hay and cornblades heaped on the ground.

In suitable places around camp large steel traps, "dead-falls," and "spring guns" are set for the Bears that prowl about.

The winter has fairly begun by the time northern blasts drive the heavy clouds of November and the feathery snowflakes pour down. The sun seldom cheers the woodcutter's hut. He envelops his body in warm flannels and dons his coonskin cap and his mooseskin leggings that reach to the girdle that secures them at his waist. In broad moccasins or snowshoes he stands from dawn till night, hacking the century-old pines which, as they tumble here and there, rustle and crackle, but then sink quietly into the deep snows. Thousands are cut each winter to afford the younger trees room to grow and supply the wants of man.

Weeks elapse. The pure white covering of the earth has become heavily crusted by the intense cold. Fallen trees have all been hewn into measured logs. The long rest of the oxen has fitted them to haul the logs to the nearest frozen stream. Gradually the ice becomes covered with masses of timber. The Lumberers begin to wait impatiently for the thaw. They pass the time in hunting the Moose, Deer, and Bear, to be shared later on with their wives and children. These excellent woodsmen create much havoc among the game. Between their winter's labors, and often under cover of darkness, they trap Sables, Martens, and Muskrats for the skins.

At last snow gives way to rain that falls in torrents. The oxen are harnessed for the return to town and to a miller's existence. Saws are filed to cut the logs that have already reached the dam by way of swollen streams.

The ground is parched again by the summer heat of the dog-days. Among the shallows of the creeks are deep holes full of Salmon and Trout. Wood Ducks and Herons breed on the sharp slimy angles of the projecting rocks. Thousands of "saw logs" remain in the pools and above and under each waterfall or rapids. The miller's dam is empty of timber. It was in the month of September that my family and I saw what steps are taken to replenish the supply. We were the guests of the hospitable Judge Theodore Lincoln and others at the pretty little village of Dennysville. Its sawmills and ponds are just above the town. The creek that conveys logs there is interrupted by many rapids and narrow-banked gorges. One gorge, about half a mile above the milldam, is so rocky and rugged at the bottom and sides as to preclude the possibility of the passing of trees along it at low water. To have moved the thousands of large logs that accumulated there in heaps so high that in some places they formed a kind of dam, would call for an army of woodmen or millers, it seemed to me. Above the gorge is a large natural reservoir that catches the headwaters of the creek. Only a small amount of water ripples through the gorge below in late summer and early autumn.

Lumberers use the refuse of the milled logs to raise a temporary barrier at the neck of the basin. They drive boards in nearly upright; the tops of trees that reach across the creek are a further support for these. Strong wooden abutments are laid against the center of the barrier to prevent its giving way to the pressure of rising waters. Wedges that hold the abutments can be knocked off when necessary.

Little or no water can escape through this barrier or temporary dam. Within three weeks the creek above it rose to the top, about ten feet high. The sheet of water extended fully a mile from the dam. We were invited to watch the effect that the breaking down of the barrier would produce. Two men threw off their jackets, tied kerchiefs round their heads, and fastened a long rope to their bodies. The other end was held by three or four other operators, braced and ready to drag their friends ashore in case of any mishap. The two walked along the abutments. At a signal they knocked out the wedges with their axes. Then they dealt the abutments a blow in unison. They had no more than escaped danger, by leaping from one cross-log to another and onto shore, than the mass of waters—frightful peril—burst forth with a horrible roar. All eyes turned towards the huge heaps of logs in the gorge below. The tumultuous burst of water instantly swept away every obstacle and rushed in foaming waves through the timber. There was a slow heaving motion in the mass of logs, as if some monster lay writhing convulsively beneath, struggling with fearful energy to extricate itself from the crushing weight. The movement increased as the waters rose. The mass of timber reached in all directions and became more and more entangled. Logs bounced and clashed, submerged, rose in the air upon sharp collision. It was like the waging of a war of destruction which the ancients describe in accounts of the Titans. To the eye of a painter the wrothy foaming, the angry curling of the water, might suggest such a scene. The tremulous, rapid motion of the logs that shot into the air might have inspired the poet to describe them as the conflict of giants.

The gorge filled to its brim. Logs rolled, reared, tossed and tumbled amid the foam as they were carried along. Many of the smaller trees broke across. Others sent up great splinters. All that had held the dam were somewhat seamed and scarred. The mingled wreck swept along until the current reached such a pitch that the logs were dashed against the rocky shores. The report was like that of distant artillery or the rumbling of thunder. Onward it rolled, the emblem of wrack and ruin, destruction and chaotic strife. It was to me like watching the rout of a vast army that had been surprised and overthrown. The roar of the cannon, the groans of the dying, the shouts of the avengers, thundered through my brain. But from out the frightful confusion of the scene came a melancholy feeling that did not entirely leave me for many days.

In a few hours almost all the timber that had lain heaped in the rocky gorge was floating in the big pond of the millers. As we walked back again into town we talked of the *Force of the Waters*.[113]

[Young Thomas Lincoln of Dennysville, who was to accompany me to Labrador the summer following my first visit to Maine, described a Moose hunt that he took part in, a few months before we sailed northward.]

The Moose were remarkably abundant in the Schoodic Lakes region the spring of 1833. The snow in the woods was so deep that few could escape the hunters. About the first of March three of us set off on a hunt with our snowshoes, guns, and hatchets and provisions enough for a fortnight. We went fifty miles the first day, in our sledge drawn by one horse, to the nearest lake and the hut of a Passamaquoddy Indian named Lewis, a farmer and forester, not to say snowshoe manufacturer. We watched his workmen make the bows of the shoes to suit themselves and the women weave in the deerskin threads.

Next day we went many miles farther on foot. Heavy rains detained us until the fourth morning out, when we went on snowshoes thirteen miles to the head of "Musquash" Lake to a deserted Lumberers' winter camp. That afternoon an Indian drove a female Moose and two yearlings close to our camp. He shot the old one, and we succeeded in capturing one of the young and shutting it up in the cattle shed. That evening we feasted on the flesh of two fine Deer killed by the dogs that day, and also on Moose which we found to be the most savory meat we had ever eaten. But a keen appetite is very apt to warp one's judgment. We spent the night on the floor near a huge fire, the most comfortable way of sleeping.

In the morning we followed the track of a Moose driven from its haunts by Indians the day before. Although the snow was five feet deep (and much deeper in some places), we had to travel three miles before reaching the spot where the Moose had spent the night. He had left the place only about an hour before, so we pushed on faster. A mile and a half along the way we took a wrong turn and had to search for his track once more, but found that an Indian was ahead of us in pursuit of the harassed animal. We heard a gun go off. There, standing in a thicket, was the wounded Moose. It had charged the Indian and forced him to hide in a thicket until we brought the six-and-a-half foot, three-year-old animal down. How it had gone at such a rate through thick-crusted snow we could not imagine. Where it had followed a brook, over which the snow had sunk somewhat because of the rising temperature of the water, we marvelled at its powerful leaps over obstacles, even over drifts—at a single bound and without leaving the least trace—ten feet high at least.

The heart of the Moose was larger than that of any animal I had ever seen. Its muzzle, which it projects when angry or frightened, is twice as large as that of a horse. Some say the Moose is shortwinded and tenderfooted. But he is certainly capable of great, prolonged exertion; and his feet seem as hard as any to me.

The young captive Moose had been too exhausted to offer any opposition to being led into camp. But the next night we were awakened by the sound of enraged commotion. It had regained its strength and was bent on getting free. If we put our hands near the openings of the shed, the yearling would spring in a fury, roaring and erecting its mane. We threw it a deerskin which it tore to pieces in a moment. We were convinced of the futility of any attempt to bring this six-foot doe back home alive in spring.

As for the other yearling, we later found that it had backtracked to a "beat" about a mile and a half away. This is a yard of about twenty acres where perhaps half a dozen Moose of a herd of fifty or so go at the approach of winter. After a snowfall the Moose divide a space of ground into well-trodden, irregular paths to which they keep. It is on the south side of some hill there that they browse on the bushes. Now and then they mark out a new path with their hoofs. A good hunter can detect a yard from a long way off, as well as its direction and distance, because of the marks of gnawing on the bark and twigs of the young maple. As he follows the marks they become more distinct and frequent. Long before he reaches the yard, however, the acute senses of the Moose will have warned them of his approach. The strongest will have led the others off in one file, unless they depart in two or three parties. If pursued, they separate. The females and their young remain together; the does break the track, and they never leave their calves, under any circumstances, unless brought down. The males are lean by now and speed off (unless the snow is too deep), and they soon outstrip the hunters. Usually they go in the direction of the wind, occasionally making short turns to keep the scent or to avoid some bad passage. Even though they may sink to the bottom at every step, they cannot be overtaken in less than three or four days. By contrast, the fat females may yield a hundred pounds of raw tallow.

We found the fugitive yearling even more intractable than the doe confined in the cattle shed. He had trampled the snow to enclose himself. When we approached he sprang with fury. Turning on snowshoes is no easy operation. We were content to let him alone and try to find a Moose less difficult to capture, knowing that he would probably injure himself fatally even if we finally took him. I am convinced that the only sound way to take them uninjured, except for the very young, is when they are exhausted and completely defenseless. They are bound securely until convinced of the futility of further resistance. If allowed limited captivity they almost always bring about their own death.

One day we came across the tracks of two young bucks which some Indians had been pursuing. We took up the trail and overtook the animals after two or three miles. In order to take them captive near camp we tried to drive them that way. We succeeded very well, until one of them, after trying to get away, turned on the member of our party nearest him, compelling a shot. The other, a little more tractable, nevertheless took enough turnings to be able to backtrack so abruptly that we were compelled to shoot him also. We dressed them, to bury the flesh in the snow. The tongues and muzzles were the parts considered the most delicate fare.

We found another yard about half a mile from this one. Our dogs overtook the fine buck we might have missed. We were not long in the sight of the female and young before she held us at bay. It is really wonderful how soon these does can beat down a hard space in the snow for their stand, making it impossible for the dogs to touch them as they stamp their forefeet with such violence that to approach them would bring certain death. This doe had only one calf with her. She would have had only one the following year, we discovered, though the usual number is two—almost invariably a male and a female.

The sagacity and spirit of the Moose puts one in mind of the horse. As we were standing by one he erected his ears, alert to our approach, yet we were at least half a mile away. The wind was away from the Moose and towards us, another sign of his wonderfully acute sense of sound and smell. He feeds on hemlock, cedar, fir or pine, but will not touch spruce. He also eats twigs of maple, birch and the soft shoots of other trees. A good imitation of his truly frightful cry, in the fall of the year, will bring him dashing towards the hunter in a tree or concealed somewhere else with his piece of rolled birch-bark that he blew on for the proper tone to decoy his prize.

The full grown Moose, nine feet in height and displaying immense branching antlers, is a most formidable sight. Like the Virginia Deer and male Caribou they shed their horns about the beginning of December. The first year they drop their antlers in spring. The Moose, when irritated, grinds his teeth, erects his mane, lays back his ears and stamps with violence. The hideous whinny of the Moose is not unlike the Camel's.

The common Deer to be seen in the lake region of our visit were so numerous that we were hard put to it to keep our dogs with us and away from the "beats." The habits of this species resemble those of the Moose.

The Caribou's very broad flat foot can be spread on the snow to the fetlock, to enable it to run on a crust barely solid enough to support a dog. When the snow is soft they go in immense droves to the larger lakes, where the crust is much harder and a safer refuge from hunters. The Caribou return to the woods if the thaw again gives way to cold. Their ability to run on snow does away with any need of yards like those of the Moose, and consequently they have no fixed place in winter. The speed of this animal is not well known, but I am inclined to believe it much greater than that of the fleetest horse.

In our camp we saw great numbers of Crossbills, Grosbeaks, Pine Martins and other small birds. Crossbills alighted on our hut with utmost familiarity. We caught five or six at a time under a snowshoe. The Wild Cat was also very abundant.[114]

With what pleasure have I, tired out and chilled through, sat beside the blazing fire in some lonely cabin! There I have seen the mother lull her babe to rest, the children surround their father just returned from the chase. A great back-log in the ample chimney, urged by lighted chips of pine, sends forth a blaze that illumines the happy family. The hunting dogs lick away trickling waters from their coats. The comfort-loving cat is busy passing her furry paws over each ear, or smoothing her glossy coat with her rough tongue.

How delightful it has been to be so kindly and hospitably received by such persons, whose means are as scanty as their generosity is great! I have received gratifying information from them on subjects of interest to me. After our humble, plentiful repast together, I have seen them take the Book of books from the shelf, for the father of the family to read a chapter aloud, before humble prayers for all friends far and near, and a goodnight. How comfortably have I lain me down on a Buffalo hide under some huge, furry bearskin! How pleasing my dreams of home and happiness as I lay sheltered from danger and inclement weather!

Once, in Maine, I spent such a night. Because of the heavy rains next morning my host persuaded me to linger. The spinning wheels began turning. One son helped another solve a ticklish arithmetic problem. The dogs lay in the corner, dreaming of plunder. Grimalkin, still close to the embers, purred in concert with the wheels, until his mistress urged him off with, "Puss, get away—you told me last night of today's rain, and I fear your tricky paws have worse news in store." Puss accordingly leaped on a bed and rolled herself in a ball for a comfortable nap.

I asked my host what his wife meant.

"She has some curious notions at times . . . she believes in all kinds of signs," he said. "Her talk to the cat refers to fires in the woods around us . . . fires that happened long ago but which still frighten her—and the rest of us—as much as ever. Indeed we all have good reason to dream about them and the calamity they bring."

I was anxious to learn more about these forest fires and their causes, having seen the mournful state of some. Willingly, my host gave me the following account.

About twenty-five years ago the larch or hackmatack trees were nearly all killed by insects. This occurred in the "black soft-growth land" of spruce, pine and fir. Evergreens are always killed by the loss of their leaves. Some years after the insects killed the larch by cutting its leaves, they attacked the evergreens which, within half a dozen years,

began to fall, until the country was strewn with the dead masses—
capital fuel, but also the start of devouring flames that have continued to
burn, intermittently, for years. The resin has helped to fuel the burning
of the deep beds of dry leaves and dead trees. Communication by road
has sometimes been cut off by such fires.

The caterpillars, about three-quarters of an inch long, were as green
as the leaves they fed on. In most places that had been burned away,
there rose a new growth of wood—hard wood that consists of anything
except pine or fir. Wherever the first natural growth is destroyed by
fire, or by the axe, or by the hurricane, another of quite a different kind
springs up.

As to the opinions of the probable cause of the fires, some believe that
the Indians set them—either to punish their enemies the Pale-faces
or to drive game for the kill. My own opinion as a woodsman and
forester is that the fires began as a result of the rubbing of one dry
trunk against another when one falls. The dry leaves on the ground are
at once ignited (particularly in the presence of much resin) then
kindled by twigs and branches, until nothing but the intervention of the
Almighty could stop the blaze. Sometimes cabins in the woods are
threatened where escape is difficult. Hundreds of families were obliged
to leave all behind if indeed they themselves escaped being burned alive.
(A rush of wind down the chimney, blowing sparks about the room,
interrupted my host's account at this point, and frightened his wife and
daughter to whom he explained the cause in reassuring tones.) He, his
wife, and his eldest daughter had had to flee.

"We were sound asleep one night in a cabin about a hundred miles
from here. About two hours before day we were wakened by the snorting
of the horses and the lowing of cattle in the woods. I took up my rifle to
go after the wild beast that I supposed was causing the hubbub. I
opened the door and was struck by the glare of light above the trees
for as far as I could see. My horses were leaping and snorting and the
cattle running among them with tails held high. At the back of the
house I could hear the crackling of burning brushwood in the near
distance and the flames coming on in a wide, extended line. I ran inside
to tell my wife and child to dress. Then I managed to catch and saddle
the two best horses in the precious moments that remained. With the
little money that we had we made off through the fire. My wife, an
excellent rider, kept close by. I held my small child in one arm. I looked
back—to see that the frightful blaze had laid hold of the house and
was close upon us. Luckily, I had a horn at my belt. I blew a blast to

bring the rest of the livestock and the dogs after us. The cattle followed for a while. But before an hour had gone by they all ran as if mad through the woods—that was the last of them. My ordinarily obedient dogs chased the herds of Deer that sprang before us—fully aware of rapidly approaching death.

"We heard blasts from our neighbors' horns and knew they were in the same predicament. In desperation I urged my wife to whip up her horse and come along with all speed toward a large lake some miles off. We jumped fallen trees and brush heaps that lay in our path like so much fuel for the terrific fires that advanced upon us in a broad front. By now we could feel the heat. We feared our horses might drop at any instant. A singular breeze passed over our heads. The glare shone over the daylight atmosphere. I myself felt slightly faint. My wife turned pale. The heat had flushed my child's face so that when she turned towards either of us our grief and perplexity increased.

"Ten miles are soon put behind, on swift horses. Nevertheless, when we neared the edge of the lake, our bodies exhausted and covered with sweat, our hearts failed us. The smoke—the insufferable heat of the blazing sheets that flew over us—were beyond belief!

"We reached the shores and moved round to the lee side after following it, uncertain, for a while. There we had to let our horses go; we never saw them again. We plunged down among the rushes at the edge of the water and lay flat, to await the chance to flee if not burned or devoured. The cool water refreshed us. But the fire rushed and crashed on through the woods. May we never see such a sight again! The very heavens were frightened, it seemed to me. The red glare above was filled with clouds of smoke, rolling and sweeping about. Our bodies were cool, but our heads were scorching. The child, now apparently aware of the danger, cried so as nearly to break our hearts.

"We grew hungry as the day wore on. Many wild animals came plunging in beside us. Others swam across to the side where we lay, and stood still. Faint and weary though I was, I managed to shoot a Porcupine for us. How the night passed I cannot tell. Smoldering fires covered the ground. The trees stood like pillars of fire, or fell across one another. The stifling, sickening smoke continued to rush over us and the burnt cinders and ashes to fall about. No, how we got through that night I really cannot tell. Much of it is beyond remembering, at any rate."

Here the forester paused for breath. The recital seemed to exhaust him. His wife proposed a bowl of milk for us before he continued:

"Towards morning the smoke lessened and some fresh air began to reach us. But the heat had not abated, and along with the dismal smoke that still filled the air there rose a smell worse than ever. Shivering as if from a fit of ague we moved out of the water to warm ourselves beside a burning log. What was to become of us I still did not know. Weeping bitterly, my wife hugged our child to her breast. But the fact God had preserved us through the worst of the danger, until the flames had passed, made me think it would be ungrateful to despair. Our hunger was easily remedied. I roasted a Deer that I shot among several still standing in the lake. We felt wonderfully strengthened.

"By now the forest fire was out of sight. But the danger of going among the burnt trees and along ground still burning in many places remained. We rested a while . . . trimmed ourselves for the march. At length I took up the child and led the way over the hot earth and rocks. Two days and nights of weary walking and of shifting for ourselves, as best we could, went by before we reached the 'hard woods' that stood free of fire. We came to a house and were kindly received.

"I have since worked constantly and hard. But thanks be to God, here we are—safe, sound and happy!"[115]

In the month of May, 1833 [while awaiting the arrival of my chartered schooner the *Ripley* for a cruise of Labrador waters], I sailed in the U.S. revenue cutter *Swiftsure* round the Bay of Fundy, from Eastport, Maine.

The vessel, her sails unfurled to the breeze, seemed to fly over the waters, under the rising sun and clouds that drifted in rich contrast with the pure azure heavens. We moved apace towards the island of Grand Manan whose stupendous cliffs emerged majestically from the deep. We passed under its craggy head that was covered with trees which, at such a height, looked scarcely larger than shrubs.

I watched the prudent Raven spread her pinions and fly away before us; the Golden Eagle soar aloft in wide circles; the Guillemots sitting on their eggs on the shelves of the precipices, or plunging and diving before surfacing again at a distance; the broad-breasted Eider Duck covering her eggs among grassy tufts; the Seal lazily basking on naked rock with its sleek sides glistening in the sun; and the shoals of swiftly gliding Porpoises, doomed to the deep, but not to a life devoid of pleasure. Far away stood Nova Scotia's bold shores. They gradually faded into the distance, a line of gray tints beautifully relieved by wing-like sails of the fishing boats.

We passed cape after cape, and through their eddies and those counter currents too terrific for description by a mere landsman, until we reached a deep cove near the shores of White Head Island. In the narrow strait beside it and Grand Manan we anchored secure from every blast that might blow. Captain Frankland, sole owner of the island of fifteen hundred acres, gave us permission to study the habits of certain Gulls that breed there in great numbers, and to seek out other treasures. We found their nests on almost every tree of one woods of several acres, quite as our Captain had assured me we would. What a treat to find birds of this kind sitting comfortably on nests of eggs in fir trees! Their cackling led us to them . . . for us to observe their habits and collect as many of them and their eggs as we deemed enough. A Rat was the only quadruped I noticed. Gooseberries, currants, raspberries, and whortleberries abounded. We spread a picnic on a summit that afforded a vast panorama of the Atlantic.

The air was filled with the melodious concerts of birds in the woods behind us. We wandered about in the tanglewood until the setting sun sent us back to the island's owner. After an excellent repast we took ourselves back to the *Swiftsure* and our hammocks.

In the morning a strange sail loomed in the distance. At once we prepared to pay her commander a visit. As we set sail, Captain Frankland and his men were flying the British flag on the island signal staff and raising three hearty cheers to which we responded. But all was found right with the other vessel. We squared our yards to bound cheerily back over the gay billows to Eastport.

On another occasion the revenue cutter *Fancy*—a charming name for so beautiful a craft—took us on board at evening for a brief cruise toward Head Harbor Bay where we were to anchor for the night. The cackling of the "old wives" [Mallards?] that covered the bay was a delight. Thousands of Gulls and Cormorants seemed anxious to pilot us as we leapt along the rugged shore to the lighthouse kept by a good, honest Englishman from Devonshire. There he and his three wild-looking lasses—as beautiful as the most finished productions of nature—spent their days in peaceful forgetfulness of the world. The fish of the bay was their principal subsistence.

Again, as so many times in life, I marveled at Nature as the dawn presented her—in richest, purest array—before her Creator. Again I was full of the desire to comprehend all I saw! The wish could not be gratified. (Yet I now feel satisfied that I have enjoyed my proper share of the wonders and beauties.) The trills of the Winter Wren rolled through the tanglewood. The Red Squirrel smacked time with his jaws. The loud notes of the Robin sounded clearly from the treetops. The Rose-breasted Grosbeak nipped the tender maple blossoms. High overhead passed Loons in pairs, wending their rapid way toward far distant shores. Would that I could have followed in their wake!

Our pilot who had been fishing for Cod up the bay was taken on board. Some of his catch was roasted on a plank before the embers as part of our breakfast. Not until afternoon did the light breeze bring us to Point Lepreaux Harbor where each one of us went his way in search of curiosities and provender. In this little harbor the myriads of Ducks that cover the Bay of Fundy are taken in a very singular manner. All water birds no longer capable of reproducing remain along these shores in July, like forlorn bachelors and old maids, to renew their plumage. At this period they are unfit for flight. Indian braves, paddled by their squaws with papooses on their backs, form a flotilla of light canoes in an extended curve. They drive the birds before them—not silently but to horrific yells, and beat the surface of the water with long poles and paddles. The birds, terrified by the noise, swim a long way off with all their might, trying to escape. At high tide every cove is filled. Thousands of Ducks were entering the one where we anchored. At low tide, when the waters receded as swiftly as they had risen, many birds remained on the beach. The braves, their squaws, and younglings alike rushed on the moulting birds with their various sticks and cudgels until all were destroyed—perhaps five hundred in all.

We spent three pleasant days about Point Lepreaux. In one harbor we fished for shells with an excellent dredge; in another we searched along the shore for eggs. I watched a Passamaquoddy chief in a canoe approach a Porpoise, stand erect, and fire. The Porpoise suddenly turned over backwards, dead. It was a creature of one hundred pounds or more. This, to the husky Indian, was nothing. With a single move— his legs spread so as to steady the canoe—he reached for the fish and threw it lengthwise at his feet; no mean feat considering the high waves of the Bay of Fundy, but one performed throughout the season that brings the Porpoises hither.

You have no doubt heard of the extraordinary tides of this bay. So had I. But like others I was loath to believe in the reports. So I went to

Windsor, a pretty town in Nova Scotia, to judge for myself. Late one day in August my companions and I were seated on the grassy, elevated bank of the river, about eighty feet or so above its bed. Almost dry, the bed extended nine miles below, like a sandy wilderness. Many vessels lay on the high banks to load gypsum, a very strange sight for us who had not arrived in time to watch the tide go out. In the morning we watched the water flow towards us, and rise with a rapidity the like of which we had never seen before. Sticks that we planted along the steep bank—sticks three feet long and placed so that the base of one touched the top of the one below—indicated a rise of three feet in ten minutes and of eighteen in an hour, about half-tide. At high-water tide the surface was sixty-five feet above the river bed! I looked about for the vessels that we had seen the night before; we were told they had gone with the night tide.

Again we boarded the *Fancy*. Captain Coolidge stood near the pilot; the pilot sat next the helmsman. A fresh breeze bore us past a succession of islands. The wind increased to a gale. With sails reefed we dashed along. We passed a heavily laden sloop that was gallantly running across our course with full sails. Suddenly we saw her upset. Staves and spars floated about. We saw three men scramble up her sides and sit on the keel, then make distress signals to our already distant boat. But the cool, prudent Coolidge gave orders to put about to the aid of the distressed. We threw them a line when we drew near, to bring them alongside. A fishing boat that had also been watching the disaster approached with long sweeps of her oars, now rising on the curling waves, now sinking from sight. By our mutual efforts we brought the men on board and towed the sloop into a safe harbor. An hour later, when we landed safely at Eastport, dense masses of fog veiled the shore. We congratulated ourselves on our escape from the Bay of Fundy.[116]

Early in June, after various delays, I departed for the coast of Labrador. Our party consisted of young George Shattuck of Boston, Thomas Lincoln of Dennysville, William Ingalls, son of Dr. Ingalls of Boston, Joseph Coolidge, son of Captain Coolidge of Eastport, my son John, and myself. The captain of the *Ripley*, Henry Emery, had been a schoolmate of my friend Lincoln. A gentleman, and a good sailor bred to the sea, Coolidge was then a fine active youth of twenty-three. My charter of the year-old, hundred-and-six-ton schooner called for three-hundred-and-fifty dollars per month to cover boat and crew. But we were to supply ourselves. (The whole outlay, in the end, ran close to two thousand dollars.) There was a floor in the hold and a big table beneath the tolerably good light under the main hatch for me to do my drawing. I intended to draw whenever possible during the long daylight of those latitudes where little sleep is needed, so pure is the air.

Strange figures indeed did we cut in our outfits . . . fishermen's boots with hobnailed soles to help us keep our footing on the seaweed; trousers of *fearnought* so coarse our legs were like a Bear's; oiled jackets and over-trousers for rainy weather; and round white hats of wool with oil-cloth flaps to the shoulders to keep the rain off our necks. We had coarse bags to strap on our backs for inland journeys, not forgetting our guns and hunting-knives.

The hardy Maine fishermen put out for the northern fishing grounds in boats of not more than thirty tons' burden. They care little in what they go. But I *did*. In any case such boats would have been too small for all of us.[117]

We left the wharf of Eastport about 1 P.M. Every one of the male population came to see the show, just as if no schooner the size of the *Ripley* had ever gone from this mighty port to Labrador. All our many friends shook hands with us as if we were never to meet again. The batteries of the garrison and the cannon of the revenue cutter saluted us with four loud, reverberating reports. Captain Coolidge was our pilot until we passed Lubec under a light head wind. Aided by the tide we drifted twenty-five miles down to Little River for the night.

The men spent the whole of the next morning, vainly trying to tow us into Little River. The party landed for a few minutes, and I shot a Hermit Thrush; but the direction of the wind led us to try putting out to sea. The wind rose at last and we cleared some dangerous rocks towards which the current had been drawing us. At 3 P.M. it became, of a sudden, so foggy that we could not see the bowsprit. I spent the night in direful apprehension of approaching ill-luck even though a smart squall decided in our favor, and day broke with a fresh wind from the northeast. By now we were dancing on the waters—and all shockingly seasick while crossing that worst of all dreadful bays, the Bay of Fundy.

We passed between the Seal Islands and the Mud Islands. Scarcely one of us was able to eat or drink, that day. The Boston schooner *Caledonia* came up and we were pretty much together all night and next day. After that the breeze turned to a gale that forced both vessels to reef. We showed ourselves superior in point of sailing . . . so good, in fact, that on the fifth day out we were about thirty miles from Cape Canso, ordinarily called Cape Cancer. I desired to pass through the "Gut" and into the harbor, where twenty fishing vessels lay. All day we had been in view of the southeastern coast of Nova Scotia, a dreary, poor, inhospitable-looking country. There was a snowfall, as we dropped anchor, from a sky unlike any I had ever seen. On going ashore we found only the low plants in bloom . . . azaleas, white and blue violets, and patches of green grass. Many birds were in full song. There was no Customs officer. No one in the dozen houses could answer my many questions in a useful way. We did not observe a single sea bird. While it snowed and rained at intervals we caught forty Lobsters simply by striking them in shallow water with a gaff hook. We returned on board and supped on fine Codfish.[118]

If I thought the abundance of fish along the Florida coast was unusual, the numbers I found in Labrador was downright astonishing. Nature's means of providing small animals to sustain the larger ones, and *vice versa,* is as ample as the grandeur of that world of hers, which is so curiously constructed.

Off the coast of Labrador both European and American fishermen have waters set apart by mutual agreement. I shall confine my observations to those of America, probably the most numerous. Boston and other eastern ports engage in the commerce. Every year Eastport sends out a fleet of schooners to catch Cod, Mackerel, Halibut, and sometimes Herring. From Maine and Massachusetts they sail from early May to early June, depending on how soon spring frees the gulf of ice. Twelve expert sailors and fishermen man vessels of a hundred tons or so. Each has its Hampton boat lashed to the deck or hung in stays. Beef, pork, biscuit, and little if anything in the way of spirits are the good, simple fare. The hold is filled with casks, some of salt, others empty for the oil to be procured. Lines, hooks and nets are furnished, along with such bait as Mussels salted for the purpose—generally used at the beginning of the season—then the less expensive Capelin fish as soon as they reach the Coast, or the flesh of Gannets and other sea birds. Wages vary from sixteen to thirty dollars per month, according to qualifications.

These men seldom rest more than three out of twenty-four hours a day except on Sunday. Only the cook fares better in this respect, although he must also help cure the fish. He makes breakfast of coffee, bread and meat for the Captain and crew, daily except Sunday, by

3 A.M., before the boats with two oars and lugsails are lowered. Each man carries his dinner, ready cooked, to eat on the fishing grounds.

The little squadron drop their anchors off likely banks, in a depth of from ten to twenty feet. At each end of the boat stands a man with two baited lines which he drops on each side of the boat. The leads touch bottom, a fish takes the hook, the fisherman gives the line a slight jerk then hauls up the prize with steady pull. He throws it athwart a small round bar of iron, near the back, forcing it to open its mouth and letting the weight of its body, no matter how small, tear out the hook. The bait is still good and over the side it and the line go again to hook another fish. Meanwhile the left line is drawn up and the catch taken. This operation at each end of the boat continues until she is so laden that her gunwale is within inches of the surface; and the time to return to the vessel in the harbor, seldom more than eight miles from the banks, has come.

The rest of the day is spent conversing about the supply of Cod, domestic affairs, politics, and the like. The whole *flotilla* enjoys the jokes that the repartee elicits, as the laughter passes from man to man. Those of one small boat compete with others for the prize haul in a given time—the source of more merriment. All return together to the harbor. Alongside the vessel each man takes his pole tipped with a bent iron that resembles the prong of a pitchfork. He pierces the fish and pitches it on deck, keeping count with a loud voice. The boats return at once to the fishing grounds, to eat their dinner and begin anew.

Meanwhile, during the morning, the Captain, four of his men, and the cook have put up long tables fore and aft the main hatchway. They have taken most of the salt barrels ashore. Now they line up the empty casks that are to be filled with the livers of the Cod. Except for a large heap of salt in the corner the hold is empty. Immediately after twelve o'clock dinner they begin cutting off the heads of the fish. A slight pull of the hand and a gash with the knife to effect this is followed by a slit up the belly. The head is thrown overboard and the rest passed along to a man who swiftly cleans it before casting all but the liver over. A third man dextrously passes his knife under the vertebrae to separate them from the flesh that he heaves through the hatchway.

In the hold the salting and packing of the fish that three men have managed to "head," "gut," and "bone" begins. Two or three more salt and pack. By the time the boats return with fresh cargo the first catch has been cleared and all hands set to work, continuing until midnight.

The men wash, put on clean clothes, hang their fishing apparel on the shrouds, and turn in to the forecastle for a sound sleep.

At 3 A.M. the Captain again calls, "All hands, ho!" A bit stiff and but half awake, the crew quickly appears on deck. Their fingers and hands may be so cramped and swollen from pulling the lines the day before that they can hardly straighten even a thumb. No matter, now. The cook who had a good nap the day before is up an hour earlier to give them breakfast. Fishing clothes are donned. Again the *flotilla* bounds off to the fishing grounds in boats swabbed the night before.

By Saturday night the three hundred or so small boats from perhaps a hundred schooners have brought about 600,000 fish back to the harbor. The salt is collected on shore and, because the fish will have grown scarce, the schooner sets sails for another harbor that it will reach well before sunset. In favorable weather the run affords the men a good Sunday's rest.

On the way they may pass a rock on which myriads of Puffins breed. The vessel will lay to for an hour or so for the gathering of eggs that are an excellent substitute for cream, or if hard-boiled as food for use at the fishing grounds. To tell if eggs are fresh, tubs of water are filled. The eggs that surface after a minute or so, or that tend to rise upward, are tossed overboard. The rest are perfectly sound and quite as palatable as any ever dropped in your barnyard by your best guinea fowl.

At the new harbor for more fishing the Captain has his least able fishermen take the salted Cod ashore and place them side by side to dry in the sun on some broad, high expanse of rock. The fish are turned several times a day. Between times the men lend a hand at clearing and stowing away the new catch on board. By evening the fish are ready to be piled up like so many haystacks, those at the top placed in such a way that the rain cannot harm them. A heavy stone keeps them from being thrown down if a blow comes up in the night. Obviously, the life of the Labrador fisherman is not one of idleness.

In July the Capelins, small fish related to Cod, approach every basin and stream along the shore in huge schools. The Cods follow, like bloodhounds after their quarry, in thick masses that literally line the shore. At this stage the fishermen follow another method. They fasten one end of a long, deep seine to the shore; the other is run out in a broad sweep over the water. A revolving capstan, or drum, hauls and winds it in, while men in boats hang onto the corked portion of the net, beat the water to frighten the fishes in the net towards the land. Others enter the water and hook the fishes with poles, flinging them onto the beach. The nearer the net comes to shore the sooner the task is over. How many Cod do you think may be taken in this way at a single haul? Thirty . . . or thirty thousand? To give you some idea, let me say that the young men of my party aboard the *Ripley* were able to catch live Cod with their bare hands. With a piece of twine and a hook baited with Mackerel, and using their gun barrels for rods, they caught heavy Trout. If two of them walked knee-deep along the rocky shore, holding a kerchief by the corners, they could sweep it full of Capelins. You have only to go to Labrador and see for yourself, should you not trust me in this.

But I believe that the seining of the Cod is not quite lawful, owing to the fact that the codlings are also dragged ashore, useless though they are. Instead of being returned to the water, as they ought to be, they are left to the Bears, Wolves, and Ravens on shore.

Fish taken along the coast or on stations only a few miles off shore are seldom more than two pounds in weight when cured, or six when caught. Parasites often render them lean and unfit for use. Some people, from laziness or for other reasons, fish with naked hooks that often wound the Cod without securing it, thus driving away shoals, much to the detriment of other anglers. Some carry their cargo off before drying them; others sell the Cod to agents from distant ports. Some have only a "pickaxe" type of fishing vessel of fifty tons; others own seven or eight vessels that size or larger. Whatever the means these fishermen are generally well compensated for their labor. I have known of men— mere "boys" at the start—to come into independent circumstances in ten years time. They have said, "How could we be content to idle at home!" I know such a person. He has quite a fleet of schooners, one with a cabin as neat and comfortable as any I ever saw in a vessel of the size of his largest and most beautiful one which, incidentally, only took fish on board when they were perfectly cured, or acted as pilot to the rest. It would now and then put into the home port with ample Halibut or a cargo of prime Mackerel.[119]

About ten o'clock the morning of June 14 a speck rose on the horizon. I was told it was Gannet Rock. At eleven I could see its top plainly; it seemed to be covered with snow several feet deep. What I saw, however, was not snow—but Gannets! I rubbed my eyes, took my spyglass to view the strangest of pictures . . . a mass of birds of such a size as I had never before cast eyes on. We all stood astounded, amazed, and agreed that such a sight, alone, was sufficient to bring anyone across the Gulf at this season. The nearer we came, the greater was our surprise at the enormous number of birds, all calmly seated on their eggs or with a newly hatched brood, their heads invariably turned windward and towards us. For a hundred yards up and for some distance around the Rock the air was filled with flying Gannets, until they looked like a heavy snowfall from where we watched.

The wind was too high for us to land. This was an unwelcome bit of news. We decided to make the attempt regardless. A whaleboat was put overboard. The pilot, two sailors, Tom Lincoln, and my son John pushed off. At the instant our vessel was brought to, the wind increased and heavy rain began to fall. Our boat went to the lee of the Rock but could not land. I could not see the birds, almost touching one another in regular lines of nests, and quite unconcerned. Our guns had no effect on those not shot, because the noise of the Gulls, Guillemots and the rest deadened the report. Others scrambled and flew in such multitudes and confusion from around those we struck that while some eight or ten were falling into the water, either dead or wounded, the eggs of many fell into the sea by the hundreds in all directions. The sea became very rough, so that the whaleboat had to return with its birds and some eggs without having climbed the Rock—to my great disappointment.

The top of the Rock is about a quarter of a mile wide from north to south and a little narrower from east to west. It rises between three and four hundred feet out of the sea which beats wildly round it except in calms. Landing is difficult, climbing even more so. The moment a boat touches, it must be hauled up on the rocks. The whole surface is perfectly covered with nests, placed a few feet apart, and in such regular order that you may look through the lines as you would through those of a patch of sweet potatoes or cabbages.

The fishermen who kill these birds for Cod bait ascend in parties of six or eight, armed with clubs. Sometimes the party is comprised of the crews of several vessels.[120]

The name of "Eggers" is given those who make a business of collecting eggs of wild birds for distant markets. Their object is to plunder every nest they can find, no matter where or at what risk. These pests often brutally destroy the poor creatures, once they have robbed them. Before I visited the coast of Labrador I could not quite believe in all their alleged cruelties which, nonetheless, gave me no little horror. But suppose I let you judge for yourself on that score.

Picture a shallop sailing slying along, like a thief who wishes to shun the very light of heaven. She steers her course under the lee of every rocky isle. Were her trade an honest one, she would not think of hiding behind the terrific rocks that seem the ordained resort of myriads of birds which every year return to rear their young far north in the peace of this desolate region. How unlike the bold, open, honest mariner whose face needs no mask—and who scorns the thought of skulking under any circumstances—are her men! With her sails patched with good canvas (probably taken from a vessel stranded on some unfriendly coast, and plundered after those on board were, perhaps, murdered by these same wretches), she is a shabby thing. Look at her sides—neither painted nor pitched, but only plastered, patched with strips of sealskin along the seams, and daubed over! Her deck has never been washed or sanded. Her hold—for no cabin has she—sends forth, though empty, an odor pestilential as that of a charnel house.

A crew of eight lies asleep at the foot of the tottering mast, oblivious of repairs needed in every part of her rigging. Still she scuds along, bent on the commission of some evil, the filthy thing!

When the afternoon is half gone the crew throw their small boat overboard, then descend to it, with their rusty guns in their hands. One skulls the skiff towards an island which for centuries has been the breeding place of countless Guillemots. Clouds of the birds rise from the rocks and fill the surrounding air, wheeling and screaming over their approaching enemies, the vile thieves. Thousands more remain quietly on the nest, over the single egg that is the hope of a pair. Muskets filled with heavy shot begin to send the dead and wounded off the rock and into the water. Instantly the sitting birds rise in their fright and join others that hover in dismay over the approaching assassins who mix shouts with oaths and curses. Exultingly the Eggers begin to trample chicks within the shell as their huge, clumsy boots move onward, until not an egg that they can find is left entire. They collect the dead birds and carry them to their boat.

Back once more in their filthy shallop, they strip the birds of their feathers with a single jerk, while the flesh is still warm, then broil them on coals. Pretty soon they begin to stuff themselves with the oily fare and with rum enough to bring on the joys of beastly intoxication . . . before tumbling on the deck for the few short hours of night in turbid slumber on their crazed craft.

"Sweet is the breath of morn," even in this desolate land. The sun rises above snow-clad summits to the east. The gay Bunting, his white crest erect, lets his brooding mate hear of his joy. A Willow Grouse on a rock crows his loud challenge. Each floweret, chilled by the night air, opens pure petals. A gentle breeze shakes heavy dewdrops from the grass. On the Guillemot Isle the birds again settle, and renew their mating. One of the Eggers, startled by the daylight, springs up and rouses his fellows who at first stare about as if to recollect their senses. With clumsy fingers they clear their drowsy eyes. Slowly they get to their feet, and, like the filthy lubbers they are, stretch and yawn from throats that might well frighten a Shark.

Their master, soon recalling to their minds that *so* many eggs are worth *so* many dollars, casts an eye in the direction of the rock of the Guillemots. Before giving orders to sail he makes a mental note of the date.

A light breeze bears the shallop a few miles onward to another harbor which, like the last, lies hidden from the ocean by another island rock. The plunder of the day before is repeated. That night the drunken brawl is reenacted. For a week, and until the last breeding place on the coast has been reached, their mischief continues. But they have not yet done their worst. They revisit every one of the islands to collect the eggs laid since their departure and to shoot as many more birds as they need. At every step the Egger picks up an egg so beautiful that one might think that a man with any feeling would pause to consider his motive for carrying it off. But nothing of the sort occurs to him—he gathers and gathers until the rock is swept bare. Dollars alone chink in his sordid mind. Assiduously he plies a trade that no man of talent, or with the industry to earn an honest living, would stoop to follow.

Now the shallop, half-filled with eggs, proceeds to the last of the islands, the one on which their depredations first began. Imagine their surprise on finding that others, desperadoes like themselves, are already there and gathering eggs as fast as they can! Enraged, they cock their guns, lower a boat, and row like fury. The first question—the firing of guns. The answer—more gunfire. Now, man to man, they fight like tigers. By the time the quarrel is settled, one man is carried back to the boat with his skull fractured. Another limps from a shot in the leg. A third feels his gums for teeth driven out through a hole in his cheek. The booty is equally divided. All have a drink together. Oaths, curses, filthy jokes are all that is to be heard while they stuff themselves with food, and reel with drink until they drop down, one by one. Groans and curses from the wounded mingle with snores from the heavy sleepers. Let the brutes lie!

Again the dawn comes, but no one stirs. The sun is high before heavy eyes are opened and limbs are stretched. At about this moment a company of honest fishermen, hungry for some eggs after months of a diet of nothing but salt meat, gallantly pull their long oars towards the rock. Every schooner of the fleet flies its nation's flag. Oars and fists are the only weapons these newcomers, dressed in their Sunday clothes, expect to use as they prepare to ascend the rock. A dozen of the Eggers defy them with guns and bludgeons. One of them, still full of rum, pulls a trigger. An unfortunate sailor reels in agony. Rallying one another with loud cheers the fishermen rush on the evildoers. A horrid fight results in the beating and bruising of every Egger left on the rock. All too often such fishermen row to the shallops of the Eggers and break every egg in the hold.

Not only do the Eggers of Labrador rob the birds in this cruel manner, but they rob the fishermen, as well, when opportunity affords. The result is quarrels without number.

None of my own party ever ventured unarmed on any of the islands claimed by these Eggers. Once we found two Eggers at their work of destruction. I explained why I had come and offered them premiums for rare birds and some eggs. Though they made affable promises, not one of the gang ever came near the *Ripley.*

These people gather all the Eider-down they can find, at the same time killing every bird in their path. They search for the eggs of Gulls, Guillemots and Ducks, massacre Puffins and others by the thousands for feathers. So ceaseless and persevering are the crimes that the birds, very abundant twenty years ago—or so the few settlers told me—have abandoned these rocks for peace and security farther north. I myself could scarcely obtain a young Guillemot while the Eggers were thereabouts. In fact it was June before I succeeded; the birds had laid three or four eggs each, instead of one. When Nature's mission was carried out in full the birds left the country. This war of extermination cannot last many years more. The Eggers themselves will be the first to regret the entire disappearance of myriads of birds that made the Labrador coast their summer home. Unless the Eggers follow the persecuted tribes northward, they will be compelled to abandon their trade.

Had the British Government not passed strict laws, long since, against the ruthless and worthless vagabonds, and laid a heavy penalty on all those caught in the act of landing their cargo in Newfoundland or Nova Scotia, I might. . . .[121]

In the spring of 1832 a Halifax party of four Eggers took nearly 40,000 eggs which they sold at twenty-five cents per dozen, a gain of more than $800 in about two months. More than twenty shallops were engaged in this rascally way. In less than half a century the wonderful nurseries will be entirely destroyed, unless some kind government will stop the shameful destruction. The birds lay again and again until Nature is exhausted, and few of the young are raised.[122]

Go where you will . . . if a shilling can be gotten there, you may expect to meet those in search of their share. I met several such on the coast of Labrador.

One morning while our schooner lay at anchor in a beautiful basin surrounded by harsh granite rocks partly covered with vegetation, I was searching for birds. I glanced towards the pinnacle of a small island separated from the mainland by a very narrow channel, the mouth of the Natashquan River. Through my telescope I could see a man on his knees, his hands clasped, his face turned towards Heaven, before him a heap of unhewn stones supporting a wooden cross. The sight of a person engaged in prayer, in a desolate region where one seldom finds humans, and where the aid of the Almighty seems more than ever necessary for subsistence, moved me deeply.

Curious, and also hopeful, I landed on the rock and then scrambled up to where the man was kneeling. After he had finished his devotions he arose and bowed to me, and spoke in very indifferent French. Why, I asked him, had he chosen such a dreary spot to pray.

"Because the sea lies before me," he answered. "From the sea comes my summer sustenance. At the approach of winter I pray facing the mountains on the mainland. The Caribou come towards the shore at that period. I kill them, feed on their flesh, and make robes of the skins."

The answer seemed reasonable enough. I longed to know more, and followed him to his small, low hut that was made of stone and mud. Inside, under the roof of thatch, weed and moss, there was a large Dutch stove that half filled the room. A small porthole or vent was stuffed with old rags. The bed was a pile of deerskins. On a rude shelf were a bowl, a jug, and an iron pot. In a corner stood three rusty old muskets, their locks fastened by thongs. Near them were skin bags of buckshot, powder, and flints. Eight Eskimo dogs yapped and leaped about us. Their strong odor, added to the smoke and filth of the place, made my visit an extremely disagreeable time.

Pierre-Jean-Baptiste Michaux had lived in this part of the world for more than ten years. He had run away from the French fishing smack that brought him when he had hopes of becoming a rich dealer in furs, seal skins, Eider Duck down, and whatever he could sell to traders who visited the place. Of medium height, but sturdy, he was active as a Wild Cat. He showed me much politeness. Without waiting for my assent to his offer of refreshment, he went off with a bowl, I knew not whither, and with his strange dogs at heel. I too stepped out for a breath of pure air and a look at the wild, majestic scenery, and the extraordinarily luxuriant plants and grasses in the scanty soil of the little valley which the Labrador Squatter had chosen for his home. The green growth reached to my waist. The flies, mosquitoes, and other insects that filled the June air were as troublesome to me as if I had been in a Florida swamp.

Michaux returned, downcast. Indeed his visage had almost a cadaverous hue. Tears ran down his cheeks. His barrel of *rum* had been stolen by the Eggers, or, perhaps by some fishermen who saw him hide it in the bushes according to the time-tried custom. Until this, his first loss, he had been happy as a lord.

"Now I can expect none until next spring," he mourned. "And God knows what will become of me in the winter without it!"

I asked how he managed to find sufficient food for his dogs.

"During summer they roam the shores and find plenty of dead fish," the man told me. "In winter they eat the flesh of Seals that I kill late in autumn, the time these animals return from the north. As for myself, everything eatable is good. When hard pushed I can, I assure you, relish the fare of my dogs as much as they do."

From there I followed the rugged line of the bay by boat with my companions of the *Ripley*. We came upon another such fortune seeker, but not until after some difficult navigation around a long point. We were pleased to see several small schooners at anchor. One lay near a sort of wharf. Several neat houses enlivened the view. On landing we were greeted with a polite welcome from the apparent owner of the settlement. The manners and dress of this man of the world were a far cry from the rude simplicity of my friend of the rum cask. Except for the handsome fur cap that covered his dark brow his clothes were similar to our own. His demeanor was that of a gentleman. I gave him my name, heartily shook hands, and was astonished, after introducing my companions, to hear him say: "My dear Sir, I have been expecting you these three weeks. I read in the papers of your intention to visit Labrador. Some fishermen told me of your arrival at Little Natashquan. Gentlemen, walk in."

We followed him to his comfortable mansion. His wife was of French extraction, handsome, and sufficiently accomplished to make an excellent companion to a gentleman. The six children were all robust and rosy. A smart girl brought us a luncheon of bread, cheese, and good port wine to which we helped ourselves with zest after having rowed fourteen or fifteen miles that morning. Our host gave us newspapers from both sides of the Atlantic and showed us his small but choice collection of books. His questions proved him on good terms with various officers of the Royal Navy.

We walked out towards his very small vegetable garden. I asked how *he* had come to seclude himself here from *the world*. "The country around is all my own, for much farther than you can see," he told me. "I do pretty much as I choose . . . pay no fees, need no lawyers, meet no taxes *here*. Through my own industry my means are ample. Vessels that come here for Sealskins and seal-oil, and for Salmon, give me all the necessities, indeed the comforts, of the life I love to follow. What else could the *world* afford me!"

I spoke of the education of his children. He replied that he and his wife were their teachers, that his sons and daughters would marry their neighbors and countrymen and, he hoped, live and die in the region.

Few birds come thereabouts in summer, according to my host. But in winter Ptarmigans by the thousands are killed, as well as great numbers of Gulls. He had a tremendous dislike for all the fishermen and Eggers. I really believe he was also glad to see the departure even of those mariners who came to carry away his Salmon, skins and oil. To repay him for his trouble I purchased a beautiful fox skin from one of his sons. As I caressed one of his more than forty huskies he said to me, "Tell my brother-in-law at Bras d'Or that we are all well here, and that I will call there to see him after I visit my wife's father!"

Seventy miles down the coast I found his father, another recluse. He had lived there for more than twenty years. His son of Bras d'Or was another one hundred and forty miles onward. Yet in winter, when snow covers the country, these families travel with ease in sledges drawn by dogs, paying visits here and there. The house of the son was imported from Quebec and fronted Belle Isle strait, with a view out over a small island and the Newfoundland coast beyond, except when fog lay over both coasts. Actually, the house was still unfinished. An immense Dutch stove was the principal feature. Her ladyship had once visited the Canadian metropolis and seemed to wish to play the part of a "bluestocking." Understanding that I knew something of the fine arts, she pointed to several of the vile prints on the bare walls. These, she said, were *elegant* Italian pictures, purchased from an Italian who had come to Bras d'Or with a trunkful. She had paid a shilling for each, frame included! I could not bring myself to answer the lady and her encomiums on this subject, but felt glad to find she possessed a feeling heart.

One of the children began to torment a captive Siskin. His mother rose to take the little fluttering thing from the boy. She kissed it, before gently launching it into the air, in a way that made me quite forget the tattle about the fine arts.

The sight of some excellent milk in clean glasses was pleasing, for not a cow had we glimpsed anywhere thus far. Asked by the lady if I played any instrument, I answered that I did, but very indifferently. Her *forte* was music, of which, indeed, she was ecstatically fond. But her instrument was away in Europe for repair. It would return by autumn, for her children to perform beautiful airs. In fact, she added, anybody could do so with ease—such as her servant when she or the children felt fatigued. Rather surprised at the extraordinary powers of this family of musicians, I asked what sort of instrument this was.

"Gentlemen, my instrument is large, longer than broad, and stands on four legs like a table," our hostess explained. "At one end is a crooked handle which, if turned round either fast or slow, makes the most excellent music, I do assure you."

I noticed the corners of my young sailing companions' mouths beginning to curl, but with one look from me they recomposed their features. I suggested to the fair one that her instrument must be a hand-organ. "Ah, that is it!" she laughed. "It is a hand-organ—I couldn't for the life of me recollect the name."

Meanwhile her husband, who had been calking an old schooner in the harbor, returned. I invited him to dine with me on board the *Ripley*. He had seen much of the world, having sailed nearly round it, and like his brother—although not such a scholar—was disgusted with it. He caught Seals, owned land, lived comfortably and happily, bartered and sold commodities as his relations did. In fine weather his recreation was to walk with his wife over the moss-covered rocks of the neighborhood. In winter he killed Ptarmigans and Caribou. His eldest son did the trapping and skinning. He owned the only horse to be found in that part of the country, as well as several head of cattle. But above all, he was kind to everyone, and everyone spoke well of him. The only disagreeable thing I could see about the place was a heap of fifteen hundred carcasses of skinned Seals. In the month of August, these sent forth a stench that might, according to some naturalists' ideas, have sufficed to attract all the Vultures in the United States.* During our stay at Bras d'Or the kindhearted couple kept us in fresh milk and butter, yet would not allow us the pleasure of making a fair return.[123]

The approaches to Little Mecatina harbor, high and horribly rugged —the highest land I had yet seen—made us beat to windward, tack after tack. About 4 P.M. on July 14, we went off in the green boat from the *Ripley,* a row of a mile and a half. The Ducks looked surprisingly small as they flew between us and the stupendously high, rough shores under whose jutting line our little bark moved along. We doubled the cape and entered the harbor—so small as to make one doubt that it was a harbor at all. The surroundings were terribly wild—fearfully high and rugged. Nothing was heard but the croaking of a pair of Ravens and their half-grown brood, mingled with the roar of the surf against the ledges that sent the angry waters foaming into the air. We watched the *Ripley* come warily in, on a fresh breeze, with her topsails reefed.

The harbor was exactly like the bottom of a large bowl. At the center, surrounded by rock cliffs fully a thousand feet high, our vessel anchored. After supper we all went ashore . . . nothing but rocks, barren rocks—wild as the wilds of the Appenines on every side; moss only inches deep; and the soil, or the decomposed matter beneath, so moist that on an incline one's feet slid for yards with the little avalanche. Walking was extremely laborious. At the bottom of each ravine the scrub intercepted our way for a considerable distance. On our return we slid down fifty feet or more into a treacherous, fairly deep pit of moss and mire. A female Blackcap [Black-poll?] Warbler started from her nest at our approach. I found four eggs in the beautiful little mansion built in the fork of a bush about three feet from the

* For years Audubon disputed the olfactory powers of the vulture.—*Ed.*

ground. I was soaked through, and again the mosquitoes were as trouble-some as those in the Floridas.[124]

The coast that we followed to Baie de Portage, then to Bras d'Or, was as crowded with rocky islands of every size and shape as the one we had been cruising. Raging waves broke against the rocks in an awesome manner. Except for Gannets we saw few birds on this run.

Bras d'Or is the grand rendezvous of the Cod fishermen. A flotilla of about one hundred and fifty of their craft, mostly from Halifax and the eastern United States, lay at anchor here. The life and stir surprised us after so many weeks of wilderness and loneliness. Boats moved to and fro, returning loaded to the gunwales, or else on their way out after fish. A hundred or so that were anchored near the *Ripley* were hauling Cod by the thousands. Their men were busily cleaning and salting while singing and joking in much the way that the fishing gentry of Billingsgate do. The owner of the Seal fishery who had known I was coming gave us a good deal of information about birds and the country. From his country seat, where snow still lay in patches on the hills, I could see the high mountains of Newfoundland with its summits rising far above the clouds. Two weeks before our coming, the ice filled the harbor of Bras d'Or, and not a vessel could approach. But now there was not a trace of the ice.

My host, Mr. Jones, gave me an account of travelling by sled in winter. He harnesses his team of seven or more Eskimo dogs with a leather collar and a back and belly band through which lines of sealskin pass on top—attached to the sled at one end but meant to act as reins at the other. The size of the team, always an odd number led by one well-broken dog, depends either on the weight of the load or the dis-tance to be covered. It is estimated that each dog draws two hundred pounds at five or six miles an hour. The draft-line of the leading dog is six to ten fathoms long, the lines of the rest gradually shorter until that of the last, which is about eight feet from the sled. They do not go in pairs, as many picture engravings suggest, but single file. In motion they are rather like a flock of Partridges, all flying loosely yet in the same course—at a gallop—no matter what the terrain. To go downhill is difficult and dangerous. At times the driver must guide the sled with his feet or a strong staff planted in the snow as the sled proceeds. When the load is heavy and the descent steep the dogs are often taken off the sled, for it to glide down alone, as the driver steers with his toes while lying flat the way boys ride sleds. The dogs know the courses well. Not even a heavy snowstorm along the way can deter them. It is safer to leave one's fate to their instinct than to rely on human judgment; more than once men who have made their dogs change course have been lost, sometimes for good. When two sleds meet, both circle around as slowly as possible towards each other, to let the packs see that their masters are acquainted. Otherwise, a dog fight is almost certain to occur. A few years earlier Jones lost a son of fourteen in a snowstorm, because the driver, a servant, imprudently turned the dogs from their course, towards Hudson's Bay. By the time the storm ended, the driver, his food supply exhausted, saw his mistake too late. The lad faltered gradually, then died in his arms.[125]

It is quite surprising to see how quickly the growth of everything, either animal or vegetable, is attained in this Labrador country. Within six weeks I saw eggs laid; birds hatched; their first moult half over; their association in flocks; and finally by early August, their preparations for leaving. That the Creator should have commanded millions of delicate, diminutive, tender creatures to cross immense spaces of country —to all appearances a thousand times more congenial to them than this—and for them to people, as it were, this desolate land for a time . . . and to enliven it with the songs of their sweet, feathered musicians for two months at most, and, by the same command, induce them to abandon it, almost suddenly . . . is as wonderful as it is beautiful.[126]

On our return from singularly wild, interesting Labrador, the *Ripley* sailed close along the northern coast of Newfoundland. The time was mid-August, the weather still mild and clear.

My young companions amused themselves on deck with various musical instruments. I gazed on the romantic scenery spread along the bold, often magnificent shores whose luxuriant growth far surpasses that to the north. In some of the valleys I thought I saw trees fairly tall. The number of dwellings increased. Many small vessels and boats danced in the coves. Sometimes a cliff would resemble the lost half of some mountain sunk in the depths of the sea. The dashing of waters at its foot was enough to make the most daring seaman wary. In the huge masses of broken rock before me, I fancied I felt a power supporting the gigantic fragments which everywhere hung as if by magic, and almost as if awaiting the proper moment to fall and crush some impious, pirate vessel. Now and again the gently swelling hills came into view, rearing their heads skyward as if desirous of existence within the azure purity.

It seemed to me that the bleat of Reindeer reached my ears. Dark clouds of Curlews were winging their southward way, and thousands of Larks and Warblers flitted over, exciting in me the wish for wings of my own on which to fly back to my country and friends.

Early one morning our vessel rounded the northern cape of the Bay of St. George. The sight of that magnificent expanse of water that reaches eighteen leagues inward (with a breadth of thirteen), and the light wind that was blowing, lifted our hearts. The long, bold range of shoreline threw deep shadows over the water, which greatly enhanced the scene. From the south banks the mildly beaming autumn sunlight played on the water, whitened the sails of small craft sailing to and fro like gulls. To see cattle feeding in cultivated meadows and the farmers at work in the fields was a welcome sight. It made up for all we had undergone in the way of wind, cold, rain and privation to the north.

The *Ripley* made for a snug harbor that suddenly came into view. A number of vessels lay at anchor before the pretty village. The appearance of our unfamiliar, warlike schooner showed we were not fishermen and caused some commotion among the villagers who were anxious to know our business. We bore our usual arms and hunting paraphernalia, but these, being half Indian and half conventional, aroused considerable suspicion on shore. The gliding of the Star-Spangled Banner to the masthead at our Captain's signal, in a salute to the French and British flags, drew a welcome.

Glad of the chance for fresh provisions and to stand once more on something like soil, we walked through and around the village in the late afternoon. Nightfall forced us back on board our floating home. After a hearty supper we serenaded the peaceful townsfolk with repeated glees.

At dawn I was on deck, admiring the industrious scene before me. Fishing boats already covered the harbor; we promptly bought some Mackerel. I noticed that the hillsides were under cultivation. A river coursed between two steep, rocky ranges. Some Micmac Indians were searching along the shores for Lobsters, Crabs and Eels, which were abundant and delicious. Two hardy Indians came alongside in their canoe to barter Reindeer meat for some of our stores.

The Indian method of cooking Lobsters was amusing to watch. They threw them alive into a great woodfire, then devoured the broiled meat while it was still so hot that not one of *us* could have touched it.

I tasted it when it was cooled and found it infinitely better-flavored than boiled Lobster.

The temperature was twenty degrees higher than that of Labrador. Yet I was told that the ice of the bay seldom breaks up before mid-May, and that few vessels attempt to visit Labrador before June 10, the date when the fisheries open.

One afternoon we were visited by a village committee which invited our whole party to a ball to be held that night. We were requested to bring our musical instruments along. Our acceptance was as unanimous as the gesture towards us was friendly. The discovery that our callers relished "old Jamaica" rum, to which they helped themselves pretty freely, also showed us that it had lost none of its energies by having visited Labrador.

We landed that night at ten o'clock. Paper lanterns lighted our way to the dance hall. One of us carried a flute and another a violin. I had a flageolet, stuck into my waistcoat pocket.

The "hall" was nothing more nor less than the ground floor of a fisherman's house. His wife who like her neighbors was quite adept at the piscatory art, curtsied—not à la Taglioni, it is true, but with a modest assurance as pleasing to me as if it had been with the airiness of that famous ballerina. But the good woman was rather unprepared, quite en negligée, and her apartment was no less so. She bustled about to try and put things in becoming order. In one hand she held a bunch of candles, in the other a lighted torch that she used to light the tapers as she placed them along the walls. This done, she emptied the contents of a large tin receptacle into glasses on a tray on the only table in the room. The black, capacious chimney was embellished with coffee pots, milk jugs, cups, saucers, knives and forks, and everything necessary for so important an occasion. Primitive wooden stools and benches were placed around.

The belles of the village began arriving. Theirs was the rosy fatness that an invigorating Northern climate produces. Their stays seemed ready to burst and their shoes equally crowded, so full of sap were these Arctic beauties. Their decoration would have vied with the noblest Indian queen of the West. Around their necks were brilliant beads that set off their ebony tresses. Their naked arms might have caused apprehension had they not been constantly busy arranging flowing ribbons, gaudy flowers, and muslin flounces.

The beaux, just back from fishing and well known to all, leaped without ceremony onto the loose boards that formed a kind of loft overhead. They changed from their dripping apparel to suit the occasion, dropped down among the company again, strutted up and down, and bowed and scraped to the ladies with as much ease (if not with as much elegance) as a Bond Street, highly-scented exquisite. Others kept coming by degrees, already dressed.

Music was called for. My son John, by way of an overture, played "Hail Columbia, Happy Land," then he fiddled the "Marseillaise," and finally, "God Save the King." A mere spectator, I ensconsed myself in a corner beside an old European, an agreeable and well-informed gentleman. Together we admired the decorum of the motley gathering. The dancers lost little time in choosing partners and falling in line. A Canadian fiddler joined my son to help create the mirth and joy that soon prevailed. Dancing, certainly, is one of the most healthful and innocent of amusements. (I have loved it a vast deal more than watching for the nibble of a Trout.) And I have sometimes thought that enjoying it with an agreeable female softened my nature as much as the pale, pure moonlight softens and beautifies a winter night. A maiden lady seated at my side—the only daughter of my talkative old companion—relished my remarks on the subject so much that she joined her tutored feet gracefully for the next set.

Refreshments were handed round by the hostess and her son between dances. I was not a little surprised to see the ladies, maids and matrons swallow a full glass of pure rum, as did their sweethearts and husbands, with evident pleasure. I perhaps forgot that in cold climates a dose of spirits does not have the effect that it produces in burning latitudes. Refinement had not yet led these healthy, robust dames to any indelicacy foreign to their nature.

The hour grew late. Knowing how much I must accomplish next day I left the party, and in a few moments reached the *Ripley*. My men were sound asleep in the boat. John and our young companions arrived towards daylight. But many of the fishermen's sons and daughters danced on, to the bowing of the Canadian's Cremona, until after our breakfast was over.

We were much surprised when some of the females who had been so perfectly free from *mauvaise honte*—shyness—the night before, now ran off into the neighboring fields and meadows at the sight of us. They were like so many young gazelles before jackals. One of them who happened to be carrying a pail of water on her head dropped it the moment she saw us, and ran to the woods to hide. Another who was out looking

for a lost cow took to the water and waded through an inlet more than
waist-deep, then made for home like a frightened hare. The only answer
that I received when I asked to know the reason for this strange conduct was a deep blush![127]

IV

Last Adventures

JOHN, my son, and my wife Lucy and I reached London on May 12, 1834, and found our Victor quite well, and we were all happy to be reunited. *The Birds of America* was going on prosperously.

Among letters of introduction given me in America by the distinguished bankers Prime, Ward & King was one to the famous London banker, Baron de Rothschild, known for his immense wealth not only as financier but jobber. Victor and I had difficulty in finding the great usurer's place of business. In London, commerce is thoroughly matter of fact. No external pomp sets the countinghouse of the Baron apart from those of men of less enormous capital. We walked into his private office without any hindrance and introduced ourselves without benefit of an announcer.

A goodlooking young gentleman told us that the Baron would be coming in a few minutes. Soon a corpulent man appeared. His face red from the exertion of walking, he hitched his trousers and without noticing anyone dropped his fat body into a comfortable chair, clearly caring for no one in this wide world but himself. While the Baron sat, we stood, our hats respectfully in hand. I stepped forward and with a bow tendered my credentials.

The man of golden consequence looked up and said, "Pray, Sir, is this a letter of business or is it a mere letter of introduction?"

Considering that I had not read the contents I could not very well answer. I was obliged to confess, rather awkwardly, that I could not tell.

Rothschild then opened it and read with the air of one interested only in the temporal side of things. "This," he said, "is only a letter of introduction, and from its contents I expect you are the publisher of some book or other, and need my subscription?"

Had a man the size of a mountain spoken to me in that arrogant style in America I would have shown some indignation and resentment.

But here it seemed best to swallow and digest it if I could. So in reply to his offensive tone I said I should be *honored* by his subscription to *The Birds of America.*

"I never, Sir, sign my name to any subscription list," he said. "But you may send in your work and I will pay for a copy of it. Gentlemen, I am busy—I wish you good morning."

We were busy men, too. So bowing respectfully we retired, pretty well satisfied with the small slice of his opulence that our labor was likely to obtain.

A few days later I sent the first volume, half-bound, plus all the parts of the second that happened to be engraved and ready. The bearer was told to take them to the house of the Baron after the latter had had a glimpse of them at his office. I continued to send part after part of the emerging publication. Eight or ten months went by before my son made out a statement for my engraver, Havell, to present at the bank of Rothschild. The Baron looked up at him with amazement after noting the amount and cried out, "What! A hundred pounds for this . . . ! Why, Sir, I will give you five pounds, and not a farthing more!" Havell made some strong representations in favor of the magnificence and expense of the work, and suggested how pleased the Baroness and children would be to have a copy. But the great financier was unrelenting.

In the end the one volume and unbound parts of its sequel were sent back to Havell's shop by the banker. As I found that instituting legal proceedings against him would come to more than it could bring, I kept the work. Afterward I sold it to a man with less money but a nobler heart. What a distance there is between two such men as the Baron de Rothschild of London and the merchant William Gaston of Savannah!*

On August 2, 1836, somewhat before sunset, John and I sailed on the packet *Gladiator* for New York, and then to make some excursions into the South for varieties of birds still needed for my great work. We laid ourselves down in those floating catacombs vulgarly known as berths. As we left St. Katharine's Dock in Portsmouth we had for company two-hundred-and-sixty live birds for the Charleston museum and friends, three hunting dogs from our noble friend the Earl of Derby for his American correspondents, and a brace of tail-less Manx

* Rothschild finally subscribed in his own good time.—*Ed.*

cats from our friend George Thackeray, retired divine and provost of
King's College. Some but not all of the birds survived the Atlantic
crossing. Wallack, the actor, was among the passengers. He amused
us with some admirable puns. The time passed pleasantly until we approached icebergs off the banks of Newfoundland. But none came near
us. Five weeks after leaving England we approached the Hook of
New York harbor.[128]

In the Choctaw Indian lands of Mississippi there was, I knew, a
large swamp abounding in rare birds, quadrupeds, reptiles and mollusks.
It begins beside those borders of the Mississippi not far from a Chickasaw
Indian village on Vanconnah Creek. Its most famous bayou, False River,
empties near the mouth of the Yazoo that follows the windings of the
swamp. The Yazoo branches off to the northeast and forms Cold
Water River where the swamp comes to an end. It was there, on the
banks of the Cold Water, that I came upon a Squatter's cabin one day.

I discovered that this man, like most of the adventurous settlers
of these wild frontier tracts, knew a good deal about hunting and the
habits of some of the larger quadrupeds. Eager to learn from him I
began to talk about the swamp. He said he thought it the very place
I ought to visit, and pointed to a heap of Bear and Deer skins, some
of which he had shot there. He agreed to let me share his cabin and
to accompany me through the great morass. Immediately I unstrapped
my drawing materials, laid up my gun, and sat down to join in a
simple but wholesome supper with the Squatter, his wife and sons.

The quiet of the evening seemed in perfect harmony with the gentle
demeanor of the family. More than once it seemed to me that the
wife and children looked upon me as a strange sort of person, going
about, as I told them I was, in search of birds and plants. Our mutual
questions would have filled a book. The Squatter, a native of Connecti-
cut, had heard of men like myself and the existence of naturalists both
in America and abroad, and he seemed pleased to have me beneath
his roof.

After supper he told me what induced him to move to this wild,
solitary spot. People were growing "too numerous now to thrive in
New England." (I could only think of some parts of Europe, so densely
populated in comparison!) The conversation turned to hunting and fishing, until we all lay down on the pallets of bearskin for the night.

At dawn I heard the Squatter calling his half-wild hogs, which he had turned loose in the woods to find part of their subsistence. The hogs and young came grunting for ears of corn tossed to them by their owner. I was not long in joining him, to look on. He said that for several weeks the animals had been disappearing one by one, and that a large Cougar was the reason. The ravenous animal was not satisfied with the flesh of the pigs, but now and then carried off one of the Squatter's calves. Attempts to shoot the villain had failed, and it had become bold enough, meanwhile, to rob the Squatter of dead Deer outside his cabin. I was intrigued by the description of the Cougar's boldness and its formidable character, and offered to help destroy it. My host was pleased but assured me that without a party made up of some of his neighbors, and their dogs as well, such an attempt would be futile.

He set a day for just such a hunting party, a fine morning as things turned out. At sunrise five neighbors rode up on horseback. Their mounts might have looked like sorry nags to the eyes of a European, but their build, strength, and speed made them better suited to chasing a Cougar or a Bear through woods and morasses than if they were thoroughbreds. A pack of large ugly curs were already becoming acquainted with those of the Squatter. He chose one of his best horses, gave me another, and left the inferior ones to his sons. Quietly we rode to the edge of the swamp, then scattered to look for fresh tracks. It was agreed that the first person who found any should blow his horn and remain on the spot until the rest of us came up.

In less than an hour the sound of the horn was clearly heard. The Squatter led the way through the thick woods towards the repeated summons of the horn. As soon as all had rallied round, the best dog was sent forward to track the Cougar. In no time the whole pack was diligently trailing him towards the swamp. Rifles were ready. We kept some distance apart but in sight of one another as we followed the dogs, determined to shoot at nothing but the "Painter" as some called him.

The dogs began to mouth and quicken their pace as if the beast might be on the ground. We put our horses into a gentle gallop behind the yelping curs whose noise increased. Suddenly they began to bark as if an animal had been "treed." The Squatter said that unless we could shoot it in the branches we could expect a long chase of it. All began to draw closer together, but on seeing the dogs at the foot of a large tree we separated to surround it. Our guns cocked, we let our bridles dangle. There was a shot—and the Cougar leaped to the ground, and it bounded off with speed that showed its unwillingness to face gunfire. Eagerly, and with a deafening cry, the dogs set off in pursuit. The hunter had struck the monster in the only place he could aim at— the forelegs, near the shoulder.

We spurred our horses towards the center of the swamp, crossing one muddy bayou after another while the dogs continued the chase. The horses began to pant at such a furious rate that we chose to leave them and advance on foot. The wounded Cougar would almost certainly take refuge in a tree and remain there for some time. So we took off the saddles and bridles and attached bells to the horses' necks, hobbled their legs, and left them to shift for themselves.

Through muddy pools, over fallen trees, and among tangled rushes we went in pursuit of the dogs. A couple of hours later we again heard barking and whining, a sign that most likely the Panther was "treed." In a moment we saw the ferocious animal outstretched on a large branch, close to the trunk of a cottonwood, his broad breast facing us and his eyes fixed first on the dogs beneath and around him then on us. One of his forelegs hung loosely by his side. He crouched with his ears close to his head as if somehow to remain unseen. The signal was given and three balls were fired at him. He sprang a few feet from the branch then tumbled headlong to the ground. Attacked on all sides by the enraged curs, he nevertheless fought with desperate valor.

The Squatter advanced almost into the midst of the dogs and with one shot just behind and beneath the left shoulder ended the Panther's career.

The sun was low in the west. Two of the party went off to shoot Deer. The Squatter sent his sons on home, to be ready to feed the hogs in the morning. We skinned the Panther and tossed its carcass to the hungry dogs. The hunters brought back a small Deer for venison steaks which we roasted on a fire. Each man brought out his "pone" of bread and a flask of spirits. After singing songs and telling stories the others lay down beneath the smoke of the fire and fell asleep. I walked around camp for a while, to enjoy the beauties of the night and think about the day's adventures. I noticed the strange effect of the phosphorescent gleam from the large decayed and fallen trees, and thought how easy it would be for a person, lost in the swamp, to think these shining masses of wood some wondrous, fearful being. The mere sight would have made his hair stand on end. At last I rejoined my companions beside the fire. I lay down, assured that no enemy could approach without rousing the dogs—still in fierce dispute over the remains of the Panther.

At daybreak we broke camp. The Squatter slung the skin of the late destroyer of his livestock over his shoulder and we retraced our steps to find the horses. They had not strayed far, and we were soon jogging along in our saddles. At my host's cabin we all had breakfast together, before the five neighbors went their way and I returned to my favorite pursuits.[129]

In March 1843, I left New York on an expedition to the Yellowstone River for the sake of my work on *The Quadrupeds of North America*. I was accompanied by my friend Edward Harris of Moorestown, New Jersey; John Bell, taxidermist; Isaac Sprague, assistant artist; and Lewis Squires, son of a neighbor of mine in Carmansville, New York City, where I settled on my return from England, though not until after two years or so in White Street.

We arrived at Fort Union in mid-June after a record journey of only forty-eight days by steamer from St. Louis, Missouri.

Next day, after dinner, the agent Alexander Culbertson told us that if a Wolf should make its appearance on the prairie near the Fort he would bring it to us, dead or alive; and he was as good as his word. The whole affair was so handsomely executed that I shall describe it in detail.

A white Wolf, alternately standing and trotting, was seen about a quarter of a mile away, but also only about a quarter of a mile from the saddle horses. I thought the men sent to drive the horses in would never reach the Fort, much less get ready to overtake the Wolf in time. We all gathered on a balcony of the Fort and peered over the palisades. I was so fidgety that I ran down twice to warn the hunters that the Wolf was making off. Culbertson told me he would see to it that it did not escape, then he rode out with gun in hand, and dressed only in shirt and breeches. A few yards out he threw his cap off and lunged forward like a jockey about to win a race. The Wolf trotted on, and ever and anon stopped to gaze at the rider and horse. Realizing— too late—he galloped off with all his might. Culbertson gained on him, fired his gun in the air, as a signal that he would bring in the Wolf. It reached the hills and dropped into a ravine. The horse dashed after, the gun went off again, and Culbertson, without dismounting, and hardly slackening his pace at all picked it up and threw it across the saddle. He returned—through a heavy shower—as swiftly as he had gone. The poor Wolf was turned over to me. The time, from start to finish, did not exceed twenty minutes. Two other riders had skirted the hills to prevent the Wolf's escape. One brought back Culbertson's gun which he had thrown to the ground as he picked up the animal. It was not quite dead when it arrived, and had scratched one of Culbertson's fingers severely.

Some Indian tribes hunt Buffalo on horseback and use arrows only. They are not expert at reloading a gun in a close race with the game. Others hunt on foot with guns, arrows or both. The Mandans start off together in parties of twenty to fifty braves, each with two horses, one for the chase and the other as a pack horse. They carry quivers of arrows—twenty to fifty depending on their wealth. Until the game is sighted they ride the pack horse, but then they jump off, leap on the other one, and start full speed for the very midst of the Buffalo herd or for its flanks. If his arrow, drawn within yards of the target, causes blood to rush from nose and mouth, the Indian knows his aim was fatal and he shoots no more. If not, he shoots another arrow, and perhaps a third, until he sees the signs.

The Buffalo carries its tail close between its legs, not erectly, when it is hunted on horseback. If the tail is carried sideways in a twisted, rolling fashion, let the rider beware of a charge at his horse. A wounded Buffalo thrashes his tail, especially if he means to fight. The hunter's horse then shies off to let the mad animal snort for a while. If the Buffalo is not shot through the heart, a dozen arrows will not stop it. It may turn suddenly around and rush upon the horse, hook it with its horns, and overthrow both horse and rider, then trample and gore his assailant to death.

Despite its great size and clumsy appearance the Buffalo can spin about like lightning. Rage goads it to seek revenge for wounds. Horse and rider have to outrun it—for their very lives—before it will give up and return to the herd. Although Mandans Indians riding together usually kill most of the herd, some of the Buffalo are pretty sure to get away.

The Gros Ventres, Black Feet and Assiniboin Indians build log pounds or "parks"—round or square, according to the ground—with a funnel-shaped passage, made of logs, brushwood and pickets, which leads to what they call a "precipice." A fleet young Indian in Buffalo robe and Buffalo headdress starts out at daybreak to overtake a herd. The moment he sees one he bellows like a calf. He begins to move slowly towards the opening of the funnel while keeping up his decoying cry. The herd begins to follow. Behind them ride a dozen yelling, galloping Indians who hem their flanks and force them into the funnel's mouth.

Behind the funnel stand women and children, waiting to frighten the Buffalo herd. As soon as the young man who decoys them is sure they will follow to the "precipice" he leaps down it and over the barricade. Headed by a bull the herd leap down after him in haste and confusion. All the Indians yell and chase the animals until every bull, cow, and calf is impounded in the "park." October and November, when hides are good and saleable, are the usual time for this chase which, however, is carried on at all seasons.

The braves assemble beside the pen. Their calumet pipes are lighted. The chief smokes to the Great Spirit, to the four points of the compass, and lastly to the Buffalo. The pipe is passed from mouth to mouth. When this ceremony is over, the destruction begins. Guns go off. Arrows fly in all directions. From the outside of the park the hunters destroy the whole herd. Even the Indian children shoot arrows to help. Then the hunters jump the log wall and begin cleaning and skinning the kill.

Sometimes the bull that leads the herd will grow uneasy when it sees the precipice. It will then turn aside, if the fence is weak, and escape with the herd. Or, when the herd crowds together to the point where their weight breaks through, the small opening in the enclosure spreads to let them scamper out again over the prairie. Cows run faster than bulls, yearlings faster than cows, and calves faster than any.

A man saw three Buffalo floating down the Missouri River on an ice cake, not far from Bismarck, North Dakota. How far they might have travelled in this way he did not know. Hundreds attempt to cross the frozen river. The ice breaks under their enormous weight. The sharp-edged ice keeps them from climbing over. Thus a whole herd may be drowned. Their hoofs slip from side to side on the ice. In their fright they spread their legs to try and support their bodies. Indians and other hunters can then easily approach them, to stab them to the heart or cut their hamstrings.

Buffalo are a hundred times harder to kill while swimming. Those in the center of the herd are protected by the others. One day I watched a man on shore shoot at a Buffalo in the river. He swam out and around the wounded animal. Then he climbed on its side and floated down-stream. The Captain of our boat sent some men down to help him with a rope, which he fastened round the Buffalo's neck. It was hoisted onto the foredeck by tackle. It measured eight feet in length, and close to five from hoof to foreshoulder. Its head was so beautiful that I made a drawing of it as well as of its powerful hoofs.

One of our Indians cut out the milk bag of the cow and ate it fresh and raw in pieces the size of a hen's egg. One of the stomachs was partly washed in a bucket of water; an Indian swallowed a large piece; one of the crew ate the rest of it uncleaned. I tasted a well-cleaned piece, though the idea was repulsive to me—no meat eater except when there is nothing else on hand. But to my utter astonishment it was very good. The choicer cuts were reserved for the cabin. Half an hour later no one would have guessed that a Buffalo had been dressed on deck.

I was only a spectator at the regular Buffalo hunts, because at fifty-eight I would hardly go at a full gallop while running and loading a gun. Lewis Squires, a member of my party, shall here relate the adventures of his first hunt:

"One morning at Fort McKenzie in Dakota I was up before daylight, along with the son of the founder of the fort, a member of the American Fur Company post there. Young Bonaventure, a hunter of the fort, rode off with us. Two carts followed to bring back the meat. After ferrying the river by flatboat we rode on toward the Buffalo country, first through a wooded bottomland, then over level prairie. This brought us to the bluffs of the western Missouri valley. A rolling prairie, quite rough, lay ahead, with steep hills and ravines at intervals as well as the dry beds of streams made by spring and fall freshets. Occasionally a broad prairie favored our progress. As soon as the carts caught up with us we dismounted and let our horses follow behind. Seated on the Buffalo robes inside the cart we approached the scene of Bonaventure's last hunt. He rode to the top of the hill but could see not a living thing on the prairie. We moved ahead. Three o'clock came. Still we saw nothing. Our appetites warned us to think about food. I took a nap while McKenzie and Bonaventure went to look for Antelope. The report of a gun woke me up. McKenzie offered me a piece of raw liver. What others could eat I could at least taste; to my surprise I found it very good. We had hardly left the spot before the Wolves and Ravens began coming from all directions where, moments before, there had not been a sign of life. We were not more than three hundred yards away from the carcass of the Antelope when eight Wolves approached it, followed by others.

"Toward sunset, Bonaventure found a Buffalo bull. We decided to camp for the night and run the herd in the morning. Near a pond that becomes quite a large lake in spring and fall, we unsaddled and hobbled our horses to graze on the good pasture. We roasted the rest of our Antelope meat on sticks before our fire. Across the pond we saw a Grizzly Bear but could not get near. We smoked our pipes; then, using our saddles for pillows, went to sleep. I was wakened in the night by a crunching sound. The fire had died down. I sat up and saw a Wolf quietly feeding on the remains of my supper. He ran off at a shot and was seen no more that night.

"At daylight we saddled our horses. After riding three or four miles we saw three Buffalo some miles ahead. When we came within two hundred yards they started. Away we went after them, up the hills and through the ravines. I was angry and disappointed when my horse gave out. My friends killed two Buffalo. Again the Wolves came up when the butchering was done. Our water keg had leaked dry. We had to drink the warm, salty water of a pond or do without.

"The next group of Buffalo we came to stood gazing at us, their heads erect and their tails lashing. As soon as they saw what we were up to, they wheeled about swiftly and flew before us. How these enormous beasts can move so swiftly is hard to understand. I doubt if one horse in ten in this country can keep up with them. I followed downhill at full speed. My horse cleared an eight-foot ditch at the bottom as I kept in the lead. I had come up to the herd and was ready to fire when my horse faltered, slackened his pace in spite of my urging, then stopped altogether. The other horses rushed by. Imagine my disappointment! I saw the others fire. Their target, a big Buffalo, swerved a little, but moved on. My horse started up again after a short rest. I joined the men in time to fire the shot that brought the Buffalo down. Never have I seen an eye so ferocious. It was inflamed and rolled wildly in its socket. The wounded Buffalo presented the wildest, most unearthly spectacle I ever gazed on. He was soon cut up and put in our cart.

"That night we burned Buffalo dung to drive away the mosquitoes that clouded about us. The impregnated water that we had been drinking that day had taken our appetites away. We went to sleep without any supper.

"Our horses, though hobbled for the night, could not be found by one of the hands in the morning, even after two hours of searching. Finally, Bonaventure found an old horse that had been lost on the prairie for months and rode it back to the fort in the belief that our own horses had been lost for good or stolen. But soon after, the runaways were found.

We overtook and passed Bonaventure. He reached camp two hours after we did."

One day McKenzie put on my Indian dress. Squires donned one belonging to Culbertson. Mrs. Culbertson, a Blackfoot Indian princess, put on her own superb dress. The cook's wife put on one that Mrs. Culbertson had given me to take home as a souvenir. Mrs. Culbertson painted the men's faces in a terrifying way. She and the cook's Indian wife rode astride like men, their hair flying in the breeze. A furious race across the mile-wide prairie began, with whips all the way. How amazed would a European lady or some of our modern belles have been to see the magnificent riding of this princess and her servant of the floating black tresses!

The men were like wild creatures from another world, but not like anything in the whole Creation. Hither and thither they dashed. Across the ravine below, they began to chase a fine Wolf. Owen tried with bow and arrow but missed. Culbertson overtook it. His gun flashed. The Wolf lay dead. Then they dashed up the hills in the intense July heat. By and by, they raced back to the gates of the fort at full speed.

Culbertson gave Harris a superb Blackfoot Indian dress and a Buffalo head. Harris, the equal of any man in the country as a rider, gave him a short gun barrel well suited to Buffalo hunting.

One day a Buffalo was sighted two miles off, grazing peacefully on the prairie. Culberston threw down his hat, bound his head with a kerchief, and was off and away at a gallop. He fired a shot as a signal to Owen who was off on the range after a Wolf. The two approached the Buffalo slowly, to give Owen's overheated horse a rest. Then they ran to overtake the bison. We ate Buffalo meat that night; but first I caught eighteen Catfish with pieces of liver for bait (as well as two Tortoises that I put back in the river).

Next day we were riding towards Fort Union. Owen sighted a bull making his way slowly towards us over the prairie. I was the only one with ammunition and would gladly have claimed the privilege of running him, but was afraid I might make out badly on my slower steed and lose the meat we needed. So I handed my gun to Owen. Bell and I went to a rise on the prairie to watch. Owen approached the bull which kept coming until it was less than a quarter of a mile away—either because it did not see or did not heed him. Owen's mare, tired after two hard runs that day, had trouble keeping up. Owen let her catch her breath before he rushed her within shooting distance. His shot seemed to check the bull's progress enough to allow him to come alongside. Owen fired his second barrel through the shoulder into the lungs, bringing the bull to a standstill.

Bell and I began to gallop towards Owen, and called to him not to shoot again. The bull, not much exhausted but too stiffened by the shot to turn quickly as we came up to him, worked himself slowly around to face us—then lunged. We drew up short and began firing our pistols but only succeeded in increasing his fury. Had we not felt satisfied that we could avoid him his appearance would have inspired terror. Nevertheless, I came very near to being finished off by him through my own folly. I stood directly in his path as he advanced, fired at his head, then ran in front of him instead of veering to one side, not thinking that he could overtake me. As I ran I glanced back and was horrified to see Mr. Bull within three feet of me, ready to give me a taste of his horns. I turned off sharply. The Buffalo was unable to wheel quickly enough to follow. Bell took the gun from Owen and shot the bull directly behind the shoulder blade. He tottered, fell forward on his horns, rolled on his side, and soon was dead.

One day a wounded bull charged Squires, then Owen and Harris. Squires rode between the Buffalo and a ravine. The animal, quite close, turned to attack. The frightened horse jumped into the ravine. Squires lost balance in the saddle. He threw his gun down and clung to the mane of his horse until he managed to pull himself up, and across its back again. He got away, but if he had fallen, the bull would have killed him in a matter of minutes. No help could have come from Owen and Harris. Their guns were empty. The bull galloped after him, but finally fell, weak from having been shot at twenty times at least.

Buffalo become so very poor during hard winters when snows cover the ground to a depth of two or three feet, that they lose their hair and are covered with scabs that the Magpies feed on. The poor beasts die by the hundreds. One can hardly conceive how it happens that so many are still to be found, regardless of the number that die and are murdered almost daily on those boundless wastes called prairies. Hosts drown in the freshets. Hundreds of calves die in spring. One sees so many that one hardly notices them more than the cattle in home pastures. They trample paths that become like wagon tracks as they cross the prairie. But this cannot last. Even now the herds are smaller. Before many years the Buffalo, like the Great Auk, will have disappeared. Surely this should not be allowed to happen. What a terrible destruction of life, and for nothing or next to it. The tongues are brought in. The flesh is left to Wolves and birds of prey, or to rot where these fine animals fell! The prairies are covered with the skulls of the victims.[130]

APPENDICES

———◆———

APPENDIX I

Audubon the Writer

Perhaps the best possible answer to the question of whether the writing of Audubon should ever have been edited for publication is suggested by the following, original, unedited version of his *"Pitting of the Wolves."* Compare it with the Macgillivray version in volume two of *Audubon and His Journals* (1897), then with the one in this book.

"Pitting Wolves"

"The whole of mankind seems to be prepossessed against the Wolf, its size, strength, agility, [?   ] of a species of cunning scarcely below that of its relation Master Reynard all tend to render it despicable especially to the Husbandman on whose flocks every body knows its keen appetite and teeth are ever bent, and all are intent on the [?   ] and destruction of both these animals in America, in many parts of which they have been very abundant, and in some are still quite so.—Traps and snares of all sorts are erected to surprise and kill the Wolf, which dogs and horses are trained to chase, overtake, and worry the other. The wolf however unless in some way incapacitated, being more powerful and perhaps better winded than the fox is rarely followed by hound or any other dogs in what is termed the chase but as its depredations are of a nature at times ferocious, and on all occasions [?   ] detrimental to the farmer, all possible exertions have been employed to exterminate the race whenever found.

"We have but few instances on record however connected with the attacks of this animal toward man, and only one of those has come under my immediate notice, which being rather unconnected with the heading of this article I shall relate to you Kind Reader in as short a manner as possible.

"Two young Negroes men who resided near the Banks of the Ohio in the lower parts of the state of Kentucky, some twenty-three years ago, had sweet hearts living on a plantation distant about ten miles from theirs. They frequently visited the fair ladies after the labour of the day had terminated with them. The [   ] way to their beloved lady directly across a [   ] canebrake, and to every lover every moment is precious, they usually travelled through this to save time. Winter once more had come dreary, sad, cold and forbidding— not a glimpse of light or of warmth one might imagine existed there after sunset except in the [?   ] bosoms [?   ] and eyes of these seminocturnal young sparks, or in that of the wolves now prowling hungry if not famishing. The snow too covered the earth and the flesh of such men could be noticed at a greater distance than at any other time. The young Beaux prudent to a certain degree lugged axes on their shoulders, and walked as likely as the narrow path before them would allow.—Brave as Caesars—On a few occasions sparkling jets of light reached their eyes but so transient were those that both men only believed these light were caused by their faces coming in contact with the [?   ] covered with the snow. Suddenly however a long fearful mingled and horrific howling reached their ears when both full well knew that the sound proceeded from a number of hungry and perhaps desperate wolves. They stopped short and placed themselves in attitude of defiance and [awaited?] the result. All was dark save a few feet of snow beneath them and the renewed silence of night was as dismal as that of the tomb. Nothing could be done to better this situation and after standing for a few minutes they resumed their march, but no sooner was this done and their axes again placed on their shoulders than one felt himself assailed by several foes. His legs were held fast in torturing pain for a moment as if pressed in a powerful screw, while the growlings and bites of other animals clung to the breast of the other and lowered him to the ground. Both fought and struggled hard against their assailants, which in fact were wolves, but one at last no longer spoke, and the other reduced in strength and perhaps in courage felt it incumbent to save himself by taking to the branches of a tree by which he reached a place of safety toward its top. The next morning the mangled remains of his companion lay scattered around on the blooded snow. Three dead wolves lay there also, the survivors were out of sight and Scipio, sliding to the earth, took up the axes and made his way homewards to retail the sad news.

"About two years after this sad event as I was travelling between Henderson and Vincennes I chanced to stop for the night at a farmer's house by the road side. My nag put away and my meal [?   ], and the talk underway, mine host asked me if I should like to pay a visit to his wolf pits about half a mile distant. Glad of the opportunity I accompanied him across his fields to the neighbourhood of a deep wood and soon saw these engines of destruction. He had three of these pits within a few hundred yards of each other They were about 8 feet deep, broader at bottom than at top in so much as to prevent the escape from them of any by the most agil and powerful animals.

The apertures were covered revolving platforms of branches of trees attached to an axle worked on lateral gugeons. on either surface of these platforms were fastened large pieces of putrid venison and other matters by no means savoury to our olfactory nerves but quite so il sauve (*sic*) to any such carnivorous animals as our wolves. My companion wished to visit them that evening as he was in the habit of doing every day merely to see that 'all was right.' He said that wolves were very abundant that autumn and that they had killed nearly the whole of his sheep and several of his colts, but that he was 'paying them in full', just now adding that if I would tally [tarry?] a few hours with him next morning he would beyond a doubt show me some sport rarely seen in those parts. We retired to rest in due time and with the dawn arose. 'I think,' said my host 'that all's right for I see my dogs are anxious to go towards the Pits and although they are nothing but curs their noses are none of the worse for that.' He took a gun, an axe, and a large knife, The dogs began howling, barking and whisking around us as if full of joy, and onward we went full of hope. When we reached the first Pit the bait was all gone, the platform much injured, and a subterranean passage had been scratched out by whatever beast had fallen in the ambush. At the next we were very fortunate, as on his peeking beneath the covering bed, he apprised me that 'three ferocious fellows were safe enough.' I also peeped and saw the three animals. Two black and the other called from after its colour a 'brindle' of [?] size sure enough. The whole lay flat on the earth, ears close over the head and eyes bespeaking more mercy than anger, but how were we to get them out of the Pit? 'Now Sir' said the Farmer 'by going down to them to be sure and hamstring the whole of them.' Being myself a novice in these matters I begged to be simply a looker on. 'With all my heart, sir, stand here and look at me through the breach' on which he glided himself down with his axe and knife given me the case of his Rifle. Once close to the wolves I was not a little surprised to see the amount of their natural cowardice. He pulled alternately the hind legs of each and with a side stroke of the knife cut asunder the principal tendon of each leg about the knee joint and came out unscathed as if he had merely been marking Lambs! 'Lo!' said the farmer 'we've forgot the rope and I'll go after it' and off he went sure enough with as much alacrity as the youthful pair of lovers before mentioned had commenced the crossing of the cane brake while intent on promising their [?] to the damsels of their choice. I now saw him returning panting and out of breath, but with his [?] hand wiping the sweat off his brow he exclaimed, 'Now for it!' I was asked to raise and hold the platform on its central balance while he with all the dexterity of an Indian threw a noose around the neck of one of the wolves when my assistance being called forth, up we hoisted the animal! Reader, it came up as if dead by fright and [motiv——]. The disabled legs swung to and fro through the air, the breath hard, the jaws open and distended, and gurglings alone evinced that it was still alive. Once on the earth, the rope was loosened by means of a stick and he was left to the dogs all of which at once infuriated worried and dispatch the murderer of this master's flocks. The second was dead within the same manner but the third which was probably the oldest as he was the blackest showed game against the curs. The moment it was left unstrangling to the furious attacks of the curs had you been there to witness its ways you would doubtless have been surprised quite as much as I myself was. This wolf (and it proved to be a female) scufled along on assisted only by its forelegs and [?   ] blood at a surprising rate, giving a [?   ] over and over to the nearest dog, which with a portion of skin from the wolf went off either howling dismally, or as if dismally mad! Indeed thinking that the wolf might escape, the Rifle was levelled at her. The trigger touched off with the bullets and with [?   ] of all dismal and death like ended the life of the savage animal."*

* The preceding appears in an edited version on pages 62–64.—*Ed.*

Sources

Below are the sources drawn upon for this "autobiography." The column on the right lists the abbreviations used in the Notes.

THE COLLECTOR. A private printing by Walter Benjamin, in 1948, of "The Fair Incognito" ("A Remarkable Femelle"). Manuscript in the American Philosophical Society collection, Philadelphia, Pennsylvania.

THE FAIR INCOGNITO

Letter from Audubon to James E. De Kay, Historical Society of Pennsylvania (Gratz Collection), Philadelphia.

JAMES E. DE KAY

EDINBURGH NEW PHILOSOPHICAL JOURNAL. 1826–28. For detailed citations see JOHN JAMES AUDUBON by Alice Ford, University of Oklahoma Press, Norman: 1964.

EDINBURGH NEW PHILOSOPHICAL JOURNAL

THE 1826 JOURNAL OF JOHN JAMES AUDUBON. Edited by Alice Ford, University of Oklahoma Press, Norman: 1967. Manuscript in the collection of Henry Bradley Martin.

JOURNAL 1826

FEATHERSTONHAUGH'S MONTHLY AMERICAN JOURNAL. Philadelphia, 1831–32.

FEATHERSTON-HAUGH'S MONTHLY AMERICAN JOURNAL

Henry Howland Papers. Buffalo Museum of Science, Buffalo, New York.

HENRY HOWLAND PAPERS

JOURNAL OF JOHN JAMES AUDUBON—1820–21. Edited by Howard Corning, Harvard University Press, Cambridge: 1929. Manuscript in the Houghton Library of Harvard College, Cambridge, Massachusetts.

JOURNAL 1820

JOURNAL OF MAMMALOGY. November, 1924; V: 223. Contains statement that Thomas Lincoln of Dennysville, Maine, provided "A Moose Hunt" by letter (unacknowledged in ORNITHOLOGICAL BIOGRAPHY).

JOURNAL OF MAMMALOGY

"Labrador Journal" in *AUDUBON AND HIS JOUR-*   LABRADOR
NALS, 2 vols. Edited by Maria R. Audubon. New   JOURNAL
York: 1897.

THE LIFE OF JOHN JAMES AUDUBON by Lucy   LIFE
Audubon. Edited by R. Buchanan in London, 1868,
and by J. G. Wilson in New York, 1869. Differs
somewhat from editing by William Macgillivray of
earlier Audubon writings on which the biography is
largely based.

"Missouri Journals" in *AUDUBON AND HIS JOUR-*   MISSOURI
NAL, 2 vols. Edited by Maria R. Audubon. New   JOURNALS
York: 1897.

"My Method of Drawing Birds" by John James Audu-   EDINBURGH
bon, in *EDINBURGH JOURNAL OF SCIENCE.*   JOURNAL OF
Edinburgh: 1828; VIII: 48–54. Other citations in   SCIENCE
JOHN JAMES AUDUBON, by Alice Ford, University of Oklahoma Press, Norman: 1964.

"Myself" in *AUDUBON AND HIS JOURNAL,* 2   MYSELF
vols. Edited by Maria R. Audubon. New York: 1897.

ORNITHOLOGICAL BIOGRAPHY, 5 vols., by John   OB
James Audubon. Edinburgh: 1831–39.

THE VIVIPAROUS QUADRUPEDS OF NORTH   QUADRUPEDS
AMERICA by John James Audubon (in collabora-
tion with John Bachman). New York: 1845–48.

REMINISCENCES . . . by Vincent Nolte. London: REMINISCENCES
1854.

A WINTER'S WREATH FOR 1829. Liverpool and   A WINTER'S
Philadelphia: 1828; 104–127.   WREATH FOR 1829

APPENDIX III

Notes

See pages 263ff for identification of sources and abbreviations.

PART ONE

1. Composite of OB: Introduction I; MYSELF; and JOURNAL 1820—with factual revision as in JOHN JAMES AUDUBON, Alice Ford, 1964.
2. OB: Pewee Flycatcher
3. MYSELF
4. OB: My Method of Drawing Birds. See bibliography for a second publication of "My Method of Drawing Birds."
5. OB: Introduction I
6. MYSELF
7. OB: Canada Goose
8. OB: Chimney Swift
9. OB: Kentucky Barbecue
10. OB: Kentucky Sports
11. OB: Colonel Boone
12. OB: Louisville in Kentucky
13. MYSELF
14. OB: Fishing in the Ohio
15. OB: The White Perch
16. OB: The American Sun Perch
17. OB: Washington Sea Eagle
18. OB: The White-headed Eagle
19. OB: A Maple Sugar Camp
20. OB: The Traveller and the Pole Cat
21. MYSELF
22. A WINTER'S WREATH FOR 1829: Journey up the Mississippi, 104–127.
23. MYSELF
24. OB: A Wild Horse
25. REMINISCENCES
26. OB: The Earthquake
27. OB: The Hurricane
28. OB: Snowy Owl
29. OB: Golden-Eye Duck
30. OB: American Avocet

INDEX

A 7746

Audubon, John James, 1785–1851.
Audubon, by himself; a profile of John James Audubon from writings selected, arranged, and edited, by Alice Ford. [1st ed.] Garden City, N. Y., Published for the American Museum of Natural History [by] the Natural History Press [1969]

xi, 276 p. illus., ports. 25 cm. 8.95

Bibliography: p. [263]–264.

I. Ford, Alice Elizabeth, 1906– comp. II. American Museum of Natural History, New York. I. Title.

QL31.A9A3 598.2'0924 [B] 71–81029
MARC

Library of Congress 69 [3]